Lecture Notes in Computer Science 13768

More information about this series at https://link.springer.com/bookseries/558

Lucas Lima · Vince Molnár (Eds.)

Formal Methods: Foundations and Applications

25th Brazilian Symposium, SBMF 2022
Virtual Event, December 6–9, 2022
Proceedings

Editors
Lucas Lima ⓘD
Federal Rural University of Pernambuco
Recife, Brazil

Vince Molnár ⓘD
Budapest University of Technology
and Economics
Budapest, Hungary

ISSN 0302-9743   ISSN 1611-3349 (electronic)
Lecture Notes in Computer Science
ISBN 978-3-031-22475-1   ISBN 978-3-031-22476-8 (eBook)
https://doi.org/10.1007/978-3-031-22476-8

This Springer imprint is published by the registered company Springer Nature Switzerland AG
The registered company address is: Gewerbestrasse 11, 6330 Cham, Switzerland

Preface

This volume contains the papers presented at SBMF 2022: the 25th Brazilian Symposium on Formal Methods. Similarly to the previous two editions, the Steering Committee had to make the hard decision to organize a virtual-only event, as the COVID-19 situation in Brazil was still concerning at the beginning of the year. Therefore, the conference was held online, from December 6 to December 9, 2022.

The Brazilian Symposium on Formal Methods (SBMF) is an event devoted to the development, dissemination, and use of formal methods for the construction of high-quality computational systems, aiming to promote opportunities for researchers and practitioners with an interest in formal methods to discuss the recent advances in this area. SBMF is a consolidated scientific-technical event in the software area. Its first edition took place in 1998, reaching the jubilee 25th edition in 2022. The proceedings of the previous editions have been published mostly in Springer's Lecture Notes in Computer Science series as volumes 5902 (2009), 6527 (2010), 7021 (2011), 7498 (2012), 8195 (2013), 8941 (2014), 9526 (2015), 10090 (2016), 10623 (2017), 11254 (2018), 12475 (2020), and 13130 (2021).

This year's conference included four invited talks, given by Dirk Beyer (Ludwig-Maximilians-Universität München, Germany), Robert Karban (NASA's Jet Propulsion Laboratory, USA), Kristin Yvonne Rozier (Iowa State University, USA), and Valdivino Santiago (Instituto Nacional de Pesquisas Espaciais, Brazil). A total of eight papers were presented at the conference and are included in this volume. They were selected from 14 submissions that came from authors in seven different countries: Brazil, Canada, Estonia, Germany, Ireland, the UK, and the USA. The Program Committee comprised 40 members from the national and international community of formal methods. Each submission was reviewed by three Program Committee members (single blind review). Submissions, reviews, deliberations, and decisions were handled via EasyChair, which provided good support throughout this process.

We are grateful to the Program Committee for their hard work in evaluating submissions and suggesting improvements. We are very thankful to the general chair of SBMF 2022, Giovanny Fernando Lucero Palma (Universidade Federal de Sergipe, Brazil), who made everything possible for the conference to run smoothly. SBMF 2022 was organized by the Universidade Federal de Sergipe (UFS), and promoted by the Brazilian Computer Society (SBC). We would further like to thank SBC for their sponsorship, and Springer for agreeing to publish the proceedings as a volume of Lecture Notes in Computer Science.

December 2022
Lucas Lima
Vince Molnár

Organization

General Chair

Giovanny Lucero   Universidade Federal de Sergipe, Brazil

Program Committee Chairs

Lucas Lima   Universidade Federal Rural de Pernambuco, Brazil

Vince Molnár   Budapest University of Technology and Economics, Hungary

Steering Committee

Adolfo Duran   Universidade Federal da Bahia, Brazil

Phillip Wadler   University of Edinburgh, UK

Gustavo Carvalho   Universidade Federal de Pernambuco, Brazil

Volker Stolz   Western Norway University of Applied Sciences, Norway

Sérgio Campos   Universidade Federal de Minas Gerais, Brazil

Marius Minea   University of Massachusetts Amherst, USA

Program Committee

Aline Andrade   Universidade Federal da Bahia, Brazil

Haniel Barbosa   Universidade Federal de Minas Gerais, Brazil

Luis Barbosa   Universidade do Minho, Portugal

Armin Biere   Albert-Ludwigs-Universität Freiburg, Germany

Manfred Broy   Technische Universität München, Germany

Sérgio Campos   Universidade Federal de Minas Gerais, Brazil

Gustavo Carvalho   Universidade Federal de Pernambuco, Brazil

Márcio Cornélio   Universidade Federal de Pernambuco, Brazil

David Déharbe   CLEARSY Systems Engineering, France

Clare Dixon   University of Liverpool, UK

Jose Fiadeiro   University of Dundee, UK

Rohit Gheyi   Universidade Federal de Campina Grande, Brazil

Juliano Iyoda   Universidade Federal de Pernambuco, Brazil

Alfons Laarman   Leiden University, The Netherlands

Thierry Lecomte   CLEARSY Systems Engineering, France

Michael Leuschel	Universität Düsseldorf, Germany
Lucas Lima	Universidade Federal Rural de Pernambuco, Brazil
Patrícia Machado	Universidade Federal de Campina Grande, Brazil
Tiago Massoni	Universidade Federal de Campina Grande, Brazil
Ana Melo	Universidade de São Paulo, Brazil
Marius Minea	University of Massachusetts Amherst, USA
Alvaro Miyazawa	University of York, UK
Vince Molnár	Budapest University of Technology and Economics, Hungary
Sidney Nogueira	Universidade Federal Rural de Pernambuco, Brazil
Marcel Oliveira	Universidade Federal do Rio Grande do Norte, Brazil
Peter Csaba Ölveczky	University of Oslo, Norway
Leila Ribeiro	Universidade Federal do Rio Grande do Sul, Brazil
Elvinia Riccobene	University of Milan, Italy
Kristin Yvonne Rozier	Iowa State University, USA
Augusto Sampaio	Universidade Federal de Pernambuco, Brazil
Adenilso Simão	Universidade de São Paulo, Brazil
Volker Stolz	Western Norway University of Applied Sciences, Norway
Sofiène Tahar	Concordia University, Canada
Leopoldo Teixeira	Universidade Federal de Pernambuco, Brazil
Máté Tejfel	Eötvös Loránd University, Hungary
Maurice ter Beek	Istituto di Scienza e Tecnologie dell'Informazione, Italy
Nils Timm	University of Pretoria, South Africa
András Vörös	Budapest University of Technology and Economics, Hungary
Tim Willemse	Eindhoven University of Technology, The Netherlands
Jim Woodcock	University of York, UK

Invited Talks

Cooperative Verification

Dirk Beyer

Ludwig-Maximilians-Universität München, Germany

Abstract. Cooperative verification is an approach where several verifiers help each other solving the verification problem by sharing artifacts about the verification task. There are many verification tools available, but the power of combining them is not yet fully leveraged. The problem is that in order to use verifiers 'off-the-shelf', we need clear interfaces to invoke the tools and to pass information. Part of the interfacing problem is to define standard artifacts to be passed between verifiers. We explain a few recent approaches for cooperative combinations and also give a brief overview of CoVeriTeam, a tool for composing verification systems from existing off-the-shelf components.

Taming Monsters with Dragons: A Fractal Approach to Digital Twin Pipelines

Robert Karban

Jet Propulsion Laboratory - NASA, USA

Abstract. This presentation will discuss how development pipelines evolve over the systems lifecycle to integrate systems and its embedded software, resulting in a digital twin to enable system qualification and auditable artifacts. We will also touch on how the Europa Clipper project leverages such pipelines.

Developing an Open-Source, State-of-the-Art Symbolic Model-Checking Framework for the Model-Checking Research Community

Kristin Yvonne Rozier

Iowa State University, USA

Abstract. Safety-critical and security-critical systems are entering our lives at an increasingly rapid pace. These are the systems that help fly our planes, drive our cars, deliver our packages, ensure our electricity, or even automate our homes. Especially when humans cannot perform a task in person, e.g., due to a dangerous working environment, we depend on such systems. Before any safety-critical system launches into the human environment, we need to be sure it is really safe. Model checking is a popular and appealing way to rigorously check for safety: given a system, or an accurate model of the system, and a safety requirement, model checking is a "push button" technique to produce either a proof that the system always operates safely, or a counterexample detailing a system execution that violates the safety requirement. Many aspects of model checking are active research areas, including more efficient ways of reasoning about the system's behavior space, and faster search algorithms for the proofs and counterexamples.

As model checking becomes more integrated into the standard design and verification process for safety-critical systems, the platforms for model checking research have become more limited. Previous options have become closed-source or industry tools; current research platforms don't have support for expressive specification languages needed for verifying real systems. Our goal is to fill the current gap in model checking research platforms: building a freely-available, open-source, scalable model checking infrastructure that accepts expressive models and efficiently interfaces with the currently-maintained state-of-the-art back-end algorithms to provide an extensible research and verification tool. We are creating a community resource with a well-documented intermediate representation to enable extensibility, and a web portal, facilitating new modeling languages and back-end algorithmic advances. To add new modeling languages or algorithms, researchers need only to develop a translator to/from the new intermediate language, and will then be able to integrate each advance with the full state-of-the-art in model checking.

This community infrastructure will be ideal for catapulting formal verification efforts in many cutting-edge application areas, including security, networking, and operating system verification. We particularly target outreach to the embedded systems (CPS) community as our new framework will make hardware verification problems from this community more accessible.

Some Applications of Formal Methods

Valdivino Santiago

Instituto Nacional de Pesquisas Espaciais - INPE, Brazil

Abstract. This talk will present some applications of formal methods for aerospace and geoinformatics systems. Firstly, it will be discussed the feasibility, in the context of space systems such as satellites, of probabilistic model checking to the mitigation problem of single event upsets (SEUs) in field-programmable gate arrays (FPGAs). Secondly, it will be presented a method for automated unit test case/data generation based on functional model checking and focusing on C++ source code. The method was applied to two geoinformatics software products. Finally, the topic will be the assessment of the safety of navigation systems for a civil commercial transport category aircraft via probabilistic model checking. Considering these applications, strengths and weaknesses of such formal methods will also be addressed during the talk.

Contents

Model Checking and Semantics

An Efficient Customized Clock Allocation Algorithm for a Class of Timed Automata

Neda Saeedloei[1(✉)] and Feliks Kluźniak[2]

[1] Towson University, Towson, USA
nsaeedloei@towson.edu
[2] RelationalAI, Berkeley, USA
feliks.kluzniak@relational.ai

Abstract. We present a new clock allocation algorithm for a fairly general class of timed automata. The algorithm is customized to take advantage of the special properties of automata in this class, and is therefore efficient.

1 Introduction

Timed automata [2] have been used as a standard formalism for modelling real-time systems. A timed automaton is a finite automaton extended with a finite set of real-valued variables called clocks. Clocks appear in constraints that accompany transitions of the automaton and express conditions on the times at which the transitions can be taken: a transition r on symbol a can be taken if the input is a and the accompanying clock constraints are satisfied. When a transition is taken, it can reset some clocks, thus making it possible for constraints to refer to the time elapsed since the clocks were last reset. All the clocks of an automaton advance at the same rate.

Model checking [6] is a popular technique for formal verification of models of complex systems, including real-time systems. When applied to timed automata, it can be computationally expensive, and the cost crucially depends on the number of clocks [3]. Although, for a given timed automaton, it is in general undecidable whether there exists a language-equivalent automaton with fewer clocks [8], the problem of decreasing the number of clocks of timed automata has been an active area of research [5,7,9,13]. The existing approaches for tackling the problem are based on either the syntactic form (e.g., [7,13]) or the semantics (e.g., [5,9]) of timed automata. Regardless of the particular approach—syntax or semantics based—the problem has been addressed mostly by constructing bisimilar timed automata [7,9].

A more recent approach [13] is not based on constructing bisimilar timed automata, but on a compiler-like static flow analysis of a given automaton $\mathcal{A}$. This approach can be applied when $\mathcal{A}$ belongs to TA_S, the class of automata that have at most one clock reset on any transition, and moreover, every clock is well-defined, i.e., on any path from the initial location to the use of a clock in a

L. Lima and V. Molnár (Eds.): SBMF 2022, LNCS 13768, pp. 3–21, 2022.
https://doi.org/10.1007/978-3-031-22476-8_1

constraint, the clock is reset before it is used. Given an automaton in TA_S, this method finds the optimal (i.e., smallest) number of clocks for the equivalence class of all automata that have the same graph and the same pattern of clock resets and uses. That is, it is impossible to use a smaller number of clocks without violating the semantics of at least one member of the class (as long as all the members have their original graphs and constraints, modulo clock renaming).

This method performs a liveness analysis of clocks, the result of which is used to construct an interference graph. It is shown that a colouring of the interference graph with a minimum number of colours is equivalent to finding an optimal clock allocation for the original timed automaton, i.e., the optimal number of clocks is the chromatic number of the graph [13]. It is also shown that for every automaton in $TA_{DS} \subsetneq TA_S$ (see Sect. 3) the interference graph is chordal (therefore perfect), hence it can be coloured in polynomial time [11], once the interference graph is constructed whose worst-case complexity is $O(n^3)$.

The class TA_{DS} was first encountered in the context of synthesizing timed automata from a set of timed scenarios [12]. This is the class of automata that satisfy two properties [13]: (i) a given clock is reset on all the outgoing transitions of a unique location, and (ii) if a clock constraint $t_j \sim a$, for some clock t_j and some $a \in \mathbb{Q}$, appears on an outgoing transition of location s, then clock t_j must be reset on an outgoing transition of a location q, where q dominates s (i.e., all paths from the initial location to s pass through q [10]).

The current paper considers the class TA_{DS} and develops a new clock allocation method which is customized for this class. Our method is based on a new liveness analysis algorithm, which is much simpler and more efficient, as it takes advantage of the properties of automata in TA_{DS}. These properties allow us to formulate a clock allocation algorithm that is also efficient. Given an automaton $\mathcal{A}$ in TA_{DS}, the algorithm computes an optimal ("optimal" in the sense used in the cited work [13]) clock allocation for $\mathcal{A}$ and replaces the original clocks with a new set of clocks, without changing the graph or the language of $\mathcal{A}$.

2   Timed automata

A *timed automaton* [2] is a tuple $\mathcal{A} = \langle \Sigma, Q, q_0, Q_f, C, T \rangle$, where Σ is a finite alphabet, Q is the (*finite*) set of locations, $q_0 \in Q$ is the initial location, $Q_f \subseteq Q$ is the set of final locations, C is a finite set of *clock* variables (clocks for short), and $T \subseteq Q \times Q \times \Sigma \times 2^C \times 2^{\Phi(C)}$ is the set of transitions. In each transition $(q, q', e, \lambda, \phi)$, λ is the set of clocks to be reset with the transition and $\phi \subset \Phi(C)$ is a set of clock constraints over C of the form $c \sim a$ (where $\sim \in \{\leq, <, \geq, >, =\}$, $c \in C$ and a is a constant in the set of rational numbers, $\mathbb{Q}$).

A *clock valuation*, ν, for C is a mapping from C to $\mathbb{R}^{\geq 0}$. ν, *satisfies* a set of clock constraints ϕ over C iff every clock constraint in ϕ evaluates to true after each clock c is replaced with $\nu(c)$. For $\tau \in \mathbb{R}, \nu + \tau$ denotes the clock valuation which maps every clock c to the value $\nu(c) + \tau$. For $Y \subseteq C$, $[Y \mapsto \tau]\nu$ is the valuation which assigns τ to each $c \in Y$ and agrees with ν over the rest of the clocks.

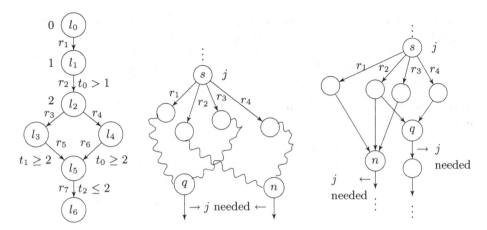

Fig. 1. In TA_{DS} **Fig. 2.** Problematic locations   **Fig. 3.** Families

A *timed word* over an alphabet Σ is a pair (σ, τ) where $\sigma = \sigma_1\sigma_2...$ is a finite [1,4] or infinite [2] word over Σ and $\tau = \tau_1\tau_2...$ is a finite or infinite sequence of (time) values such that (i) $\tau_i \in \mathbb{R}^{\geq 0}$, (ii) $\tau_i \leq \tau_{i+1}$ for all $i \geq 1$, and (iii) if the word is infinite, then for every $t \in \mathbb{R}^{\geq 0}$ there is some $i \geq 1$ such that $\tau_i > t$. A run ρ of $\mathcal{A}$ over a timed word (σ, τ) is a sequence of the form $\langle q_0, \nu_0 \rangle \xrightarrow[\tau_1]{\sigma_1} \langle q_1, \nu_1 \rangle \xrightarrow[\tau_2]{\sigma_2} \langle q_2, \nu_2 \rangle \xrightarrow[\tau_3]{\sigma_3} \ldots$, where for all $i \geq 0$, $q_i \in Q$ and ν_i is a clock valuation such that (i) $\nu_0(c) = 0$ for all clocks $c \in C$ and (ii) for every $i > 1$ there is a transition in T of the form $(q_{i-1}, q_i, \sigma_i, \lambda_i, \phi_i)$, such that $(\nu_{i-1} + \tau_i - \tau_{i-1})$ satisfies ϕ_i, and ν_i equals $[\lambda_i \mapsto 0](\nu_{i-1} + \tau_i - \tau_{i-1})$. The set $inf(\rho)$ consists of $q \in Q$ such that $q = q_i$ for infinitely many $i \geq 0$ in the run ρ.

A run over a finite timed word is *accepting* if it ends in a final location [4]. A run ρ over an infinite timed word is *accepting* iff $inf(\rho) \cap Q_f \neq \emptyset$ [2]. The *language* of $\mathcal{A}$, $L(\mathcal{A})$, is the set $\{(\sigma, \tau) \mid \mathcal{A}$ has an accepting run over $(\sigma, \tau)\}$.

3   The Class TA_{DS}

Most of the definitions in this section and Sect. 5.1 are taken from our earlier work [13].

Assume $TA = \langle E, Q, q^0, Q_f, V, R \rangle$ is the original timed automaton. If $r = (q, q', e, \lambda, \phi) \in R$, then $source(r) = q$ and $target(r) = q'$. The outgoing/incoming transitions of a location $s \in Q$ are denoted by $out(s) = \{r \in R \mid s = source(r)\}$ and $in(s) = \{r \in R \mid s = target(r)\}$.

Let $\mathcal{A}$ be a timed automaton with a unique initial location. If s and q are locations in $\mathcal{A}$, then s *dominates* q if and only if all paths from the initial location to q pass through s [10]. We follow the conventions of the cited work [13] and denote the *dominance relation* between locations in $\mathcal{A}$ by $\succeq$: $s \succeq q$ iff s dominates q (we also say that q is dominated by s). We write $s \succ q$ to denote that $s \succeq q$ and $s \neq q$. The definition of dominated locations can be extended to *dominated transitions*: a transition r is *dominated* by location s iff $s \succeq source(r)$.

In the timed automaton of Fig. 1, l_0, l_1, l_2, l_5 and l_6 are all the locations that dominate l_6. Transition r_7 is dominated by l_0, l_1, l_2 and l_5.

In the rest of the paper we assume that every timed automaton $\mathcal{A}$ has an associated injective partial labelling function $L : Q \to N_L$, where $N_L \subset \{0, 1, 2, ...\}$ is the set of labels (values of L) used for $\mathcal{A}$.

Definition 1. *A timed automaton belongs to the class* TA_{DS} *if and only if it satisfies the following three restrictions:*

1. *It has a unique initial location,* q^0, *from which every location can be reached.*
2. *Clock* t_j *is reset on all the transitions in* $out(s)$, *where* $L(s) = j$.[1]
3. *A clock constraint on a transition* r *can contain an occurrence of* t_j *only if* $j \in N_L$ *and* $L^{-1}(j) \succ source(r)$.

Restriction 3 is called *the dominance assumption*, and it means that if $t_j \sim a$ is a clock constraint on a transition $r \in out(s)$, then the value of t_j represents the amount of time that has elapsed since leaving a location q, where $q \succ s$ and $L(q) = j$. This guarantees that all clocks are *well-defined*: a reference to t_j in a clock constraint on r is always preceded by a reset, on every path from q^0 to r.

4   The Notion of Optimality

To make the paper self-contained, in this section we describe the notion of optimality used in our earlier work [13].

Assume $\mathcal{A} = \langle E, Q, Q_0, Q_f, V, R \rangle$ is the original timed automaton, where $Q_f \neq \emptyset$.[2] We assume that the clocks in $\mathcal{A}$ belong to the set $V = \{t_0, t_1, t_2, ...\}$. Our clock allocation method will replace these with a disjoint set of clocks.

Let $N = \{j \mid t_j \sim a \in \phi_r$, where $r \in R\}$. This is the set of *clock numbers*, i.e., of the indices of all the clocks that are referred to on some transitions in R. Notice that $N \subseteq N_L$.

For a transition $r = (s, q, e, \lambda, \phi) \in R$, we use ϕ_r to denote the set of clock constraints on r.

Definition 2. $clock\_ref : R \to 2^N$ *maps transition* r *to the set* $\{j \mid t_j \sim a \in \phi_r\}$. *Intuitively,* $clock\_ref(r)$ *is the set of (indices of) clocks that are referred to in the constraints on* r.

Given a timed automaton $\mathcal{A}$, we abstract from the specific syntax of the constraints and consider only the identities of the clocks that are used in them. This concept is formalized as follows:

Definition 3. *Let* $\mathcal{A} = \langle E, Q, Q_0, Q_f, V, R \rangle$. *The syntactic abstraction of* $\mathcal{A}$ *is defined as* $AbsSynt(\mathcal{A}) = \langle E, Q, Q_0, Q_f, V, R_c \rangle$, *where*

$$R_c = \{(s, q, e, \lambda, clock\_ref(r)) \mid r = (s, q, e, \lambda, \phi) \in R\}.$$

---

[1]   If a transition leads only to paths on which t_j is not used, the reset (and the clock that is reset) will be eliminated by our algorithms.

[2]   One could argue that the optimal number of clocks of a timed automaton is zero when the accepted language is empty.

Let TA be a given set of timed automata. The function $AbsSynt$ induces a "natural" division of TA into equivalence classes[3] (of course, this has nothing to do with the equivalence of automata in the usual sense). We will use $C(\mathcal{A})$ to denote the equivalence class of $\mathcal{A} \in TA$, i.e., $C(\mathcal{A}) = \{a \in TA \mid AbsSynt(a) = AbsSynt(\mathcal{A})\}$.

Given a timed automaton $\mathcal{A} \in TA$, our method of clock allocation is carried out on $AbsSynt(\mathcal{A})$. It will be clear from the construction that the clock allocation is correct and optimal for the entire equivalence class of $\mathcal{A}$, in the following sense:

1. *Correctness:* if we systematically replace the clocks (as prescribed by the computed allocation) in any timed automaton belonging to $C(\mathcal{A})$, then the resulting automaton will accept the same language as the original one.
2. *Optimality:* any allocation with fewer clocks would be incorrect, i.e., there would exist at least one timed automaton $\mathcal{B} \in C(\mathcal{A})$, for which it would change the accepted language.

The reason we perform this abstraction is that in our analysis we do not want to concern ourselves with "pathological" cases in which the required number of clocks is strongly affected by some particular form of the constraints. An example of such a pathological case is an automaton with a clock c, such that all the clock constraints on c are of the form $c \geq 0$, which is always true. Clearly, in an optimal clock allocation clock c can be safely removed.

5   Finding an Optimal Allocation of Clocks

Our objective is to transform a timed automaton $\mathcal{A} \in TA_{DS}$ to an equivalent automaton $\mathcal{A}'$ with the same graph and the same set of constraints (modulo clock renaming), but with a number of clocks that is *optimal* in the sense defined in Sect. 4. This is done in four steps:

1. *Liveness analysis* identifies the *ranges* of clocks in $\mathcal{A}$.
2. The original clocks are replaced with new clocks in a way that takes ranges into account but minimizes the number of clocks.
3. Old clock resets are deleted and new clock resets are generated.
4. Existing clock constraints are rewritten in terms of the new clocks.

5.1   Liveness Analysis of Clocks

Assume $\mathcal{A} = \langle E, Q, \{q^0\}, Q_f, V, R \rangle \in TA_{DS}$ is the original timed automaton and L is the aforementioned labelling function.

If $r = (s, q, e, \lambda, \phi) \in R$, then λ_r is used to denote the set of clocks to be reset on r. Notice that $|\lambda_r| \leq 1$ (since $\mathcal{A} \in TA_{DS}$).

If $p = r_1...r_k$ is a path, then $transitions(p) = \{r_1, ..., r_k\}$.

We use the following functions:

---

[3] Let $f : X \to Y$ be a total function. For any $D \subseteq X$, $\{(a,b) \in D^2 \mid f(a) = f(b)\}$ is an equivalence relation.

- $active : R \rightarrow 2^N$ maps transition r to the set $\{j \mid$ there is a path $rr_1...r_k$, $k \geq 1$, such that $j \in clock\_ref(r_k)$ and $t_j \notin \lambda_{r_i}$ for $1 \leq i < k\}$. Intuitively, $active(r)$ identifies clocks that are "alive" on r (i.e., their values may be subsequently used).
- $born : R \rightarrow 2^N$ maps transition r to the set $\{j \mid t_j \in \lambda_r \wedge j \in active(r)\}$. Intuitively, $born(r)$ identifies a clock that is reset on r whose value can be used on some transition reachable from r. Notice that $born(r) \subseteq active(r)$.
- $last\_ref : R \rightarrow 2^N$ maps transition r to $clock\_ref(r) \backslash active(r)$.
- $needed : R \rightarrow 2^N$ maps transition r to $active(r) \cup last\_ref(r)$.

A clock t_j is needed (or is active) on a transition r if $j \in needed(r)$ (or $j \in active(r)$).

Let r be a transition such that $j \in last\_ref(r)$. Then in the target timed automaton a (new) clock c that has been assigned to the old clock t_j can be reassigned to another (old) clock and be reset on r.

In the automaton of Fig. 1, 0 is in both $active(r_2)$ and $clock\_ref(r_2)$, but not in $last\_ref(r_2)$. On r_6, $0 \in clock\_ref(r_6)$, but $0 \notin active(r_6)$, so $0 \in last\_ref(r_6)$.

Lemma 1. *For a timed automaton in TA_{DS} with its set of locations Q, we have*

$$\forall_{q \in Q} \forall_{r_i, r_k \in in(q)} \ active(r_i) = active(r_k).$$

Proof. Assume $j \in active(r_i)$. Then there is a transition r in $out(q)$ such that $j \in needed(r)$. But r can be reached from r_k, therefore $j \in active(r_k)$. The rest of the proof follows from symmetry.   □

Definition 4. *A path $p = r_0...r_n$ is a path for clock t_j iff $born(r_0) = \{j\}$ and $j \in needed(r_i)$ for $0 \leq i \leq n$.*

In the automaton of Fig. 1, $r_1 r_2 r_4 r_6$ is a path for clock t_0, as is $r_1 r_2 r_4$, $r_1 r_2$ or just r_1. Similarly, $r_2 r_3 r_5$ is a path for clock t_1. Finally, $r_3 r_5 r_7$ and $r_4 r_6 r_7$ are paths for clock t_2.

Definition 5. *$range : N \times R \rightarrow 2^R$ maps (j, r) to $\{r' \mid r' \in transitions(p)$, where p is a path for clock t_j that starts at $r\}$.*

Intuitively, $range(j, r)$, where $j \in born(r)$, is the set of transitions in all the paths for clock t_j that begin at r. If $range(j, r) \neq \emptyset$, then we say it is a *range for clock t_j.*

In the automaton of Fig. 1, $range(0, r_1) = \{r_1, r_2, r_4, r_6\}$, $range(1, r_2) = \{r_2, r_3, r_5\}$, $range(2, r_3) = \{r_3, r_5, r_7\}$, and $range(2, r_4) = \{r_4, r_6, r_7\}$.

We will use the term *active range* to denote that set of transitions in the range on which the clock in question is active.

Liveness analysis of clocks is performed by Algorithm 1. Given an automaton $\mathcal{A} \in TA_{DS}$, the algorithm determines, in effect, the ranges of all the clocks in $\mathcal{A}$.

We assume the existence of the following four functions:

- $ancestor\_transitions : R \rightarrow 2^R$ maps transition r to the set of transitions from which it can be reached by some non-empty path.

Algorithm 1: Computing *active* and *born*

Input : A timed automaton $\mathcal{A} = \langle E, Q, \{q^0\}, Q_f, V, R \rangle$, a labelling
function L, functions *ancestor_transitions* and *dominated*.
Output: Functions *active* and *born*.

foreach *transition* $r \in R$ *in* $\mathcal{A}$ **do**
   $born(r) := active(r) := \emptyset$;

foreach *clock number* $j \in N$ **do**
   $active\_on(j) := \emptyset$;

foreach *transition* $r \in R$ *in* $\mathcal{A}$ **do**
   foreach *clock number* $j \in clock\_ref(r)$ **do**
     /* Dealing with cycles.   */
     $tmp := ancestor\_transitions(r) \setminus trans\_to\_source(r)$;
     $tmp := tmp \cap dominated(L^{-1}(j))$;
     if $tmp \cap out(target(r)) \neq \emptyset$ **then**
       $tmp := tmp \cup \{r\}$;
     $active\_on(j) := active\_on(j) \cup tmp$;

foreach *transition* $r = (s, q, e, \lambda, \phi) \in R$ *of* $\mathcal{A}$ **do**
   if $L(s) = j$ *and* $r \in active\_on(j)$ **then**
     $born(r) := \{j\}$;

foreach *clock number* $j \in N$ **do**
   foreach *transition* $r \in active\_on(j)$ **do**
     $active(r) := active(r) \cup \{j\}$;

- *dominated* : $Q \to 2^R$ maps location q to the set of transitions that are dominated by q.
- *active_on* : $N \to 2^R$ maps clock number j to the set of transitions on which j is active.
- *trans_to_source* : $R \times N \to 2^R$ maps transition r and clock number j to the set of transitions on all paths that begin with r and end at $L^{-1}(j)$.

Assuming that sets are implemented as bit vectors and that bit vector operations take constant time, the worst-case complexity of Algorithm 1 is $O(|R||N|)$.

For the automaton of Fig. 1, we show the values of *active* and *born* obtained by Algorithm 1 for two transitions: $born(r_4) = \{2\}$, $active(r_4) = \{0, 2\}$ and $born(r_6) = \emptyset$, $active(r_6) = \{2\}$. Notice that both clocks t_0 and t_2 are needed at r_4 and r_6.

5.2 Clock Allocation

After liveness analysis has generated the annotations in our automaton, the next step is to use these annotations to allocate new clocks. This is done by an algorithm that replaces the clocks of the original timed automaton with new ones, while minimizing their number. The general idea is that, once a clock is reset on a transition on which it is born, it should never be reset again within the relevant active range; however, the clock can be reused outside that active range, provided that certain consistency requirements are satisfied.

We begin by introducing some additional notation.

Let A, B and C be sets and let $r \subset A \times B \times C$. The relation r can be applied to an argument $a \in A$ by using the left-associative operator ".": $r.a = \{(b, c) \mid (a, b, c) \in r\}$. Similarly, for $b \in B$, $r.a.b = \{c \mid (b, c) \in r.a\}$.

If, for every $(a, b) \in A \times B$, $r.a.b$ is either a singleton or the empty set, then r is a function of two arguments: $r : A \times B \to C$. If $r.a.b$ is never the empty set, then the function is total, otherwise it is partial.

If r is a function of two arguments, then $r.a.b = \{c\}$ is often written as $r(a, b) = c$ and $r.a.b = \{\}$ as $r(a, b) = \bot$.

Next, we formally define clock allocations. We assume the existence of a set $\mathcal{C}$, disjoint from V, with $|R|$ clock variables (this is enough, since at most one clock is reset on any given transition).

Definition 6. *Given a timed automaton $\mathcal{A}$ with the set R of transitions and the set N of clock numbers, a clock allocation for $\mathcal{A}$ is a relation $alloc \subset R \times \mathcal{C} \times N$ such that $(r, c, j) \in alloc \Rightarrow j \in active(r)$.*

Inclusion of (r, c, j) in *alloc* represents the fact that on transition r clock c is associated with the old clock t_j (i.e., c will eventually replace t_j on r).

Definition 7. *A clock allocation alloc is* inconsistent *iff there exist two overlapping paths for some clock t_j, p and p' (which need not be different), some $c \in \mathcal{C}$ and $r_k, r_l \in transitions(p) \cup transitions(p')$ such that*
$$j \in active(r_k) \wedge j \in active(r_l) \wedge (r_k, c, j) \in alloc \wedge (r_l, c, j) \notin alloc.$$
alloc is consistent *iff it is not inconsistent.*

(Notice that the paths may overlap on a transition r on which the clock is not active, i.e., we may have $t_j \in last\_ref(r)$.)

Definition 8. *A clock allocation alloc is* correct *if:*

- *alloc is a function, i.e., $alloc : R \times \mathcal{C} \to N$;*
- *alloc is consistent.*

Intuitively, the fact that *alloc* is a function means simply that, on any given transition, a clock c can be associated with at most one (old) clock t_j. Note that it is possible for a correct allocation to associate two or more (new) clocks with the same (old) clock on the same path. It is also possible for different clocks to be associated with the same (old) clock t_j on different paths for t_j, as long as the paths are disjoint.

Definition 9. *A clock allocation is* lean *if it is an injective function.*

Intuitively, a lean allocation does not associate a clock on a transition with more than one (new) clock.

Definition 10. *A clock allocation alloc is* complete *iff, for every transition $r \in R$ and every $j \in active(r)$, there is a clock $c \in \mathcal{C}$ such that $(r, c, j) \in alloc$.*

Observation 1. *Let $\mathcal{A}$ be a timed automaton with the set of transitions R, and let alloc be a complete, correct and lean clock allocation for $\mathcal{A}$. Then the following holds:* $\forall_{r \in R} |alloc.r| = |active(r)|$.

Definition 11. *We define the number of clocks used in an allocation by:*
$$cost(alloc) = |\{c \in \mathcal{C} \mid \exists_{r \in R} \exists_{j \in N} (r, c, j) \in alloc\}|.$$

Definition 12. *Let $\mathcal{A}$ be a timed automaton and let alloc be a complete and correct clock allocation for $\mathcal{A}$. The allocation alloc is* optimal *if there is no complete correct allocation alloc′ for $\mathcal{A}$ such that $cost(alloc') < cost(alloc)$* [13].

Theorem 1. *Let $\mathcal{A}$ be a timed automaton with the set of locations Q, and let alloc be a complete and correct clock allocation for $\mathcal{A}$. Then the following holds:*
$$\forall_{s \in Q} \forall_{r_i, r_k \in in(s)} alloc.r_i = alloc.r_k.$$

Proof. $alloc.r_i = alloc.r_k$ is equivalent to

$$\forall_{j \in N} \forall_{c \in \mathcal{C}} ((r_i, c, j) \in alloc \Leftrightarrow (r_k, c, j) \in alloc).$$

Let $s \in Q$ and $r_i, r_k \in in(s)$. Let j and c be such that $(r_i, c, j) \in alloc$. This implies that $j \in active(r_i)$. But then, from Lemma 1, we have $j \in active(r_k)$. Therefore there is some $r \in out(s)$ such that both the sequences $r_i r$ and $r_k r$ belong to paths for clock t_j (because j is needed on r). Since the paths overlap on r, from consistency of *alloc* we must have $(r_k, c, j) \in alloc$. The rest of the proof follows from symmetry. □

In the timed automaton of Fig. 1, assume that c_0 is associated with clock t_0, c_1 with clock t_1 and c_2 with clock t_2. Then,

$$\alpha = \{ r_1, c_0, 0), (r_2, c_0, 0), (r_2, c_1, 1), (r_3, c_1, 1), (r_3, c_2, 2),$$
$$r_4, c_0, 0), (r_4, c_2, 2), (r_5, c_2, 2), (r_6, c_2, 2) \}$$

is a lean, correct and consistent allocation. Notice that $1 \in last\_ref(r_5)$, so $active(r_5)$ does not include clock number 1. Similarly, clock t_0 is not active on transition r_6. So $\alpha.r_5 = \alpha.r_6 = \{(c_2, 2)\}$, in accordance with Theorem 1.

The theorem has two important implications for an algorithm that computes a clock allocation:

- Information about the allocations on all the incoming transitions of a location can be stored in the location itself.
- The exact order in which the transitions of the automaton are traversed need not be important.

These points will become clear as we present our clock allocation algorithm.

5.3   The Clock Allocation Algorithm

We describe our algorithm in two steps: in the first step we present the algorithm for tree-shaped automata, where the root of the tree is the initial location; in the second step we extend the algorithm to allocate clocks for an arbitrary timed automaton in TA_{DS}. We do so not because we think that tree-shaped automata are particularly important, but in the hope of helping the reader's intuition.

The Clock Allocation Algorithm for Tree-Shaped Automata. The tree variant is presented as Algorithm 2, which begins with an initial pool of available clocks, $\mathcal{C}$, and the set of used clocks, $\mathcal{U}$, which is initially empty. We assume that the clocks in $\mathcal{C}$ are numbered: the algorithm always allocates that available clock which has the smallest number.

The algorithm performs a depth first walk of the automaton, beginning at the initial location, and annotates each location with a set of available clocks and a set of *clock assignments*. An assignment is a pair (c, j), where c is the clock that replaces the (old) clock t_j. More precisely, we define the following functions:

- $pool : Q \rightarrow 2^{\mathcal{C}}$ maps a location s to the set of clocks available at s;
- $assignments : Q \rightarrow 2^{\mathcal{C} \times N}$ maps s to the set of clock assignments at s.

As the algorithm annotates each location s with $assignments(s)$ and $pool(s)$, it ensures that every (old) clock t_j and every (new) clock c appear at most once in $assignments(s)$, and a clock c appears either in $assignments(s)$ or in $pool(s)$.

Every time the algorithm visits a transition where a clock, e.g., t_j is born, it associates a clock, say c, with j. If c has never been used before, it is added to $\mathcal{U}$. When the algorithm visits a transition r where $j \in last\_ref(r)$, it restores c to the pool of available clocks. When the algorithm stops, $\mathcal{U}$ contains the clocks of the target automaton: $|\mathcal{U}|$ can be significantly smaller than $|\mathcal{C}|$.

Observe that the resulting allocation is obviously complete. Also, the following theorem holds:

Theorem 2. *The allocation found by Algorithm 2 is correct and lean.*

Proof. On any transition where a clock, say t_j, of the original timed automaton is born, one (new) clock, e.g., c, is assigned to j. Moreover, c is not, on that transition, assigned to any other i (corresponding to clock t_i). A clock is assigned to a clock number i only when t_i is born. So the allocation is always an injective function, i.e., it is lean.

To see that the allocation is consistent, take any path p for some clock t_j. A clock c is assigned to j only on the first transition of p. At that point c is removed from the pool and is not returned there before p ends. It is therefore impossible for c to be assigned to any i on any transition r of p such that $j \in active(r)$.

Observe that if there is another path for t_j, say p', that shares a transition with p, then p and p' will have a common initial transition, because the graph of the automaton is a tree. In that case c will be assigned to j on that transition, and will not be assigned to another clock number on any transition r of p or p' such that $j \in active(r)$.   □

We now turn our attention to the general case, i.e., when the timed automaton $\mathcal{A}$ is not necessarily a tree.

The Clock Allocation Algorithm for General Automata. Algorithm 2, when applied to general automata, would trace out a spanning tree of $\mathcal{A}$, and the resulting allocation would still be an injective function. It might not, however, be consistent. An inconsistency can arise only in a situation similar to the one illustrated in Fig. 2. Two paths for a clock t_j have different initial transitions:

Algorithm 2: Assigning clocks to a tree-shaped automaton in TA_{DS}

Input : A timed automaton $\mathcal{A} = \langle E, Q, \{q^0\}, Q_f, V, R \rangle$, the initial pool of
available clocks $\mathcal{C}$, and functions *active* and *born*.
Output: Functions *pool* and *assignments*, and the set $\mathcal{U} \subseteq \mathcal{C}$ of clocks used.

$\mathcal{U} := assignments(q^0) := \emptyset$;
$pool(q^0) := \mathcal{C}$;
foreach $r = (s, q, e, \lambda, \phi) \in R$, *in a depth first order* **do**
$\quad$ **if** *q has not been visited yet* **then**
$\qquad$ $tmp\_pool := pool(s)$;
$\qquad$ $tmp\_assignments := assignments(s)$;
$\qquad$ $source\_active := \{j \mid (c, j) \in assignments(s),$ for some $c\}$;
$\qquad$ **foreach** $j \in source\_active \backslash active(r)$ **do**
$\qquad\quad$ /* $j \in$ last_ref(r) */
$\qquad\quad$ $tmp\_assignments := tmp\_assignments \backslash \{(c, j)\}$, where
$\qquad\qquad$ $(c, j) \in assignments(s)$;
$\qquad\quad$ $tmp\_pool := tmp\_pool \cup \{c\}$, where $(c, j) \in assignments(s)$;
$\qquad$ **if** $born(r) \neq \emptyset$ **then**
$\qquad\quad$ $tmp\_pool := tmp\_pool \backslash \{d\}$, where d is the clock in tmp_pool
$\qquad\qquad$ which has the smallest number;
$\qquad\quad$ $tmp\_assignments := tmp\_assignments \cup \{(d, j)\}$,
$\qquad\qquad$ where $born(r) = \{j\}$;
$\qquad\quad$ $\mathcal{U} := \mathcal{U} \cup \{d\}$;
$\qquad$ $pool(q) := tmp\_pool$;
$\qquad$ $assignments(q) := tmp\_assignments$;

---

r_1 and r_3. If on each of those transitions j were associated with a different (new) clock, then the values of the allocation on the paths that join at location q, in particular, on the transitions belonging to $in(q)$ would be different. So, Theorem 1 would not hold, even though the allocation would be complete and lean. We will call location q a *problematic location with respect to* j. Note that j is needed in the outgoing transition of q. The algorithm must be augmented to ensure that the same clock is assigned to j on all transitions in $out(s)$ (where $L(s) = j$) that can lead to the same problematic location q.

These considerations can be formalised as follows:

Definition 13. *Let $R_0 = range(j, r_0)$ and $R_1 = range(j, r_1)$ be two ranges of a clock t_j that start on some transitions r_0 and r_1. R_0 is related to R_1 iff (1) R_0 and R_1 intersect, or (2) R_1 intersects with some range of clock t_j, say R_2, and R_2 is related to R_0.*

Definition 14. *Let S be a range of clock t_j. We use $Rel(j, S)$ to denote the set of all ranges of t_j that are related to S.*

Notice that a range is related to itself, and $Rel(j, S)$ can be a singleton. Moreover, the set of ranges of clock t_j is partitioned by sets of the form $Rel(j, p)$, where p is a range for clock t_j.

Definition 15. *Let $A = Rel(j, S)$ for some j and S. The set of all those transitions belonging to members of A on which t_j is active is a* family for t_j.

In Fig. 1, $range(2, r_3) = \{r_3, r_5, r_7\}$ and $range(2, r_4) = \{r_4, r_6, r_7\}$ are related. If we choose, say, $S = range(2, r_3)$, then $Rel(2, S) = \{\{r_3, r_5, r_7\}, \{r_4, r_6, r_7\}\}$. The only family for t_2 is $\{r_3, r_4, r_5, r_6\}$ (t_2 is not active on r_7).

Observe that each family for a clock t_j must begin at the same location: location s, where $L(s) = j$. It is easy to determine whether two initial transitions for some clock t_j belong to the same family: we must check whether they can lead to the same problematic location.

In the automaton of Fig. 2 we see two families for clock t_j. The first is generated by paths for t_j that begin with r_1 and r_3: those transitions in these paths on which t_j is active form a family, because of the problematic location q. The second family is generated by paths that begin with r_2 and r_4.

Figure 3 illustrates the transitive nature of a family: r_1, r_2 and r_3 belong to the same family, because of the problematic location n. Similarly, r_2 and r_4 belong to the same family on account of the problematic location q. Therefore r_1, r_2, r_3 and r_4 all belong to the same family.

Observation 2. *Let F be a family for some clock t_j, and let alloc be a complete correct allocation. Then there must exist a clock variable $c \in C$ such that $alloc.r.c = \{j\}$ for every transition $r \in F$ on which t_j is active. Otherwise alloc would be inconsistent. We say that c is* allocated to F.

In the automaton of Fig. 2, t_j must be associated with the same (new) clock, say c, on paths for clock t_j that begin at transitions r_1 and r_3. Similarly, t_j must be associated with the same clock (which can, but need not, be c) on paths that begin at r_2 and r_4, as their transitions belong to the same family.

Observation 3. *The number of families to which a transition r belongs is $|active(r)|$.*

Proof. Assume the number of families to which transition r belongs is n. Therefore, there are exactly n families for different clocks that share transition r (two families for the same clock cannot share r, or they would be the same family). Since t_j is active on all the transitions of a family for t_j, it follows that $active(r)$ contains exactly one element for each of the n families. □

Definition 16. *Two families, F_1 and F_2, belong to the same* cluster *iff $F_1 \cap F_2 \neq \emptyset$. A cluster cl is a maximal set of such families, i.e., every family outside cl does not overlap with at least one of the families in cl.*

Observe that the members of a cluster must be families for different clocks (otherwise they would not overlap). Observe also that a family can belong to more than one cluster.

We say transition r *belongs* to cluster $\mathcal{F}$, if there is a family $F \in \mathcal{F}$, such that $r \in F$. Notice that if $active(r) = \emptyset$, then r does not belong to any family; therefore, it does not belong to any cluster.

Since each pair of families in a cluster shares some common transition, we immediately see the following:

Observation 4. *Every family in a cluster must be allocated a different clock.*

In the automaton of Fig. 1, there is only one cluster, and it contains all the three families: $\{r_1, r_2, r_4\}$ for clock t_0, $\{r_2, r_3\}$ for clock t_1 and $\{r_3, r_4, r_5, r_6\}$ for clock t_2. Obviously, a correct allocation for the automaton requires three clocks, even though no more than two clocks are needed on any particular transition.

Definition 17. *The* size *of a cluster is the cardinality of the set of families that form the cluster.*

Theorem 3. *Let alloc be a complete correct allocation for a timed automaton $\mathcal{A}$. Then cost(alloc) cannot be smaller than the size of the largest cluster in $\mathcal{A}$.*

Proof. This is a direct consequence of Observations 2 and 4.   □

We are now ready to return to a detailed description of the general algorithm.

To take into account the problematic locations, at each location s labelled with some j, the outgoing transitions of s are divided into two sets: (i) the set of "mother" transitions, i.e., $\{r \in out(s) \mid born(r) = \{j\}\}$ and (ii) the set of "other" transitions, i.e., $\{r \in out(s) \mid born(r) = \emptyset\}$. Observe that the mother transitions are the initial transitions of all the families for clock t_j. The mother transitions require special attention, while the other transitions are processed as before. The set of mother transitions is divided into groups. Each group is the set of initial transitions of a family for clock t_j. *All transitions belonging to the same group must obtain the same clock assignment for clock number j* (see Observation 2). Notice that if for some clock, say t_i, $i \in last\_ref(r)$ for *every* transition r in the group, then the clock previously assigned to i becomes available and can be assigned to j.

It is a direct consequence of Theorem 1 that the choice of the path taken by the algorithm to reach location s has no effect on the values of *assignments(s)* and *pool(s)* (assuming that the algorithm produces a correct allocation).

A status is assigned to each location which will advance through the following sequence: *Unseen, Seen,* and *Visited.* Whenever a location is visited for the first time, all its immediate successors are annotated, and thus become *Seen.* A location is visited only after it has been annotated (and its status is *Seen*). To start the process and establish the invariants, the algorithm begins by annotating the initial location. We assume the existence of the following two functions:

- *reachable* : $Q \rightarrow 2^Q$ maps location q to the set of locations that are reachable from q by some non-empty path.
- *reachable_from* : $Q \rightarrow 2^Q$ maps location q to the set of locations from which it can be reached by some non-empty path.

The general clock allocation is implemented by Algorithm 4, which consists of a collection of procedures. To make the algorithm more efficient, for every clock t_i of $\mathcal{A}$, the set of *potentially* problematic locations with respect to i, i.e., $pp(i)$, is computed in advance by Algorithm 3.

Algorithm 3: Identifying potentially problematic locations

Input : A timed automaton $\mathcal{A} = \langle E, Q, \{q^0\}, Q_f, V, R \rangle$, function *active*, and the set N of clock numbers.

Output: A mapping from each clock number to the set of potentially problematic locations with respect to that clock number.

foreach $j \in N$ **do**
    $pp(j) := \emptyset$;

foreach $q \in Q$ **do**
    foreach j *such that there are two different transitions* $r, r' \in in(q)$
    where $j \in active(r) \cap active(r')$ **do**
       $pp(j) := pp(j) \cup \{q\}$;

Algorithm 4: allocating clocks to a general automaton in TA_{DS}

Input : A timed automaton $\mathcal{A} = \langle E, Q, \{q^0\}, Q_f, V, R \rangle$, the initial pool of available clocks $\mathcal{C}$, and functions *active* and *born*.

Output: Annotations for locations.

foreach *location* $s \in Q$ **do**
    Set the status of s to *Unseen*;

$annotate(q^0, \mathcal{C}, \emptyset)$;
$visit(q^0)$;

Procedure annotate(location q, set of clocks p, set of assignments a)

```
/* Invoked only when status of q is Unseen. */
```
$pool(q) := p$;
$assignments(q) := a$;
Set the status of q to *Seen*;

Procedure visit(location q)

```
/* Invoked when the status of q is Seen or Visited. */
```
if *status of* q *is not Visited* **then**
    Set the status of q to *Visited*;
    annotate-immediate-successors(q);
    foreach $r \in out(q)$ **do**
       $visit(target(r))$;

After the clock allocation algorithm has terminated, the value of *alloc.r*, for every transition r, is given by *assignments*($target(r)$). The information is easily used to generate new resets and rename clocks in the constraints.

The time complexity is quadratic in the size of the graph.

Procedure annotate-immediate-successors(location q)

Partition $out(q)$ into *mothers* and *others*;

foreach $r \in others$ **do**

   if *status of target(r) is Unseen* **then**

      propagate($q, r, \emptyset$);

   /* Otherwise target(r) is already annotated: Theorem 1. */

if *mothers* $\neq \emptyset$ **then**

   $Groups :=$ *partition-into-a-set-of-groups*($q, mothers$);

   foreach *group* $\in Groups$ **do**

      $c :=$ *find-clock*($q, group$);

      foreach $r \in group$ **do**

         /* The target of r is Unseen: dominance assumption. */

         propagate($q, r, \{c\}$);

Procedure find-clock(location q, set of transitions *group*)

/* Find a clock for L(q) on transitions in group. */

$live\_on\_entry := \{j \mid (c, j) \in assignments(q)\}$;

$dying\_all := \bigcap_{r \in group}(live\_on\_entry \setminus active(r))$;

/* Clocks whose ranges end in all the transitions in group: */

$released\_all := \{c \mid (c, j) \in assignments(q) \wedge j \in dying\_all\}$;

$available := released\_all \cup pool(q)$;

Return the clock with the smallest number in *available*;

Procedure propagate(location q, transition r, set of clocks *sc*)

/* Invoked only when the target of r is Unseen. q is the source
of r. Propagate assignments(q) and pool(q) to target(r),
taking into account that some clock ranges may end on r. If sc
is not empty, it must be a singleton: assign its member to
clock number L(q). */

$freed\_assignments := \{(d, j) \mid (d, j) \in assignments(q) \wedge j \notin active(r)\}$;

$freed\_clocks := \{d \mid (d, j) \in freed\_assignments\}$;

$tmp\_pool := pool(q) \cup freed\_clocks$;

$tmp\_assignments := assignments(q) \setminus freed\_assignments$;

if $sc \neq \emptyset$ **then**

   $tmp\_pool := tmp\_pool \setminus sc$;

   $tmp\_assignments := tmp\_assignments \cup \{(c, L(q))\}$, where $c \in sc$;

$annotate(target(r), tmp\_pool, tmp\_assignments)$;

The resulting allocation is obviously complete. Also, the algorithm satisfies the following theorem:

Procedure partition-into-a-set-of-groups(location q, set of transitions *mothers*)

$mother\_targets := \{target(r) \mid r \in mothers\}$;
/* Initially, each mother is in its own group. */
$Groups := \emptyset$;
foreach $r \in mothers$ **do**
  $\lfloor$ $Groups := Groups \cup \{r\}$;

/* Those locations in pp(L(q)) that can be reached from more than
   one mother are the problematic locations. */
foreach $s \in pp(L(q))$ **do**
  | $targets := reachable\_from(s) \cap mother\_targets$;
  | Merge those members of *Groups* that contain transitions whose target is
  $\lfloor$ in *targets*;
return *Groups*;

Theorem 4. *The computed allocation is correct and lean.*

Proof. All the paths for a clock t_j begin at the same location. The initial transitions of these paths (the "mother" transitions) are partitioned into groups. The members of a group are exactly the initial transitions of a family for t_j. The algorithm associates some clock with a group: the association is propagated to all the transitions of the paths for t_j that begin in the group, therefore there is no pair of transitions that satisfies the definition of inconsistency.

When some clock c is assigned to j on the transitions of a group, t_j is the only clock that is born, so c is not, on those transitions, assigned to any i such that $i \neq j$. Moreover, after c is assigned to j, it is removed from the pool and returned only on transitions on which t_j is not active. Therefore c cannot be assigned to any other i on any transition r such that $j \in active(r)$. So the allocation is always an injective function, i.e., it is lean. □

Lemma 2. *Assume alloc is a complete, correct and lean allocation. Then, for any transition r, the number of clocks in alloc.r is not greater than the size of the largest cluster to which r belongs.*

Proof. Assume cluster $\mathcal{F}$ with size n is the largest cluster to which r belongs. Suppose that $|alloc.r| > n$. By Observation 1, $|active(r)| = n' > n$. By Observation 3, the number of families to which r belongs is n'. This implies that r belongs to a cluster $\mathcal{F}'$ whose size is n', which contradicts the assumption. □

Theorem 5. *The computed allocation is optimal.*

Proof. This is a direct consequence of Lemma 2, Theorem 3, Theorem 4 and the fact that the algorithm always allocates the available clock with the smallest number, i.e., a new clock is added to the set of used clocks only when none of those already in the set will do. □

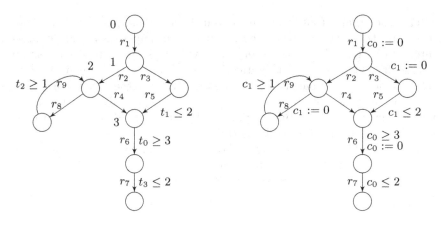

Fig. 4. Two equivalent timed automata

5.4   Generating Clock Constraints and Clock Resets

The final step of our clock allocation method is to generate clock resets and constraints and assign them to the transitions. This step is performed as follows.

Let $r = (s, q, e, \lambda, \phi) \in R$ be a transition, and let $t_j \sim a$ be a constraint on r. Then the constraint will be transformed into $c \sim a$, where $(c, j) \in assignments(q)$.

Clock resets are generated by identifying transitions at which ranges begin. For a transition $r = (s, q, e, \lambda, \phi) \in R$, the clock reset $d := 0$ will be added to transition r if $born(r) = \{i\}$ and $(d, i) \in assignments(q)$.

Figure 4 shows a timed automaton in TA_{DS} along with an equivalent automaton obtained by our clock allocation method: the set of clocks $\{t_0, t_1, t_2, t_3\}$ of the original automaton is replaced by the set $\{c_0, c_1\}$. Observe that the range of clock t_0 that begins at transition r_1 ends on transition r_6 where clock t_3 is born, so the same clock, namely c_0, is assigned to both t_1 and t_3. On transition r_6 the value of clock c_0 is used to check the satisfiability of clock constraint $c_0 \leq 2$ before it is assigned to t_3.

6   Related Work and Conclusions

We study the problem of optimal clock allocation for TA_{DS} (see Definition 1 on p. 4). TA_{DS} is a class of timed automata with some interesting properties. The characteristics of automata belonging to this class allowed us to formulate a particularly efficient clock allocation method, based on liveness analysis of clocks. Given a timed automaton $\mathcal{A} \in TA_{DS}$, the method finds an optimal (in the sense used in our earlier work [13]) clock allocation for $\mathcal{A}$ and replaces the original clocks of $\mathcal{A}$ with a new set whose size is minimal, without changing the graph or the form of the constraints in $\mathcal{A}$.

Our approach is different from our earlier method [13], in which the optimal clock allocation problem for automata in $TA_S \supsetneq TA_{DS}$ is solved by colouring an interference graph that is obtained from liveness analysis. That method is more general than the one developed in the current paper, as it can be applied to automata in $TA_S \setminus TA_{DS}$. However, our new liveness analysis is much simpler and more efficient, as it takes advantage of the properties of automata in TA_{DS}.

The worst-case complexity of liveness analysis in the cited work [13] is $O(|Q|^4)$, where Q is the set of locations. The liveness analysis in the current paper has the worst-case complexity of $O(|R||N|)$, where R is the set of transitions and $|N|$ is the number of clocks that are *used*.

Being customized for automata in TA_{DS}, the clock allocation algorithm itself is simple and efficient. Even though the interference graph for automata in TA_{DS} is chordal and can be coloured in $O(|R| + |Q|)$, the cost of constructing the interference graph is $O(|Q|^3)$. The complexity of our clock allocation is $O(|Q|^2)$.

References

1. Abdulla, P.A., Deneux, J., Ouaknine, J., Worrell, J.: Decidability and complexity results for timed automata via channel machines. In: Caires, L., Italiano, G.F., Monteiro, L., Palamidessi, C., Yung, M. (eds.) ICALP 2005. LNCS, vol. 3580, pp. 1089–1101. Springer, Heidelberg (2005). https://doi.org/10.1007/11523468_88
2. Alur, R., Dill, D.L.: A theory of timed automata. Theor. Comput. Sci. **126**(2), 183–235 (1994)
3. Alur, R., Madhusudan, P.: Decision problems for timed automata: a survey. In: Bernardo, M., Corradini, F. (eds.) SFM-RT 2004. LNCS, vol. 3185, pp. 1–24. Springer, Heidelberg (2004). https://doi.org/10.1007/978-3-540-30080-9_1
4. Baier, C., Bertrand, N., Bouyer, P., Brihaye, T.: When are timed automata determinizable? In: Albers, S., Marchetti-Spaccamela, A., Matias, Y., Nikoletseas, S., Thomas, W. (eds.) ICALP 2009. LNCS, vol. 5556, pp. 43–54. Springer, Heidelberg (2009). https://doi.org/10.1007/978-3-642-02930-1_4
5. Bengtsson, J., Larsen, K., Larsson, F., Pettersson, P., Yi, W.: UPPAAL—a tool suite for automatic verification of real-time systems. In: Alur, R., Henzinger, T.A., Sontag, E.D. (eds.) HS 1995. LNCS, vol. 1066, pp. 232–243. Springer, Heidelberg (1996). https://doi.org/10.1007/BFb0020949
6. Clarke, E.M., Jr., Grumberg, O., Peled, D.A.: Model Checking. MIT Press, Cambridge (1999)
7. Daws, C., Yovine, S.: Reducing the number of clock variables of timed automata. In: Proceedings of the 17th IEEE Real-Time Systems Symposium (RTSS 1996), 4–6 December 1996, Washington, DC, USA, pp. 73–81 (1996)
8. Finkel, O.: Undecidable problems about timed automata. CoRR abs/0712.1363 (2007)
9. Guha, S., Narayan, C., Arun-Kumar, S.: Reducing clocks in timed automata while preserving bisimulation. In: Baldan, P., Gorla, D. (eds.) CONCUR 2014. LNCS, vol. 8704, pp. 527–543. Springer, Heidelberg (2014). https://doi.org/10.1007/978-3-662-44584-6_36
10. Lengauer, T., Tarjan, R.E.: A fast algorithm for finding dominators in a flowgraph. ACM Trans. Program. Lang. Syst. **1**(1), 121–141 (1979)
11. Pereira, F.M.Q., Palsberg, J.: Register allocation via coloring of chordal graphs. In: Yi, K. (ed.) APLAS 2005. LNCS, vol. 3780, pp. 315–329. Springer, Heidelberg (2005). https://doi.org/10.1007/11575467_21

12. Saeedloei, N., Kluźniak, F.: From Scenarios to Timed Automata. In: Proceedings of the Formal Methods: Foundations and Applications - 20th Brazilian Symposium, SBMF 2017, Recife, Brazil, 29 November–1 December 2017, pp. 33–51 (2017)
13. Saeedloei, N., Kluźniak, F.: Clock allocation in timed automata and graph colouring. In: Proceedings of the 21st International Conference on Hybrid Systems: Computation and Control (Part of CPS Week), HSCC 2018, Porto, Portugal, 11–13 April 2018, pp. 71–80 (2018). http://doi.acm.org/10.1145/3178126.3178138

Formalization of Functional Block Diagrams Using HOL Theorem Proving

Mohamed Abdelghany$^{(\boxtimes)}$ and Sofiène Tahar$^{(\boxtimes)}$

Department of Electrical and Computer Engineering, Concordia University,
Montreal, QC, Canada
{m_eldes,tahar}@ece.concordia.ca

Abstract. Functional Block Diagrams (FBD) are commonly used as a graphical representation for safety analysis in a wide range of complex engineering applications. An FBD models the stochastic behavior and cascading dependencies of system components or subsystems. Within FBD-based safety analysis, Event Trees (ET) dependability modeling techniques are typically used to associate all possible failure/success events to each subsystem. In this paper, we propose to use higher-order logic theorem proving for the formal modeling and step-analysis of FBDs. To this end, we develop a formalization in HOL4 enabling the mathematical modeling of the graphical diagrams of FBDs and the formal analysis of subsystem-level failure/reliability. The proposed FBD formalization in HOL4 is capable of analyzing *n-level* subsystems with *multi-state* system components and enables the formal FBD probabilistic analysis for any given probabilistic distribution and failure rates.

Keywords: Functional block diagrams · Event trees · Safety analysis · Higher-order logic · Theorem proving · HOL4

1 Introduction

In many safety-critical complex systems, a catastrophic accident may happen due to the coincident occurrence of multiple sudden events in different subsystem components. These undesirable accidents in safety-critical systems may result in huge financial losses and sometimes severe injury or fatalities. Therefore, the central safety inquiry in many complex systems is to identify the possible consequences given that one or more sudden events could happen at a subsystem level. For that purpose, several dependability modeling techniques have been developed for safety analysis of critical-systems, such as Fault Trees (FT) [14], Reliability Block Diagrams (RBD) [21] and Event Trees (ET) [18]. FTs and RBDs are used to either analyze the factors causing a complete system failure or the complete success relation ships of a system only, respectively. In contrast to FTs and RBDs, ETs provide a complete analysis for all possible complete/partial failure and success consequence scenarios that can occur in a system. Moreover, ET analysis can be used to associate failure and success events to all subsystems of a safety-critical system in more complex hierarchical structures, such as

© The Author(s), under exclusive license to Springer Nature Switzerland AG 2022
L. Lima and V. Molnár (Eds.): SBMF 2022, LNCS 13768, pp. 22–35, 2022.
https://doi.org/10.1007/978-3-031-22476-8_2

Functional Block Diagrams (FBD) [9]. An FBD is a graphical representation of the detailed system functionality and the functional relationship between all its subsystems that are represented as Functional Blocks (FB). Each FB describes the failure characteristics of a subsystem by modeling its component failure and success relationship in terms of an ET structure [18]. All these subsystem level ETs associated with their corresponding FBs are then composed together to build a complete subsystem-level ET model of a complex system.

Papazoglou [9] was the first researcher to lay down the mathematical foundations of ETs and FBDs in the late 90s, where the analysis is done purely manually using a paper-and-pencil approach. A major limitation in the manual approach is the possibility of human error-proneness. On the other hand, there exist several simulation ET tools, such as ITEM [11], Isograph [10], and EC Tree [20], which have been widely used to determine all possible failure and success consequence scenarios of realistic systems, like electrical power grids [16], nuclear power plants [19] and Electric railways [12]. However, simulation based analysis approaches lack the rigor of detailed proof steps and may not be scalable for large systems due to an explosion of the test cases. To the best of our knowledge, these tools have not been used for FBD modeling and analysis. On the other hand, such simulation approaches generally use approximate random-based algorithms, such as MATLAB Monte-Carlo Simulation (MCS) for ET analysis [13], for faster computation, which could introduce undesirable inaccuracies that can be deemed fatal for safety-critical systems.

Following the recommendations of safety standards, such as IEC 61850 [15], EN 50128 [6], and ISO 26262 [17], we propose to use formal techniques based on theorem proving for the safety analysis of complex systems. In particular, we use the HOL4 theorem prover [8], which provides the ability of verifying probabilistic mathematical expressions constructed in higher-order logic (HOL). Prior to our work, there were two notable projects for building frameworks to formally analyze FTs and RBDs. For instance, HOL4 has been previously used by Ahmad et al. in [5] to formalize Static FTs and RBDs. Furthermore, Elderhalli et al. in [7] had formalized Dynamic FTs and RBDs in the HOL4 theorem prover. All these formalizations are basically required to formally analyze either a system static/dynamic failure or static/dynamic success only. Therefore, in [2], Abdelghany *et al.* developed a HOL4 theory to reason about ETs considering both failure and success states of system components simultaneously. The authors proposed a new datatype EVENT_TREE consisting of ET basic constructors that can analyze large scale ET diagrams. Based on [2], Abdelghany *et al.* have also developed the formalizations of cause consequence diagrams (CCD) in HOL4 to enable formal failure analyses combining, respectively, ETs with FTs [3] and ETs with RBDs [4]. These works allow the reasoning about all possible complete/partial failure and success consequences events that can occur at the subsystem level. However, a limitation of CCD analysis is that we can only assign two states to each subsystem (failure or success). While for realistic systems, safety and reliability engineers need to assign *multi-states* to subsystem components (e.g., partial failure, partial success, complete failure, complete success). To this end, Functional Block Diagrams (FBD) would be the graphical representation of choice for the reliability analysis of *n-level* multi-state critical systems.

In this paper, we provide a formalization of Functional Block Diagrams that can mathematically model FBDs based on our ET theory in HOL4 to analyze multi-state subsystem components and obtain all possible consequence classes (e.g., partial failure, partial success, etc.) that can occur in the whole system at the subsystem level. The proposed formalization in HOL4 defines a basic FBD constructor *Functional Block* (FB), which can be used to build the mathematical expressions of *n-level* FBDs based on *multi-state* subsystem components. Also, the formalization of FBDs, in this paper, enables a formal probabilistic risk assessment of scalable graphical diagrams of FBDs that provides the reasoning support for formal safety analysis of complex systems at the subsystem-level based on any arbitrary probabilistic distribution and failure rates.

The rest of the paper is organized as follows: In Sect. 2, we review the recently developed ET theory in HOL4. Section 3 introduces the fundamentals of FBDs. In Sect. 4, we detail our proposed HOL4 formalization of FBDs. Lastly, Sect. 5 concludes the paper.

2   Preliminaries

Event Tree (ET) is a well-known probabilistic reliability and risk assessment technique, which provides all possible risk consequence scenarios that can occur in a safety-critical system, i.e., complete/partial failure and reliability [18]. An ET diagram starts by an *Initiating Node* from which all possible consequence scenarios of a sudden event that can occur in the system are drawn as *Branches* connected to *Proceeding Nodes* so that *only one* of these risk scenarios can occur, i.e., all possible ET consequence paths are *disjoint* and *distinct*.

2.1   Formal ET Modeling

The ET constructors are formally modeled using a new recursive datatype EVENT_TREE, in HOL4 as follows [1]:

Hol_datatype EVENT_TREE = ATOMIC of (event)|
                          NODE of (EVENT_TREE list)|
                          BRANCH of (event) (EVENT_TREE)

The type constructors NODE and BRANCH are recursive functions on EVENT_TREE-typed. Also, a semantic function is defined over the EVENT_TREE datatype that can yield a corresponding ET model as [1]:

Definition 1: *Event Tree*

⊢ ETREE (ATOMIC X) = X ∧
  ETREE (NODE (h::L)) = ETREE h ∪ (ETREE (NODE L)) ∧
  ETREE (BRANCH Y Z) = Y ∩ ETREE Z

The function ETREE takes a success/fail event Y, identified by an ET type constructor ATOMIC and returns the event Y. If the function ETREE takes a list XN of type EVENT_TREE, identified by a type constructor NODE, then it returns the union of all elements after applying the function ETREE on each element of the given list. Similarly, if the function ETREE takes a success/fail event X and a proceeding ET Z, identified by a type constructor of EVENT_TREE type, then it performs the intersection of the event Y with the ET Z after applying the function ETREE. A complete ET model should draw all possible consequence scenarios, called *paths*. Each *path* consists of a unique consequence of branch events associated with it. A function ET_{PATH} is defined to obtain a specific path in the ET model consisting of M branch events. This was done in HOL4 by using the HOL4 recursive function FOLDL that recursively applies the BRANCH ET constructor on a given list of different M branch events as [2]:

Definition 2: *ET Path of M Events*

⊢ ET_{PATH} p (EVENT$_1$::EVENT$_M$) =
   FOLDL (λa b. ETREE (BRANCH a b)) EVENT$_1$ EVENT$_M$

A function $\otimes_L$ is defined that can model an ET diagram with all possible scenarios for two consecutive node lists L_1 and L_2, as shown in Fig. 1a, based on the mathematical Cartesian product $\otimes$ concept, in HOL4 as [2]:

Definition 3: *Two Stair ET Generation*

⊢ $L_1 \otimes_L L_2$ =
   MAP (λa. MAP (λb. ETREE (BRANCH a b)) L_2) L_1

where the function $\otimes_L$ takes two different EVENT_TREE-typed lists and returns an EVENT_TREE-typed list by recursively mapping the BRANCH constructor on each element of the first NODE list paired with the entire second NODE list using the HOL4 mapping function MAP.

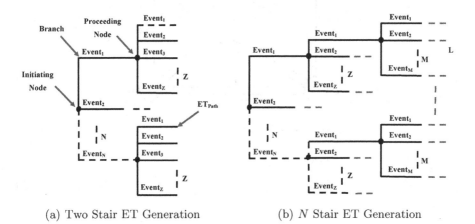

(a) Two Stair ET Generation   (b) *N* Stair ET Generation

Fig. 1. Generic ET model generation

Also, a function $\bigotimes_{L}^{N}$ is defined that generates a sequential and a complex ET model (see Fig. 1b) consisting of N components of a given system and each component is represented by a different M *multi-state* model for reliability studies (i.e., 2-state model, 3-state model, ..., M-state model), as shown in Fig. 2. in HOL4 as follows [2]:

Definition 4: N *Stair ET Generation*

$\vdash$ L $\bigotimes_{L}^{N}$ L$_N$ = FOLDR (λL$_1$ L$_2$. L$_1$ $\bigotimes_L$ L$_2$) L$_N$ L

where L is a *list* of all component states till $N - 1$ (i.e., L = [[$\mathcal{C}_1$]; [$\mathcal{C}_2$];...; [$\mathcal{C}_{N-1}$]]) and L$_N$ = [$\mathcal{C}_N$].

Moreover, a reduction function $\boxtimes^N$ is defined in [2] to reduce the generated complete ET model. Lastly, a partitioning function $\boxplus$ is defined to extract a collection of ET paths specified in the index list N from the reduced ET model L representing the possibilities of an accident event, in HOL4 as [2]:

Definition 5: *ET Paths Partitioning*

$\vdash$ N $\boxplus$ L = MAP (λa. EL a L) N

where the HOL4 function EL extracts a specific element from the given list.

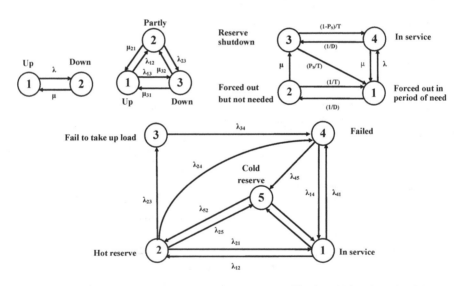

λ: Failure Rate   T: Average reserve shut-down time   P$_s$: Probability of starting failure

μ: Repair Rate   D: Average in-service time

Fig. 2. Multi-state models for safety studies

2.2   Formal ET Probabilistic Analysis

For the formal ET probabilistic analysis, Abdelghany *et al.* verified, in [2], several mathematical ET probabilistic formulations, as presented in Table 1.

Table 1. ET HOL4 probabilistic theorems [2]

EventTrees	ProbabilisticTheorems
	Theorem1: `probp` $\quad$`(ETREE` $\qquad$`(NODE(` $E_1::E_N$`)))` $= \sum$ `(Pr`$_L$ `p` $(E_1::E_N))$
	Theorem2: `probp` $\quad$`(ETREE` $\qquad$`(BRANCH Event`$_X$ $\qquad$`(NODE(` $E_1::E_Z$`))))` $=$`(probp` $\quad$ E_X`)` $\times \sum$ $\left(\text{Pr}_L \text{ p}(E_1::E_Z)\right)$
	Theorem3: `probp` $\quad$$\left(\text{ET}_{PATH} \text{ p}(E_1::E_M)\right)$ $= \prod$ $\left(\text{Pr}_L \text{ p}(E_1::E_M)\right)$
	Theorem4: `probp` $\quad$`(ETREE` $\qquad$`(NODE` $\qquad\quad$`(MAP(` λ`a. ET`$_{PATH}$ `pa)` $\qquad\qquad$`(Path`$_{1M}$`::Path`$_{NM}$`))))` $= \sum$ $\quad$`(MAP` $\qquad$`(`λ`a.` $\prod$ `(Pr`$_L$ `pa))(` `Path`$_{1M}$`::Path`$_{NM}$`)`

The probability of N events in an ET initiating node is verified as the sum of probabilities associated with the events of the given list. The probability of a branch success/fail event connected to a proceeding node is verified as

the multiplication of the branch event probability with the sum of the probabilities for the next proceeding node events. Also, the probability of ET_{PATH}
consisting of M ET branch events is verified as the multiplication of the individual probabilities of all the branch events associated with it. Moreover, a
two-dimensional probabilistic formulation is verified for extracting a collection of N paths and each of M success/fail events from an ET model, where
each path consists of an arbitrary list of events, as the sum of the individual
probabilities of all the paths associated with it. These mathematical expressions (Theorems 1–4) are verified under the ET constraints defined by Papazoglou [18] (a) all associated events in the given list X_N are drawn from the events
space p ($X_N \in$ events p); (b) p is a valid probability space (prob_space p);
(c) the events in the given list X_N are independent (MUTUAL_INDEP p X_N);
(d) each pair of elements in a given list X_N is distinct (ALL_DISTINCT X_N);
and lastly (e) each pair of elements in the given list X_N is mutually exclusive
(disjoint X_N). The elements in a list are intrinsically finite and thus all ET
constraint requirements are satisfied. The function Pr_L takes an arbitrary list
$[Z_1, Z_2, Z_3, \ldots, Z_N]$ and returns a list of probabilities associated with the elements of the list $[Pr(Z_1), Pr(Z_2), , \ldots, Pr(Z_{N-1}), Pr(Z_N)]$, while the function
$\prod$ takes a list $[Y_1, Y_2, Y_3, \ldots, Y_N]$ and returns the product of the list elements
$Y_1 \times Y_2 \times Y_3 \times \cdots \times Y_N$. The function $\sum$ takes a list $[X_1, X_2, X_3, \ldots, X_N]$ and
returns the sum of the list elements $X_1 + X_2 + X_3 + \cdots + X_N$.

3   Functional Block Diagrams

Functional Block Diagrams (FBDs) are a probabilistic risk assessment technique that can construct hierarchical ET structures to perform subsystem-level
reliability analysis for complex systems. A Functional Block (FB) is the basic
constructing element of an FBD graph that represents the stochastic behavior
of each subsystem in a safety-critical system. To present a clear understanding
of FBD-based safety analysis, consider a turbine governor system of a steam
power plant that controls the position of a steam inlet valve (V), which in turn
regulates the steam flow to the turbine and thus controls the output power. The
valve operates with an induction motor (IM) that is energized by a power supply (PS), as shown in Fig. 3. The main objective of the valve is to control the
Steam Flow (SF) at point B given the flow situation at point A and a command
signal C that dictates the required function of the valve, i.e. open or close. The
FBD *six* step-wise analysis, defined by Papazoglou [9], are as:

1. *FBD Construction*: A system FBD (decomposed into FBs) is constructed
   based on the engineering knowledge to describe the subsystem-level behavior,
   as shown in Fig. 4.
2. *ET Generation*: Construct a complete ET model corresponding to each subsystem FB. Assuming each subsystem component is represented by two operating states only, i.e., Success (S) or Fail (F). Figure 5 depicts the subsystem complete ETs, i.e., $ET_{1(Complete)}$, $ET_{2(Complete)}$ and $ET_{3(Complete)}$ corresponding to FB_1, FB_2 and FB_3, respectively, of the steam-turbine governor.

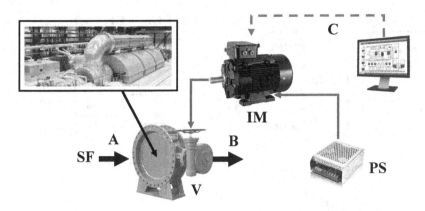

Fig. 3. Steam-turbine governor of a power plant

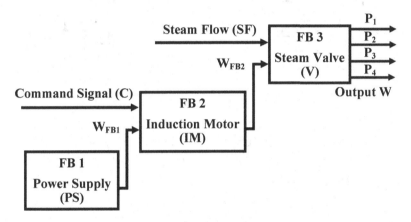

Fig. 4. FBD of steam-turbine governor

3. *ET Composition*: All ETs associated with their corresponding FBs are composed together considering the functional behavior of the governor system to form a complete subsystem-level ET model. For instance, $ET_{1(Complete)}$, $ET_{2(Complete)}$ and $ET_{3(Complete)}$ are composed to form the subsystem-level $ET_{Governor}$, as shown in Fig. 5, with all possible complete/partial failure and reliability ET consequence paths that can occur.

4. *Probabilistic Analysis*: Lastly, evaluate the probabilities of the system complete ET paths based on the occurrence of a certain event. These probabilities represent the likelihood of each unique sequence at the component-level that is possible to occur in a system so that *only one* can occur. For example, the probability of IM Complete Failure (CF) and Governor Complete Success (CS) shown in Fig. 5, i.e., $\sum_{probability(Paths\ 4-31)}$ and $Path_0$, respectively, can be expressed mathematically after shorthand as:

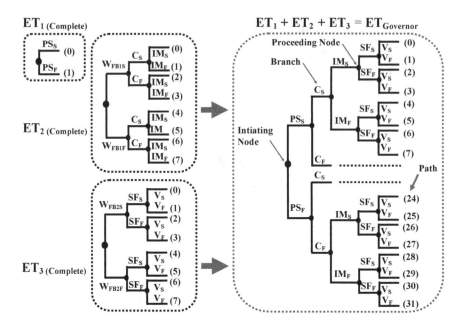

Fig. 5. Steam-turbine governor ET diagrams

$$Pr(\text{IM}_{CF}) = Pr(\text{PS}_S) \times Pr(\text{C}_S) \times Pr(\text{IM}_F) +$$
$$Pr(\text{PS}_S) \times Pr(\text{C}_F) + Pr(\text{PS}_F)$$
$$Pr(\text{Governor}_{CS}) = Pr(\text{PS}_S) \times Pr(\text{C}_S) \times Pr(\text{IM}_S) \times$$
$$Pr(\text{SF}_S) \times Pr(\text{V}_S)$$

$$(1)$$

where $Pr(X_F)$ is the probability of failure for a component X and $Pr(X_S)$ represents the correct functioning of the component, i.e., $1 - Pr(X_F)$.

4   FBD Formalization

In this section, we describe, in detail, our proposed FBD formalization in the HOL4 theorem prover.

4.1   Formal FBD Modeling

We start the formalization of FBDs by defining a modeling function for its basic element FB, using Definition 4, as shown in Fig. 6, in HOL4 as follows:

Definition 6: *Functional Block*

$\vdash \mathcal{FB}\ (\mathcal{S}::\mathcal{I}_N) = \mathcal{I}_N \otimes_L^N \mathcal{S}$

where $\mathcal{S}$ is a list of all subsystem internal components failure and success states and $\mathcal{I}_N$ is a *two-dimensional* list of all inputs states that affect the subsystem FB, i.e., $\mathcal{I}_N = [[\mathcal{I}_1]; [\mathcal{I}_2]; [\mathcal{I}_3]; \ldots; [\mathcal{I}_n]]$. Also, we can obtain the ET model of a specific functional block $\mathcal{FB}_j$ by defining a function $\mathcal{FB}_{ET}$, in HOL4 as follows:

Definition 7: *Functional Block ET*

$\vdash \mathcal{FB}_{ET} \; \mathcal{FB}_j$ = ETREE (NODE $\mathcal{FB}_j$)

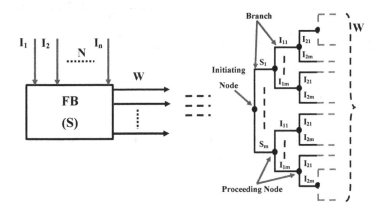

Fig. 6. An FB equal to a complete ET model

To construct multiple consecutive N FBs, we define the following recursive function $\mathcal{FB}_{ET}^N$, in HOL4 as follows:

Definition 8: *Multiple Functional Block ET*

$\vdash \mathcal{FB}_{ET}^N \; (\mathcal{FB}_1 :: \mathcal{FB}_N)$ = $(\mathcal{FB}_{ET} \; \mathcal{FB}_1) :: (\mathcal{FB}_{ET}^N \; \mathcal{FB}_N)$

In order to verify the correctness of the above-mentioned functions, we formalize the following FBD modeling properties, in HOL4 as follows:

Property 1: An ET diagram of an FB model having N input lists $\mathcal{I}_N$ and an internal state list $\mathcal{S}$ can be *split* as connected individual FBs for all lists associated with the FB model, as shown in Fig. 7, in HOL4 as:

Theorem 5: *Splitting Single Functional Block*

$\vdash \mathcal{FB}_{ET} \left(\mathcal{FB} \left(\mathcal{S} :: \mathcal{I}_N \right) \right) = \mathrm{ET}_{PATH} \; \mathrm{p} \left(\mathcal{FB}_{ET}^N \left(\mathcal{S} :: \mathcal{I}_N \right) \right)$

Property 2: The *commutativity* and *associativity* properties of two consecutive FBs consisting of N input lists $\mathcal{I}_N$, as shown in Fig. 8, in HOL4 as:

Theorem 6: *Commutativity and Associativity of Two FBs*

$\vdash \mathcal{FB}_{ET} \left(\mathcal{FB} \left(\mathcal{I}_1 :: \mathcal{I}_N \right) \otimes_{\mathrm{L}} \mathcal{I}_2 \right) = \mathcal{FB}_{ET} \left(\mathcal{I}_1 \otimes_{\mathrm{L}} \left(\mathcal{FB} \left(\mathcal{I}_2 :: \mathcal{I}_N \right) \right) \right)$

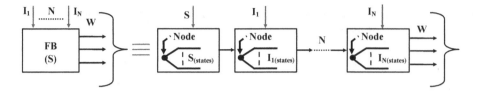

Fig. 7. An FB of N inputs split into individual FBs

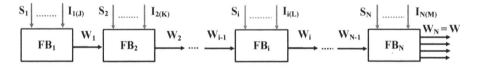

Fig. 8. Commutativity and associativity of two FBs

Now, we can define a *three-dimensional* function $\mathcal{FB}_N$ that takes N FBs, where each FB takes an arbitrary list of n-inputs and then generates the corresponding complete FBD model to obtain all possible risk consequences of failure and reliability, as shown in Fig. 9, in HOL4 as:

Definition 9: *Three Dimensional N Functional Blocks*

$\vdash \mathcal{FB}_N \ (\mathcal{SI}_1::\mathcal{SI}_2::\mathcal{SI}_N) = \mathcal{FB} \ (\texttt{MAP} \ (\lambda \texttt{a}. \ \mathcal{FB} \ \texttt{a}) \ (\mathcal{SI}_1::\mathcal{SI}_2::\mathcal{SI}_N))$

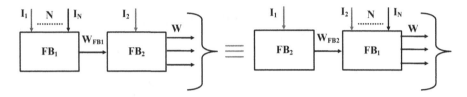

Fig. 9. Complete FBD model of multi-level FBs connected together

The next steps of the FBD analysis are to reduce and partition the ET model for each FB. Since the outcome of $\mathcal{FB}$ is a list of all risk events, we can use the same reduction function $\boxtimes^N$ and partitioning function $\boxplus$ for ET analysis to reduce the ET model and partition a collection of consequence events that end with the same risk events.

4.2 Formal FBD Probabilistic Analysis

The last step in the FBD analysis is to determine the probability of each ET consequence possible scenario at the subsystem-level that could occur in the complex system. Based on the ET probabilistic theorems (Theorems 1–4 in Table 1) and the formal FBD modeling theorems (Theorems 5 and 6), we have verified some FBD probabilistic theorems, in HOL4 as:

Property 3: The probability of the Cartesian product function $\bigotimes_L$ for two $\mathcal{FB}$ lists X_N and Y_N, as shown in Fig. 10a, is verified as the multiplication of the sum of the individual probabilities of all the events associated with each list, in HOL4 as:

Theorem 7: *Two FBs of One Inputs*

$$\vdash \texttt{prob p} \left(\mathcal{FB}_{ET} \left(X_N \bigotimes_L Y_M\right)\right) = \sum \left(\text{Pr}_L \texttt{ p } X_N\right) \times \sum \left(\text{Pr}_L \texttt{ p } Y_M\right)$$

where the function $\sum$ takes a list Y_M and returns the sum of the elements of a list, i.e., $Y_1 + Y_2 + Y_3 + Y_4 + \cdots + Y_{N-1} + Y_N$ while the function Pr_L returns the probabilities of the elements of a list, i.e., $[Pr(Z_1), Pr(Z_2), , \ldots, Pr(Z_{N-1}), Pr(Z_N)]$.

Property 4: A generic probabilistic formulation for one $\mathcal{FB}$ associated with N component multi-state lists, as shown in Fig. 10b, is verified as the product of the sum of each component list probabilities, in HOL4 as:

Theorem 8: *One FB of N Inputs*

$$\vdash \texttt{prob p} \left(\mathcal{FB}_{ET} \left(\mathcal{FB} \left(L_1::L_N\right)\right)\right) = \prod \left(\sum\nolimits_{\text{prob}} \texttt{ p } \left(L_1::L_N\right)\right)$$

where the function $\sum_{\text{prob}}$ is used to recursively apply the functions Pr_L and $\sum$ on a given *two-dimensional* list L_N, i.e., $[[L_1]; [L_2]; [L_3]; \ldots; [L_n]]$.

Property 5: A probabilistic formulation for two FBs of one list and N lists, as shown in Fig. 10c, is verified as the multiplication of their probabilities, in HOL4 as:

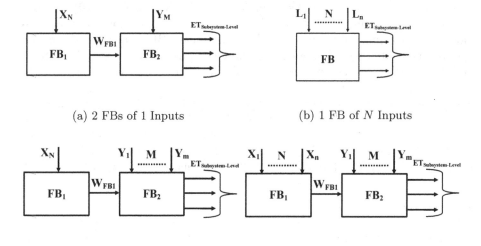

(a) 2 FBs of 1 Inputs   (b) 1 FB of N Inputs

(c) 2 FBs of 1 and N Inputs   (d) 2 FBs of 2 N Inputs

Fig. 10. Different configurations of connected FBs

Theorem 9: *Two FBs of One Input and N Inputs*

$\vdash$ **prob p** $\left(\mathcal{FB}_{ET} \ (X_N \ \bigotimes_L \ (\mathcal{FB} \ (Y_1::Y_m))))\right)$ =
$\sum \ (Pr_L \ p \ X_N) \times \prod \ (\sum_{prob} p \ (Y_1::Y_m))$

Property 6: A probabilistic formulation for two FBs of N input lists, as shown in Fig. 10d, is verified as the multiplication of both probabilities, in HOL4 as:

Theorem 10: *Two FBs of Two N Inputs*

$\vdash$ **prob p** $\Big(\mathcal{FB}_{ET}$

$\left(\mathcal{FB} \ (X_1::X_m) \ \bigotimes_L \ \mathcal{FB} \ (Y_1::Y_m))\right)\Big)$ =
$\prod \ (\sum_{prob} p \ (X_1::X_n)) \times \prod \ (\sum_{prob} p \ (Y_1::Y_m))$

The prime purpose of the above-developed formalization of FBDs is to build a reasoning support for the subsystem-level formal safety analysis of complex systems within the sound environment of HOL4. Our proposed formalization is capable of enabling the verification of safety properties of complete/partial failure of critical systems of any size and compute their reliability events simultaneously. For instance, our FBD formalization framework can handle systems consisting of multi-level decomposition subsystems, where each subsystem is composed of multiple components and each component is associated with multi-state failure and success consequence events [1].

5   Conclusions

In this paper, we described the formalization of FBDs step-analysis in HOL theorem proving using a generic list data-type. Our proposed formalization provides the mathematical verification of the graphical FBDs diagrams of complex systems associated with multi-state components and based on any given probabilistic distribution. The proposed formal approach enables safety engineers to perform FBD-based safety analysis of n-level complex systems within the sound environment of HOL4. We believe that our work will help safety design engineers to meet the desired quality requirements. As future work, we plan to apply the proposed the FBD formalization in the safety analysis of real world case studies. We also intend to develop an integrated framework with a GUI for FBD modeling and linking ET tools with the FBD formalization in HOL4.

References

1. Abdelghany, M.: Formal probabilistic risk assessment using theorem proving with applications in power systems. Ph.D. thesis, Concordia university, Montreal, QC, Canada (2021)
2. Abdelghany, M., Ahmad, W., Tahar, S.: Event tree reliability analysis of safety-critical systems using theorem proving. IEEE Syst. J. **16**(2), 2899–2910 (2022)

3. Abdelghany, M., Tahar, S.: Cause-consequence diagram reliability analysis using formal techniques with application to electrical power networks. IEEE Access **9**, 23929–23943 (2021)
4. Abdelghany, M., Tahar, S.: Formalization of RBD-based cause consequence analysis in HOL. In: Kamareddine, F., Sacerdoti Coen, C. (eds.) CICM 2021. LNCS (LNAI), vol. 12833, pp. 47–64. Springer, Cham (2021). https://doi.org/10.1007/978-3-030-81097-9_4
5. Ahmad, W., Hasan, O., Tahar, S.: Formal reliability and failure analysis of ethernet based communication networks in a smart grid substation. Formal Aspects Comput. **31**, 321–351 (2019)
6. Boulanger, J.L.: CENELEC 50128 and IEC 62279 Standards. Wiley, Hoboken (2015)
7. Elderhalli, Y., Hasan, O., Tahar, S.: A framework for formal dynamic dependability analysis using HOL theorem proving. In: Benzmüller, C., Miller, B. (eds.) CICM 2020. LNCS (LNAI), vol. 12236, pp. 105–122. Springer, Cham (2020). https://doi.org/10.1007/978-3-030-53518-6_7
8. HOL Theorem Prover. https://hol-theorem-prover.org
9. Papazoglou, I.: Functional block diagrams and automated construction of event trees. Reliab. Eng. Syst. Saf. **61**(3), 185–214 (1998)
10. Isograph (2022). https://www.isograph.com
11. ITEM (2021). https://itemsoft.com/eventtree.html
12. Ku, B.H., Cha, J.M.: Reliability assessment of catenary of electric railway by using FTA and ETA analysis. In: Environment and Electrical Engineering, pp. 1–4. IEEE (2011)
13. Li, W.: Reliability Assessment of Electric Power Systems Using Monte Carlo Methods. Springer, Heidelberg (2013)
14. Limnios, N.: Fault Trees. Wiley, Hoboken (2013)
15. Mackiewicz, R.E.: Overview of IEC 61850 and benefits. In: Power Systems Conference and Exposition, pp. 623–630. IEEE (2006)
16. Muzik, V., Vostracky, Z.: Possibilities of event tree analysis method for emergency states in power grid. In: Electric Power Engineering Conference, pp. 1–5. IEEE (2018)
17. Palin, R., Ward, D., Habli, I., Rivett, R.: ISO 26262 safety cases: compliance and assurance. In: IET Conference on System Safety, pp. 1–6 (2011)
18. Papazoglou, I.: Mathematical foundations of event trees. Reliab. Eng. Syst. Saf. **61**(3), 169–183 (1998)
19. Peplow, D.E., Sulfredge, C.D., Sanders, R.L., Morris, R.H., Hann, T.A.: Calculating nuclear power plant vulnerability using integrated geometry and event/fault-tree models. Nucl. Sci. Eng. **146**(1), 71–87 (2004)
20. Sen, D.K., Banks, J.C., Maggio, G., Railsback, J.: Rapid development of an event tree modeling tool using COTS software. In: Aerospace Conference, pp. 1–8. IEEE (2006)
21. Trivedi, K., Bobbio, A.: Reliability block diagrams. In: Reliability and Availability Engineering: Modeling, Analysis, and Applications, pp. 105–149. Cambridge University Press (2017)

Generation and Synthesis

A Sound Strategy to Compile General Recursion into Finite Depth Pattern Matching

Maycon J. J. Amaro[1]($\boxtimes$) (ID), Samuel S. Feitosa[2] (ID), and Rodrigo G. Ribeiro[1] (ID)

[1] Universidade Federal de Ouro Preto, Ouro Preto, MG, Brazil
maycon.amaro@aluno.ufop.edu.br
[2] Universidade Federal da Fronteira Sul, Chapecó, SC, Brazil

Abstract. Programming languages are popular and diverse, and the convenience of programmatically changing the behavior of complex systems is attractive even for the ones with stringent security requirements, which often impose restrictions on the acceptable programs. A very common restriction is that the program must terminate, which is very hard to check because the Halting Problem is undecidable. In this work, we proposed a technique to unroll recursive programs in functional languages to create terminating versions of them. We prove that our strategy itself is guaranteed to terminate. We also formalize term generation and run property-based tests to build confidence that the semantics is preserved through the transformation. Our strategy can be used to compile general purpose functional languages to restrictive targets such as the eBPF and smart contracts for blockchain networks.

Keywords: Program transformation · Recursion · Program generation

1 Introduction

Looping statements and recursion are one of the most common features of programming languages, but they also require a lot of caution. Non-termination is at best an annoying situation, and at worst a serious security or logical concern. Some compilers and technologies put a lot effort in guaranteeing that no program will run forever, inevitably being very restricted due to the undecidability of the Halting Problem [22]. Some examples include dependently typed languages that are used as proof assistants, such as Coq [13] and Agda [18]; smart contract languages for blockchain systems [14] and the technology to run sandboxed programs in the Linux Kernel—the eBPF (extended Berkeley Packet Filter).

eBPF [7] is an interesting case to explore, because its verifier will reject any program that has a back jump. In other words, it will reject any form of repetition[1], be it iterative or recursive. Their motivation in doing so is understandable: running programs in the Operating System's kernel requires a lot of caution. One

---

[1] Version 5.3 and higher has support for bounded loops only.

© The Author(s), under exclusive license to Springer Nature Switzerland AG 2022
L. Lima and V. Molnár (Eds.): SBMF 2022, LNCS 13768, pp. 39–54, 2022.
https://doi.org/10.1007/978-3-031-22476-8_3

mistake could bring the system down. Allowing potential non-terminating programs is a breach that ill-intentioned users could explore to perform Denial of Service attacks.

While imperative languages have additional constructs for repetition, functional languages can only count with recursion for repeating computations. Bounded loops are one easy way to walk around the restriction that all programs must terminate, but using functional languages to write programs targeting eBPF requires better strategies. Notice that ensuring termination alone is not sufficient. A program with repetition, even with a proof that it terminates, would still be rejected by eBPF. Termination must be syntactically assured.

In this work, we present an algorithm to transform recursive functions into finite depth pattern matching functions with an *equivalent* semantics, in the sense that both functions must yield the same results when the recursive function halts and the non-recursive function, with the given input, has enough nested pattern matching constructions to produce a value. We also present a sound strategy to generate random terminating programs so our algorithm can be properly tested. More specifically, we make the following contributions:

- We present System R, a core language with recursion and its unrolling algorithm.
- We present System L, a core language with no recursion and show how to compile system R programs into equivalent System L programs.
- We describe a sound algorithm to generate random well-typed terminating programs for the System R language.
- We formally demonstrate some properties regarding the presented algorithms. Property-based tests are applied otherwise.

2   Basic Definitions

We consider the simply typed λ-calculus, frequently represented as $\lambda_\rightarrow$ [20], extended with natural numbers, pattern matching over naturals and recursion, as defined in [23]. Its syntax is described by the following context-free grammar:

$$\tau ::= \mathbb{N} \mid \tau \rightarrow \tau$$
$$e ::= \text{zero} \mid \text{suc } e \mid v \mid \lambda v : \tau.e \mid e\,e \mid \text{match } e\,e\,(v, e) \mid \mu v : \tau.e$$

We use the metavariable v to range over variable names, τ to range over types and e to range over expressions. We use *expressions* and *terms* interchangeably. $\lambda_\rightarrow$'s type system is described by the following set of rules:

$$\frac{}{\Gamma \vdash \text{zero} : \mathbb{N}}\ \{znat\} \qquad\qquad \frac{\Gamma \vdash e : \mathbb{N}}{\Gamma \vdash \text{suc } e : \mathbb{N}}\ \{snat\}$$

$$\frac{\Gamma, v : \tau \vdash e : \tau'}{\Gamma \vdash (\lambda v : \tau.e) : \tau \rightarrow \tau'}\ \{lam\} \qquad\qquad \frac{v : \tau \in \Gamma}{\Gamma \vdash v : \tau}\ \{var\}$$

$$\frac{\Gamma \vdash e : \tau \rightarrow \tau' \quad \Gamma \vdash e' : \tau}{\Gamma \vdash e\,e' : \tau'}\ \{app\} \qquad\qquad \frac{\Gamma, v : \tau \vdash e : \tau}{\Gamma \vdash (\mu v : \tau.e) : \tau}\ \{rec\}$$

$$\frac{\Gamma \vdash e_1 : \mathbb{N} \quad \Gamma \vdash e_2 : \tau \quad \Gamma, v : \mathbb{N} \vdash e_3 : \tau}{\Gamma \vdash \text{match } e_1 \, e_2 \, (v, e_3) : \tau} \; \{match\}$$

Rule *znat* types zero as a natural number in any context. Rule *snat* types suc as a natural number as long as its argument is also a natural number. Rule *var* types any element of the context with its typing information. Rules *lam* and *app* type abstractions and applications. Rule *match* requires its first argument to be a natural number and the others to have the same type. The third argument expression is bound to a variable name intended to refer to the predecessor of the first argument, if it is not zero. Finally, rule *rec* types recursive expressions (fixpoint operator).

The semantic style considered in this work is the small step, *call by value* semantics following [23]. In the text, capture-avoiding substitution of variable x by term y in term e is represented by $[x \mapsto y]e$.

3   Expansion and Transformation

Transformation of recursive functions into terminating versions is done considering the two core calculi we defined: System R, which is a subset of the presented λ-calculus also featuring some form of recursion; and the strongly normalizing System L. Translating programs from System R to System L implies recursion elimination. In order to still be able to perform non trivial computations, System R's expressions are expanded before the translation, unrolling the recursive definitions up to a factor we called *fuel*[2]. In this way, the output functions still computes something identical to the original function, although they can never have the same exact semantics, since one is recursive and the other has no automated repetition at all.

System R's syntax establishes two levels for expressions, reserving the top level for recursive definitions and applications only. The bottom level is constituted of the same constructs seen in λ-calculus, except for the μ operator. We made this choice to prevent nested fixpoint expressions. For example, we want to avoid expressions of the form $\mu v_1 : \tau.(\mu v_2 : \tau.e)$. In functional languages such as Haskell and Racket, the programmer is able to define several functions before defining a main expression. Those definitions can be compiled into derived forms, abstracting the main expression and applying it to the function definitions. The semantics of those applications will create nested μ functions. As a syntatic transformation, our unrolling is intended to happen before semantic evaluation. Our choice to allow recursive functions only at top level is just a matter of presentation: we can allow several definitions to be unrolled separately with some minor tweaks (by using a `let in` construction and several fuel values, for example). Once semantic evaluation nests them, they will be already expanded. With some extra effort, the core ideas in this paper should apply to the traditional $\lambda_{\rightarrow}$ as well, although it is a conjecture at this point.

---

[2] The term "fuel" is inspired by Petrol Semantics. It is presented, for instance, in [16].

Recursive definitions also require a functional type, so trivial loops of type $\mathbb{N}$ cannot be expressed (for example, the term $\mu v : \mathbb{N}.v$). The following context-free grammar describes System R's syntax:

$$\tau ::= \mathbb{N} \mid \tau \to \tau$$
$$p ::= \mu v : \tau \to \tau.e \mid p\, e$$
$$e ::= \text{zero} \mid \text{suc}\, e \mid v \mid \lambda v : \tau.e \mid e\, e \mid \text{match}\, e\, e\, (v, e)$$

Meta-variable p ranges over top-level expressions. For convenience, we assume every program will contain a recursive definition, regardless if it is involved in a application or not. Typing rules remain the same as $\lambda_\to$ except for *rec* rule that now requires the functional type. The new *rec* rule is:

$$\frac{\Gamma, v : \tau \to \tau' \vdash e : \tau \to \tau'}{\Gamma \vdash (\mu v : \tau \to \tau'.e) : \tau} \; \{rec\}$$

Alternatively, the typing rule for recursive functions in System R could require the expression to have an ocurrence of the variable that was added to the context. This is convenient for proving theorems but is burdensome for random program generation and real life implementations. Variable ocurrence are inductively defined following Definition 1.

Definition 1 (Variable ocurrence). *A variable $v : \tau$ occurs in some term e, denoted by $v : \tau \in_v e$, if e is v or if $v : \tau$ occurs in any of the subterms of e. Otherwise, $v : \tau$ does not occur in e, denoted by $v : \tau \notin_v e$.*

Informally, the semantics of System R is the same of $\lambda_\to$. But since System R's syntax won't allow a fixpoint inside a bottom-level term, the conventional evaluation rule for recursive functions cannot be applied. The solution is to elaborate System R to $\lambda_\to$, which is straightforward, given System R programs are a subset of $\lambda_\to$. In this way, only during evaluation recursive definitions are allowed to bypass the syntactic restrictions. Notice that there is no need to modify the rule to reflect the constraint of fixpoints having functional type, because that is just a particular case of the more general rule already present in $\lambda_\to$.

3.1 Unrolling

The inlining of a function f means to replace the ocurrences of f for its body, and is largely used by developers of compilers to increase performance of their programs [6]. By inlining recursive definitions into themselves, we create an equivalent expression that performs fewer recursive calls. As Rugina and Rinard [21] point out, we need to be careful to not super-exponentially grow the code of the functions. For example, consider this pseudo-Haskell function for adding two numbers in Peano notation:

```
sum :: Nat → Nat → Nat
sum = \x y → case x of
   Zero  → y
   Suc w → sum w (Suc y)
```

The idea in this expression is to match the first number x over the patterns zero or suc. If it is zero, we simply answer with the second number y. Otherwise we name w the predecessor of x and recursively call the function over w and the successor of y. Inlining this function with itself once would give us the following expression:

```
sum :: Nat → Nat → Nat
sum = \x y → case x of
  Zero  → y
  Suc w → (\x y → case x of
    Zero  → y
    Suc w → sum w (Suc y)) w (Suc y)
```

We had one match (**case of**, in Haskell) before and now we have two. If we inline this last expression with itself we would end up with four matches, because the definition of *sum* now contains two of them:

```
sum :: Nat → Nat → Nat
sum = \x y → case x of
 Zero  → y
 Suc w → (\x y → case x of
 Zero  → y
 Suc w → (\x y → case x of
  Zero  → y
  Suc w → (\x y → case x of
   Zero  → y
   Suc w → sum w (Suc y)) w (Suc y)) w (Suc y)) w (Suc y)
```

Doubling the number of matchings every step in a simple term like this is not in our best interest. Instead, we want to increase these matches just by one in each step. Inlining the original expression 2 times should actually give us the following term:

```
sum :: Nat → Nat → Nat
sum = \x y → case x of
  Zero  → y
  Suc w → (\x y → case x of
    Zero  → y
    Suc w → (\x y → case x of
     Zero  → y
     Suc w → sum w (Suc y)) w (Suc y)) w (Suc y)
```

If the original function had two recursive calls, then we would want to increase the number of matches by two in each step, and that would still be better than having 2^{m+1} matches after m steps. So, we have to always keep track of the original expression and inline its body inside the output expressions. Definition 2 formalizes this behavior.

Definition 2. *The n-expansion of a System R expression e is the result of the nth cumulative inlining of e, described by exp in the following algorithm:*

$$inl(v, v', e) = \begin{cases} e & if \ v \equiv v' \\ v & otherwise \end{cases}$$

$$inl(zero, v', e) = zero$$
$$inl(suc \ e', v', e) = suc \ (inl(e', v', e))$$
$$inl(e_1 \ e_2, v', e) = (inl(e_1, v', e)) \ (inl(e_2, v', e))$$
$$inl(\lambda v : \tau.e', v', e) = \lambda v : \tau.(inl(e', v', e))$$
$$inl(match \ e_1 \ e_2 \ (w, e_3), v', e) = match \ (inl(e_1, v', e)) \ (inl(e_2, v', e))$$
$$(w, (inl(e_3, v', e)))$$

$$exp'(e', \_, \_, 0) = e'$$
$$exp'(e', v, e, n) = inl(exp'(e', v, e, n - 1), v, e)$$

$$exp(\mu v : \tau \to \tau'.e, n) = \mu v : \tau \to \tau'.(exp'(e, v, e, n))$$
$$exp(p \ e, n) = (exp(p, n)) \ e$$

Function $inl(e', v, e)$ performs the inlining of e inside e' replacing the ocurrences of v. This is only allowed between bottom-level expressions, so the fixpoint construction can never appear here. Function $exp'(e', v, e, n)$ accumulates the inlinings n times, always using the original e instead of previous result with itself. Function $exp(e, n)$ expands a recursive function v by n-expanding its body replacing the ocurrences of v. Functions inl, exp' and exp halt for every input (Lemmas 1 and 2) and the resulting term is still a recursive function (Lemma 3), whose recursive calls must be now eliminated.

Lemma 1 (Inlining Halts). *For all bottom-level terms e, e' of System R, and every variable v, there exists a bottom-level term e'' such that $inl(e', v, e) = e''$.*

Proof. By induction on the structure of e. Base cases for variable and zero immediately produce a term. In the other cases inlining is merely propagated to subterms, which are strictly smaller. □

Lemma 2 (Expansion Halts). *For every $n \in \mathbb{N}$ and System R expression e, there exists an expression e' such that $exp(e) = e'$.*

Proof. The expansion of bottom-level terms, done in the exp' function, always halts because inlining halts and n is always decreasing towards 0, in which case the expression is left unchanged. Top-level expressions come in two cases.

- Case 1: $e = \mu v : \tau \to \tau'.e_b$. Its body e_b, which is a bottom-level expression, is expanded.

– Case 2: $e = (p)(e_r)$. The top-level p is expanded with the same n, bottom-level e_r is left unchanged. By the structure of the grammar, a top level expression will always end with a recursive definition, falling in case 1.

$\square$

Lemma 3 (Occurrence Preserving Expansion). *For every $n \in \mathbb{N}$, term e and variable $v : \tau$, if $v : \tau \in_v e$ then $v : \tau \in_v exp(e, n)$.*

Proof. Inlining substitutes all ocurrences of a variable v_1 by some e_1 inside some e_2. If v_1 occurs in e_1 and in e_2, then by induction, v_1 occurs in $inl(e_2, v_1, e_1)$. The expansion of a recursive definition $\mu v : \tau \to \tau'. e$ inlines e within e replacing v in every step. So if v occurs in e then it follows that v still occurs after each cumulative inlining, and thus after the expansion. $\square$

3.2   Recursion Elimination

System L's syntax offers no way to express any kind of recursion, but offers a construction for abnormal termination, namely the term error:

$$\tau ::= \mathbb{N} \mid \tau \to \tau$$
$$e ::= \text{zero} \mid \text{suc } e \mid v \mid \lambda v : \tau.e \mid e\ e \mid \text{match } e\ e\ (v, e) \mid \text{error}$$

Its type system is identical to $\lambda_\to$ minus the rule for recursion, and adding the rule for typing error with an arbitrary type:

$$\frac{\forall \tau}{\Gamma \vdash \text{error}\ : \tau}\ \{error\}$$

The semantics for System L is the same as $\lambda_\to$'s but including three rules for propagating errors and removing the $\{rec\}$ rule. The error construction, although a normal form, is not considered a value. In this way, the semantics remains deterministic [20]. The included rules are:

$$\frac{}{\text{suc error} \longrightarrow \text{error}}\ \{esuc\} \qquad\qquad \frac{}{\text{error } e_2 \longrightarrow \text{error}}\ \{eapp_1\}$$

$$\frac{}{v_1 \text{ error} \longrightarrow \text{error}}\ \{eapp_2\} \qquad \frac{}{\text{match error } e_1\ e_2\ (v, e_3) \longrightarrow \text{error}}\ \{ematch\}$$

Since System L has no way of expressing recursion or any form of repetition there is no way a program in System L loops forever. Translating a term from System R to System L will produce a program that will surely terminate. To achieve this, we must eliminate the remaining recursive calls, i.e., the occurrences of the function name in the expression. Definitions 3 and 4 formally describe recursion elimination and translation.

Definition 3. *Ocurrence elimination of a variable v from a bottom-level term e is the translation of e to System L, replacing v ocurrences by error. It is defined by this algorithm:*

$$elim(v', v) = \begin{cases} error & if\ v \equiv v' \\ v' & otherwise \end{cases}$$

$$elim(zero, v) = zero$$
$$elim(suc\ e, v) = suc\ (elim(e, v))$$
$$elim(\lambda v' : \tau.e, v) = \lambda v' : \tau.(elim(e, v))$$
$$elim(e_1\ e_2, v) = (elim(e_1, v))\ (elim(e_2, v))$$
$$elim(match\ e_1\ e_2\ (v', e_3), v) = match\ (elim(e_1, v))\ (elim(e_2, v))$$
$$(v', elim(e_3, v))$$

Definition 4. *The translation of a System R expression e is the ocurrence elimination of the recursive function's name from its own body:*

$$tsl(\mu v : \tau \rightarrow \tau'.e) = elim(e, v)$$
$$tsl(p\ e) = (tsl(p))\ e$$

The second case of *tsl* leaves the right term of application unchanged, since bottom-level System R expressions are a subset of System L. In an actual implementation, an auxiliary function is necessary to simply translate bottom-level terms into their System L's counterparts. The composition of unrolling and translation gives us the transformation algorithm, which always halts (Theorem 1):

$$transform(e, f) = tsl\ (exp(e, f))$$

Lemma 4 (Ocurrence Elimination Halts). *For every bottom-level System R term e and variable v, there exists a System L expression e' such that* $elim(e, v) = e'$.

Proof. Ocurrence elimination behaves similar to inlining. In inlining, the ocurrences of v are replaced by some term e_1. In occurence elimination, the ocurrences of v are replaced by the term *error*. By induction, if the term is a variable or a zero, it is immediately translated by error or its counterpart in System L and then halts. If not, the ocurrence elimination is propagated to the subterms, which are strictly smaller.   □

Theorem 1 (Transformation Halts). *For every* $f \in \mathbb{N}$ *and System R expression e, there exists a System L expression e' such that* $transform(e, f) = e'$.

Proof. Translation erases the μ construction, which is absent in System L, and then eliminates the ocurrences of the recursive function's name from the body. Transformation composes n-expansion and translation. Since both functions always halt, their composition always halts too.   □

In the example program for adding two numbers x and y, when the ocurrences of the function's name are eliminated in the translating process, the resulting expression can still answer with y if x is 0: $\mu s : \mathbb{N} \rightarrow \mathbb{N} \rightarrow \mathbb{N}.\lambda x : \mathbb{N}.\lambda y : \mathbb{N}.match\ x\ y\ (w, (error\ w)\ (suc\ y))$.

If we expand the expression f times before translating, the System L version would be able to successfully compute the sum whenever $x \leq f$, reducing to error otherwise. There can be no general way of guessing f, since it could solve the halting problem. One disadvantage of our approach is to rely on the programmer to inform the fuel for the function, similar to what they have to do when using bounded loops in imperative languages. One advantage of this approach is that some infinite loops are immediately reduced to error. No matter how high is f, if we transform $\mu v : \mathbb{N} \to \mathbb{N}.v$ the output program will always be one simple error.

4 Term Generation

Property-based testing is an interesting approach to testing, because it relies on generating random programs to check properties, avoiding the bias when developers create manual test cases. But using this approach when checking properties of compilers is not easy, because it is necessary to define how to generate valid programs of that language. In this work, since we are directly dealing with termination, we are also interested in generating terminating programs.

To accomplish this, we define for our generation procedure a superset of types, in which our base type $\mathbb{N}$ is indexed by natural numbers. Those indexes are related via subtyping, such that $\mathbb{N}^x <: \mathbb{N}^y$ whenever $x \leq y$. Functions are related in the usual way, being covariant in return type and contravariant in the argument type. Our generation judgment $\Gamma; d; r; \tau \rightsquigarrow e$ means that expression e of type τ can be generated from context Γ, given limits d for expression depth and r for type indexes. The relation $\rightsquigarrow$ is annotated with a letter to distinguish the form of the expressions it generates. $\xi(xs)$ selects a random element from a non-empty list xs. Our first rules are the generation of zero and terms that are variables. A zero can be generated in every scenario where a $\mathbb{N}$ is expected, regardless of the index. Variables can be picked from a non empty list of candidates. Those candidates are the variables from the context that are a subtype of the expected type.

$$\frac{}{\Gamma; d; r; \mathbb{N}^x \rightsquigarrow_z zero} \; \{zero\} \qquad \frac{cs = \{v \mid v : \tau' \in \Gamma \wedge \tau' <: \tau\} \quad cs \neq \emptyset}{\Gamma; d; r; \tau \rightsquigarrow_v \xi(cs)} \; \{var\}$$

The successor construction can be also generated in every scenario where a $\mathbb{N}^x$ is expected, as long as index x is not already 0. Its argument can be zero, a variable or another successor construction. The index limit is decreased for the generation of its subterm. When we generate pattern matchings inside recursive definitions, the first branch must be a constant, so it is useful to not include the other rules as possible subterms for this construction. The notation $\psi, \phi, \cdots = \xi(\{a, b, c, d, \dots\})$ means that rules annotated with ψ, ϕ, etc., are an alias to rules annotated with any letter in the list inside ξ, and are meant to be selected randomly for each letter on the left side.

$$\frac{\Gamma; d; r; \mathbb{N}^x \rightsquigarrow_\psi e \quad \psi = \xi(\{z, v, s\})}{\Gamma; d; r + 1; \mathbb{N}^{x+1} \rightsquigarrow_s suc\ e} \quad \{suc\}$$

Abstractions need to generate an expression of the return type before inserting a λ. The function *fresh* generates a variable name that is not present in the given context. Operator $\lfloor \tau \rfloor$ erases index from indexed type τ.

$$\frac{v = fresh(\Gamma) \quad \Gamma, v : \tau_1; d; r; \tau_2 \rightsquigarrow_\psi e \quad \psi = \xi(\{z, v, s, a\})}{\Gamma; d; r; \tau_1 \rightarrow \tau_2 \rightsquigarrow_a \lambda v : \lfloor \tau_1 \rfloor.e} \quad \{abs\}$$

Applications of type τ need the generation of a function that results in that τ, applied to an appropriate argument, which has also to be generated. Operator Θ generates a type given the limits d and r, and never associates to the left. This operator is defined by randomly selecting one out of two more specific versions: $\Theta^\rightarrow$ that generates only function types and $\Theta^\mathbb{N}$ that generates only indexed $\mathbb{N}$ types.

$$\Theta^\mathbb{N}(r) = \mathbb{N}^{\xi(\{1,...,r\})}$$
$$\Theta^\rightarrow(0, r) = (\Theta^\mathbb{N}(r)) \rightarrow (\Theta^\mathbb{N}(r))$$
$$\Theta^\rightarrow(2d, r) = (\Theta^\mathbb{N}(r)) \rightarrow (\xi(\{\Theta^\mathbb{N}(r), \Theta^\rightarrow(d, r)\}))$$
$$\Theta(d, r) = \xi(\{\Theta^\mathbb{N}(r), \Theta^\rightarrow(d, r)\})$$

If limits are high enough, both base and functional types can be generated. Otherwise, it will force the generation of a base type ($\mathbb{N}$ is our only base type here). Generating applications will cut the d limit to half for generating its subterms.

$$\frac{\tau' = \Theta(d, r) \quad \Gamma; d; r; \tau' \rightarrow \tau \rightsquigarrow_\phi e_1 \quad \Gamma; d; r; \tau' \rightsquigarrow_\psi e_2 \quad \phi, \psi = \xi(\{z, v, s, a\})}{\Gamma; 2d; r; \tau \rightsquigarrow_a e_1\ e_2} \quad \{app\}$$

Match constructions need to generate a term of type $\mathbb{N}$ and two terms of the expected type. For the third term e_3, a fresh variable is added to context with a decreased index limit, and this limit is decreased for e_3 as well. The operator $\downarrow$ decreases the index of the type. If it is a function, only the leftmost atom is decreased. Matches can only be introduced when limit d is greater than 1.

$$\frac{\begin{array}{ll} v & = & fresh(\Gamma) \quad \Gamma; d; r; \mathbb{N}^r \rightsquigarrow_\phi e_1 \\ \phi, \psi, \rho = \xi(\{z, v, s, a\}) & \Gamma; d; r; \tau \rightsquigarrow_\psi e_2 \quad \Gamma, v : \mathbb{N}^{r\downarrow}; d; r\downarrow; \tau \rightsquigarrow_\rho e_3 \end{array}}{\Gamma; 2d; r; \tau \rightsquigarrow_a match\ e_1\ e_2\ (v, e_3)} \quad \{match\}$$

The generation of recursive functions and applications involving them require more caution. Generating a recursive function needs the generation of a proper body, which means it has to be well-typed and must terminate.

$$\frac{v = fresh(\Gamma) \quad \Gamma, v : (\tau_1 \rightarrow \tau_2)_\downarrow; d; r\downarrow; \tau_1 \rightarrow \tau_2 \rightsquigarrow_b e}{\Gamma; 2d; r + 1; \tau_1 \rightarrow \tau_2 \rightsquigarrow_f rec\ v : \lfloor \tau_1 \rightarrow \tau_2 \rfloor.e} \quad \{rec\}$$

The simplest way of guaranteeing this is inserting λs until we are left with the generation of a $\mathbb{N}$, and then generate a match. This match will generate an immediate natural number on its first branch and it will allow a recursive call on the second. The expression being matched needs to be zero or a variable. The expression being generated for the second branch needs to be standardized, i.e., modified to make sure that, if there is a recursive call, then its first argument will be the predecessor of the matching expression.

$$\frac{\begin{array}{l} v = \mathit{fresh}(\Gamma) \\ \rho = \xi(\{z, v, s, a\}) \quad \Gamma; d; r; (\mathbb{N}^x)_\downarrow \rightsquigarrow_\psi e_1 \quad \Gamma, v : (\mathbb{N}^x) \downarrow; d; r; \mathbb{N}^x \rightsquigarrow_\rho e_3' \\ \phi, \psi = \xi(\{z, v, s\}) \quad \Gamma; d; r; \mathbb{N}^x \rightsquigarrow_\phi e_2 \quad e_3 = \mathit{stdz}(e_3'; \Gamma, v : (\mathbb{N}^x)_\downarrow) \end{array}}{\Gamma; d; r; \mathbb{N}^x \rightsquigarrow_b \mathit{match}\ e_1\ e_2\ (v, e_3)} \quad \{\mathit{buildBody1}\}$$

$$\frac{v = \mathit{fresh}(\Gamma) \quad \Gamma, v : \tau_1; d; r; \tau_2 \rightsquigarrow_b e}{\Gamma; d; r; \tau_1 \rightarrow \tau_2 \rightsquigarrow_b \lambda v : \lfloor \tau_1 \rfloor . e} \quad \{\mathit{buildBody2}\}$$

The standardization process is defined by the following algorithm, where bottom is a function that returns the first variable name added to the context, i.e., the bottom of the scope stack; and top is a function that returns the last variable name added to the context, i.e., the top of the scope stack.

$$std(e_1\ e_2, v_1, v_2) = \begin{cases} e_1\ v_2 & e_1 \equiv v_1 \\ (std(e_1, v_1, v_2))\ (std(e_2, v_1, v_2)) & \mathit{otherwise} \end{cases}$$

$$std(\lambda v : \tau.e, v_1, v_2) = \lambda v : \tau.(std(e, v_1, v_2))$$

$$std(\mathit{match}\ e_1\ e_2\ (v, e_3), v_1, v_2) = \mathit{match}\ (std(e_1, v_1, v_2))\ (std(e_2, v_1, v_2))$$
$$(v, std(e_3, v_1, v_2))$$

$$std(e, \_, \_) = e$$

$$stdz(e, \Gamma) = std(e, bottom(\Gamma), top(\Gamma))$$

Applications involving recursive definitions are most useful if they yield a number as a final value, and so we force this to happen. After generating a functional type and a recursive definition of this type, we generate proper arguments and apply them to the function.

$$\frac{\tau = \Theta^\rightarrow(d, r) \quad \Gamma; d; r; \tau \rightsquigarrow_f e' \quad \Gamma; d; r; e'; \mathit{revargs}(\tau) \rightsquigarrow_c e}{\Gamma; 2d; r; \mathbb{N}^x \rightsquigarrow_g e} \quad \{\mathit{apprec}\}$$

$$args(\mathbb{N}^x) = []$$
$$args(\mathbb{N}^x \rightarrow \tau_2) = \mathbb{N}^x :: (args(\tau_2))$$
$$\mathit{revargs} = \mathit{reverse} \circ args$$

For this, we build a list of arguments and extend the judgement to contain them. We must build the applications of the outer arguments first, applying the recursive definition to the first argument as the innermost application. For this, we need to assume our list of arguments is reversed.

$$\frac{\psi = \xi(\{z,v,s,a\}) \quad \Gamma;d;r;\mathbb{N}^x \rightsquigarrow_\psi e'}{\Gamma;d;r;e;[\mathbb{N}^x] \rightsquigarrow_c e\,e'} \ \{bdA1\} \qquad \frac{\Gamma;d;r;e;ts \rightsquigarrow_c e_1 \quad \psi = \xi(\{z,v,s,a\}) \quad \Gamma;d;r;\mathbb{N}^x \rightsquigarrow_\psi e_2}{\Gamma;d;r;e;\mathbb{N}^x :: ts \rightsquigarrow_c e_1\,e_2} \ \{bdA2\}$$

Finally, generating a System R expression means to generate a type and generate a term accordingly:

$$\frac{\Gamma;d;r;\mathbb{N}^x \rightsquigarrow_\psi e}{\Gamma;d;r;\mathbb{N}^x \rightsquigarrow e} \qquad \frac{\Gamma;d;r;\tau_1 \to \tau_2 \rightsquigarrow_\phi e}{\Gamma;d;r;\tau_1 \to \tau_2 \rightsquigarrow e}$$

If we want only top terms of System R, then it is enough to use $\psi = g$ and $\phi = f$. But it is interesting to allow the generation of bottom level terms when testing properties, since recursive functions are optional in real-life implementations. In that case, $\psi = \xi(\{z,v,s,a,g\})$ and $\phi = \xi(\{a,f\})$.

4.1   Soundness of Term Generation

Lemma 5 (Bottom level generation is sound). *For every context Γ, natural numbers d and r, type τ and $\psi \in \{a,s,z,v\}$, if $\Gamma;d;r;\tau \rightsquigarrow_\psi e$ then $e : \tau$.*

Proof. The rule for $\{zero\}$ can only be used to generate terms of type $\mathbb{N}$, which is the type of zero and the rule for $\{var\}$ pick a value of type τ' from the context if available, where τ' and τ are equal up to erasure of indices. Rules $\{suc\}$, $\{abs\}$ and $\{match\}$ directly represent their counterparts in the type system, generating subterms of the appropriate type. The rule for $\{app\}$ generates a random type to construct a functional type with return of type τ and then generates both the function and its argument, building an application with them.   □

Lemma 6 (Bottom level generation halts). *For every context Γ, natural numbers $d \geq 2$ and r, and type τ, there exists a term e such that $\Gamma;d;r;\tau \rightsquigarrow_a e$.*

Proof. Type τ is either $\mathbb{N}$ or a function type. The first case has rules $\{match\}$ and $\{app\}$ available (since $d \geq 2$) and the other is generated by $\{abs\}$. When generating subterms for $\{match\}$, $\{abs\}$ or $\{app\}$, the rules $\{zero\}$, $\{var\}$ and $\{suc\}$ can be used. Rules $\{zero\}$ and $\{var\}$ trivially halt. Rule $\{suc\}$ decreases r and the index of $\mathbb{N}$ by 1 for the generation of its subterms and cannot be used when those values are 0. The subterm generated by rule $\{abs\}$ has a type strictly smaller then τ and it cannot be used once τ becomes $\mathbb{N}$. Rules $\{app\}$ and $\{match\}$ decrease the d limit by half for the generation of their subterms, and cannot be used when $d < 2$. Therefore, some value in the triple (d,r,τ) will always decrease for the generation of a subterm. The rule $\{zero\}$ can be used to generate a trivial term whenever rules $\{app\}$, $\{match\}$ and $\{abs\}$ cannot be used anymore and there are no candidates for using $\{var\}$.   □

Theorem 2 (Top level generation is sound). *For every context Γ, natural numbers d and r, type τ and $\psi \in \{f, g\}$, if $\Gamma; d; r; \tau \rightsquigarrow_\psi e$ then $e : \tau$.*

Proof. If τ is a functional type, e is generated using $\{\text{rec}\}$. This rule creates a fresh var of type τ and adds it to the context when generating a subterm of type τ, satisfying the corresponding typing rule. The subterm is generated using a special procedure that builds an adequate body for the recursive function. This procedure generates well-typed λ abstractions until τ is a single $\mathbb{N}$, generating a well-typed pattern matching right away. If τ is already $\mathbb{N}$, a functional type and a recursive function p of this type are generated by rule $\{\text{apprec}\}$, then the type of each argument is used to generate bottom-level values and build nested applications until p has all arguments necessary to generate a $\mathbb{N}$. □

Theorem 3 (Top level generation halts). *For every context Γ, natural numbers $d \geq 2$ and r, and type τ, there exists a term e such that either $\Gamma; d; r; \tau \rightsquigarrow_f e$ or $\Gamma; d; r; \tau \rightsquigarrow_g e$.*

Proof. If τ is a functional type, it must follow that $\Gamma; d; r; \tau \rightsquigarrow_f e$. Rule $\{\text{rec}\}$ depends on $\rightsquigarrow_b$ for generating its subterm. By using $\{\text{buildBody2}\}$, τ is decreasing for the generation of the subterms of the λ inserted abstractions. When it reaches $\mathbb{N}$, bottom level terms are generated for the insertion of the match. If τ is already $\mathbb{N}$, bottom level terms are generated for each argument type of the generated functional type, finishing with the application of the recursive function when the list of arguments contains only the last one. □

5 Quick-Checking Properties

We implemented Ringell [10], an interpreter for both System R and System L. When given only a source-code file, it will parse the text, typecheck the abstract syntax tree, use System R as the internal representation and run it using the $\lambda_{\rightarrow}$ interpreter as seen in [23]. When given a source-code file and a nonnegative integer number n, it will transform the System R representation into System L, using n as fuel for expansion, and then run it using the $\lambda_{\rightarrow}$ interpreter as seen in [20]. Ringell's syntax, inspired in Haskell and $\lambda_{\rightarrow}$, is simple and support just a few syntactic constructions, making it close to both System R and System L syntax.

The term generation procedure is implemented in Ringell's test modules. We specified some properties using Quick Check [19], invoking modules from Ringell for validation. The properties are as follows:

- Property 1: All generated System R programs are well typed
- Property 2: All generated System R programs terminate
- Property 3: For every generated System R term e of type $\mathbb{N}$, if e terminates with value v doing at most f recursive calls, then $transform(e, f)$ yields v.
- Property 4: For every generated System R term e of type $\mathbb{N}$ and some fuel f, if $transform(e, f)$ yields a value v, then e terminates resulting in v.

Property 2 is only true because of our generation procedure, it is obviously not a property of System R. Properties 3 and 4 are our desired semantic properties for the transformation technique: the output function results in the same value of the original if enough fuel is given and the output function yielding a value implies the original function terminates with the same value. Both properties concern only programs of the base type ℕ, because there are two syntatic constructors for programs of functional type in System R and only one in System L, and we prefer using propositional equality instead of creating a more complex equivalence relation for this purpose. Figure 1 presents the coverage results generated by Haskell Stack coverage flag, after running thousands of successful tests for each property.

	Top Level Definitions		Alternatives		Expressions	
	%	covered / total	%	covered / total	%	covered / total
ExpL	100% 8/8		88% 31/35		86% 155/180	
ExpR	88% 16/18		94% 52/55		89% 350/393	
Unroll	100% 7/7		100% 30/30		89% 130/145	
	93% 31/33		94% 113/120		88% 635/718	

Fig. 1. Test coverage results

The first column are for modules names, in which ExpR and ExpL are the interpreters and Unroll is where the functions involved in transformation are. Most of non-reached code concerns error control and arguments of functions that were not used in all cases of the function (for example, context is not needed for evaluating a zero).

6 Related Work

There are some papers closely related to ensuring termination of functional programs, although the systems they describe do not focus on syntactically transforming the programs.

Abel's foetus [1–4] is a simplification of Munich Type Theory Implementation, and features a termination checker for simple functional programs. It builds an hypergraph of function calls, computes its transitive closure and tries to find a decreasing lexicographic order in the recursive functions' arguments. Foetus is pretty limited, forcing the programmer to construct several auxiliary, often mutually recursive, functions to convince the checker.

Barthe's Type based termination [5, 8, 9] is a strategy in which the language's types carries more information so the type system can serve as a proof system that the programs terminate. It is an elegant but complicated approach, and since it does not transform the programs syntactically, targets with stringent security requirements would still not accept the functions.

Also, LLVM's Clang [15] offers a macro to unroll bounded loops in languages of C family, which is largely used when using pseudo-C code to compile for eBPF.

GCC [12] has a command line option to unroll loops in C programs. The features in both compilers are unable to deal with recursion. At the time of this paper, Microsoft's MSVC [17] has no way to directly instruct the compiler to unroll a loop.

Finally, our generation procedure and test approach are based on the work in [11]. It formalizes a type-directed algorithm to generate random programs of Featherweight Java, which is used to verify several properties using QuickCheck.

7 Conclusion

It is quite useful to allow the dynamic change of behavior in computing systems. This level of adaptation is essential to complete several tasks with efficiency, being attractive even for systems with stringent security requirements, such as the Linux kernel. Because infinite loops can bring a whole system down, a very common restriction in those systems is that the programs must terminate, which is impossible to check in general. Although imperative languages have bounded loops to walk around this limitation, functional languages are left empty-handed. In this work, we proposed a technique to unroll recursive programs in functional languages. For this task, we defined two core languages: one with recursion (System R) and one without recursion but with syntax for errors (System L). We defined an expansion algorithm for System R and a translation algorithm from System R to System L. Our strategy is guaranteed to terminate, and can be used to create compilers from general purpose functional languages to restricted scenarios such as eBPF or smart contracts for blockchain networks. Our prototype implementation of the strategy, Ringell, is available to public access.

References

1. Abel, A.: Foetus—termination checker for simple functional programs. Technical report, Ludwigs-Maximilians-University, Munich (1998)
2. Abel, A.: Specification and verification of a formal system for structurally recursive functions. In: Coquand, T., Dybjer, P., Nordström, B., Smith, J. (eds.) TYPES 1999. LNCS, vol. 1956, pp. 1–20. Springer, Heidelberg (2000). https://doi.org/10.1007/3-540-44557-9_1
3. Abel, A., Altenkirch, T.: A semantical analysis of structural recursion. In: Fourth International Workshop on Termination WST, pp. 24–25. Darmstadt University of Technology, Dagstuhl, Germany (1999)
4. Abel, A., Altenkirch, T.: A predicative analysis of structural recursion. J. Funct. Program. **12**(1), 1–41 (2002)
5. Barthe, G., et al.: Type-based termination of recursive definitions. Math. Struct. Comput. Sci. **14**(1), 97–141 (2004)
6. Appel, A.: Modern Compiler Implementation in ML. Cambridge University Press, New York (2004)
7. Authors of eBPF: eBPF - Introduction, Tutorials and Community Resources (2022). https://ebpf.io/

8. Barthe, G., Grégoire, B., Riba, C.: A tutorial on type-based termination. In: Bove, A., Barbosa, L.S., Pardo, A., Pinto, J.S. (eds.) LerNet 2008. LNCS, vol. 5520, pp. 100–152. Springer, Heidelberg (2009). https://doi.org/10.1007/978-3-642-03153-3_3

9. Barthe, G., Grégoire, B., Riba, C.: Type-based termination with sized products. In: Kaminski, M., Martini, S. (eds.) CSL 2008. LNCS, vol. 5213, pp. 493–507. Springer, Heidelberg (2008). https://doi.org/10.1007/978-3-540-87531-4_35

10. Ringell Developers: Ringell (2022). https://github.com/mayconamaro/ringell

11. Feitosa, S., Ribeiro, R., Du Bois, A.: A type-directed algorithm to generate random well-typed Java 8 programs. Sci. Comput. Program. **196**, 102494 (2020)

12. GNU: GCC, the GNU Compiler Collection (2022). https://gcc.gnu.org/

13. Huet, G., Kahn, G., Paulin-Mohring, C.: The CoQ proof assistant a tutorial. Rapport Technique **178** (1997)

14. Le, T.C., Xu, L., Chen, L., Shi, W.: Proving conditional termination for smart contracts. In: Proceedings of the 2nd ACM Workshop on Blockchains, Cryptocurrencies, and Contracts, BCC 2018, pp. 57–59. Association for Computing Machinery, New York (2018). https://doi.org/10.1145/3205230.3205239

15. LLVM Project: Clang C Language Family Frontend for LLVM (2022). https://clang.llvm.org/

16. McBride, C.: Turing-completeness totally free. In: Hinze, R., Voigtländer, J. (eds.) MPC 2015. LNCS, vol. 9129, pp. 257–275. Springer, Cham (2015). https://doi.org/10.1007/978-3-319-19797-5_13

17. Microsoft: Visual Studio Compiler for Windows (2022). https://visualstudio.microsoft.com/cplusplus/

18. Norell, U.: Towards a practical programming language based on dependent type theory. Ph.D. thesis, Chalmers University of Technology and Göteborg University, Sweden (2007)

19. O'Sullivan, B., Goerzen, J., Stewart, D.: Real World Haskell. O'Reilly, Sebastopol (2008)

20. Pierce, B.C.: Types and Programming Languages. MIT Press, Cambridge (2002)

21. Rugina, R., Rinard, M.: Recursion unrolling for divide and conquer programs. In: Midkiff, S.P., et al. (eds.) LCPC 2000. LNCS, vol. 2017, pp. 34–48. Springer, Heidelberg (2001). https://doi.org/10.1007/3-540-45574-4_3

22. Sipser, M.: Introduction to the Theory of Computation, 3rd edn. Cengage Learning, Cambridge (2012)

23. Wadler, P., Kokke, W., Siek, J.G.: Programming language foundations in Agda (2020). http://plfa.inf.ed.ac.uk/20.07/

Automatic Generation of Verified Concurrent Hardware Using VHDL

Luciano Silva and Marcel Oliveira[✉]

Universidade Federal do Rio Grande do Norte, Natal, RN, Brazil
`marcel@dimap.ufrn.br`

Abstract. The complexity of development and analysis is inherent to systems in general, especially in concurrent systems. When working with critical systems this becomes much more evident, as inconsistencies are usually associated with a high cost. Thus, the sooner we can identify an inconsistency in the design of a system and remove it, the lower its cost. For this reason, it is common to use strategies to reduce the difficulty and problems faced in this process. One of these strategies is the use of formal methods, which can, for instance, make use of process algebras to specify and analise concurrent systems, improving its understanding and enabling the identification of eventual concurrency problems and inconsistencies even in the initial stages of the project, ensuring the accuracy and correction of the system specification. This article presents a strategy for automatically translating the main operators of the process algebra CSP (Communicating Sequential Processes) into the VHSIC hardware description language (VHDL). The former is a language that allows us to make a formal description of a concurrent system and the latter is a hardware description language that can be compiled on a Field Programmable Gate Arrays (FPGA) board. Our automatic translator is validated by a case study of a smart elevator control system. We present its formal specification in CSP and then its translation into VHDL code, generated by our tool, which we synthesised on an FPGA board.

Keywords: Concurrency · CSP · VHDL · Code synthesis

1 Introduction

The process of developing a system, whether hardware or software, is not a simple task, especially when working with concurrent systems. This development process usually involves several steps, each one supported by a set of methodologies, techniques and tools.

There are important differences between the development of hardware systems and the development of software systems. When implementing software systems, high-level languages are usually used. These languages offer a high level of

This work is partially supported by INES, CNPq grant 465614/2014-0, CAPES grant 88887.136410/2017-00, FACEPE grants APQ-0399- 1.03/17 and PRONEX APQ/0388- 1.03/14.

abstraction, removing from the programmer the responsibility on aspects such as the use of memory, generated code optimisation, and concurrency management. However, when we work with hardware systems, the entire development process is guided by issues such as memory usage and code optimisation. Thus, the languages used for this purpose generally offer resources that allow the developer to have greater control over these aspects and this ends up generating some limitations in the development process. In addition, when we work with hardware systems, we have several particularities and we need to consider some factors, such as customer requirements, hardware requirements, and commercial and project scalability factors.

In the development of concurrent systems, the difficulties encountered are further increased, as the control aspects that are specific to parallel environments are not trivial. Associated with all this, some systems become even more complex, as they work with critical tasks. These, according to Sommerville [18], are the so-called critical systems and require a higher level of correctness in their functioning. There is no margin for errors. Thus, it is necessary to use methodologies, techniques and tools that guarantee a higher level of correctness so that the implemented system reflects exactly its specification.

With the increase in the number of critical systems, some techniques proved to be efficient to assist in the development of such systems. Among these techniques, we have the formal methods, which make use of mathematical principles that guarantee the accuracy in the design of a system. They can be used in the specification, refinement, synthesis and prototyping steps. In this way, we can make a specification of the project's requirements and, from there, make several refinements of it, always preserving the behaviour of the initial specification [18]. This preservation is guaranteed through proof of correctness or exhaustive verification of the generated models. However, at the end of this process, the result will be a formal refinement, and not an executable code, which ideally should have a behaviour that indeed refines the formal specification.

CSP [7] is a process algebra aimed at describing concurrent systems. This language provides constructs that can be used to describe the behaviour of a concurrent system in a more natural way. With a clear notation, CSP is an appropriate solution for formal specification of concurrent and distributed systems [17]. Using this language, we can abstract a system as a composition of units (processes) that have some behaviour and communicate with each other and with the environment [7,16]. This interaction takes place through an event interface [17]. The FDR [6] model checker allows the automated analysis of aspects of a specification, such as determinism, the absence of deadlocks and livelocks, and the correctness of refinements. Languages like CSP increase the reliability of systems as they use a set of strategies to ensure properties and requirements. However, despite increasing the reliability of the specified systems, we are not able to execute a CSP code: a translation to a programming language is required.

When we work with hardware systems, the VHDL language presents itself as a possibility of hardware description, with which we can easily work on the design (design/conception) of digital circuits in FPGA [3]. With VHDL we can describe a digital system in three ways, namely: behavioural, data-flow and structural descriptions. When working with complex digital systems, the most recommended descriptions are the behavioural ones, as they allow the transformation between inputs and outputs from the process specification, where sequential instructions are defined in a similar way to high-level programming languages. Code compilation and simulation is achieved using tools like Intel's Quartus II.

Translating a formal specification into a programming language keeping the faithfulness of the implementation with respect to the specification is far from a simple task and is usually an error-prone time consuming task. For this reason, it is imperative to find alternatives that help us to accelerate the development process and mitigate errors in the resulting code.

Motivated by this scenario, this work proposes the translation of the main CSP operators into VHDL. This translation is automated by the tool csp2vhdl, another contribution of this paper.

This article is organised as follows. In Sect. 2 we present CSP and VHDL and describe their main constructors and operators. Section 3 presents the proposed translation from CSP into VHDL. Section 4 presents the automatic translator we developed in this work. The translation process is illustrated in Sect. 5, in which we describe the development of an intelligent elevator controller system, which was translated by the tool developed and executed on an FPGA board. Finally, in Sect. 6, we present our final remarks.

1.1   Related Work

Other researchers have already considered the translation of process algebras into programming languages. For instance, in [8], the refinement of CSP specifications into occam-2 and Ada 9X [1] code was presented. The intention, however, is to illustrate the translation; no tool support is available.

The translation of CSP into imperative and object-oriented programming languages is also the subject of [15], where Raju *et al.* present a tool that translates a small subset of CSP into Java and C, with the help of libraries that provide models for processes and channels and allows programmers to abstract from basic constructs of these languages (i.e., JCSP [20] for Java and CCSP [10] for C). Using this approach, we have an automatic translation into software.

In [11], we extend this work and provide a translation from a subset of Circus, a combination of CSP with Z [21] and Dijkstra's command language that has an associated refinement theory [4], into JCSP. In [5], that authors extended [11] and implemented a tool that automatically applies this translation strategy.

Most of the translations between CSP and a programming language available in the literature target the generation of software. In [8], occam-2, which is the native programming language for a line of transputer microprocessors, is the target language. Unfortunately, it is not supported by any tool.

Our work is strongly based on Oliveira and Woodcock's [9,12,13] approach for generating hardware projects based on a high-level formal description, using Handel-C, a procedural language, rather like occam, but with a C-like syntax.

Although targeting hardware, Handel-C is a programming language with hardware output rather than a hardware description language. This makes Handel-C different from VHDL [2]. A hardware design using Handel-C is more like programming than hardware engineering; this language is developed for programmers who have no hardware knowledge at all. In [13], we achieve an automatic generation of verified hardware. In the literature, as far as we know, only [14](probably based on [19]) present tools that convert a subset of CSP into Handel-C code. Their methodology is very similar to ours, but the subset of CSP considered is relatively small. In this paper, we take a different approach and provide a direct translation to VHDL, avoiding the need of acquiring an additional Handel-C compiler to generate hardware.

2   Theoretical Background

In this section, we will present the concepts necessary for understanding the work. First, the source language of our translation process, CSP, is presented. Then, we present the target language, VHDL.

2.1   CSP

CSP is a process algebra designed to describe synchronisations and communications between various processes. Processes that are described using CSP can go through a series of verifications, some of which are non-determinism, absence of deadlock and livelock, and refinement correctness against a formal specification through the use of tools such as FDR. A CSP script can be used as a basis for implementing code in a high-level language, and it can also be used as a starting point for hardware projects. The main CSP operators can be seen in Table 1. In this paper, we use the ASCII version of CSP, called CSP_M.

New data types can be defined using the keyword **datatype**. When defining a new type, the values it can take must be unique, so they cannot be part of the set of values that have already been defined. Each value must be separated by the pipe character, as seen in the following example:

```
datatype StatusDoor = open | close
```

The simplest process of all is STOP. This process is never prepared to engage in any of its interface events. Another simple process is SKIP, which indicates that the process has reached successful termination. A prefixing c -> P describes a process that first engages in the event c and then behaves as described by P. In CSP, a channel can be used for input or output of values. To represent a channel c outputting a value v we use the expression c!v and to represent a channel c receiving an input value we use the notation c?x, where the value received will be assigned to the variable x which is implicitly declared. The process P [] Q is an external choice between process P and Q: it allows the environment to resolve the choice by communicating an initial event to one of the

Table 1. CSP main operators

Operator	Description
STOP	A process that simply deadlocks
SKIP	A process that successfully terminates
c -> P	Event prefix
P [] Q	External choice (deterministic)
P |~| Q	Internal choice (non-deterministic)
g & P	Guarded process
if g then P else Q	Conditional choice
P ; Q	Sequential composition
P [| cs |] Q	Generalised parallelism
P [A || B] Q	Alphabetised parallelism
P ||| Q	Interleaving
P / Q	Interrupt
P \cs	Channel abstraction

processes. When the environment has no control over the choice (i.e. the choice is resolved internally), we have an internal choice, which is written P |~| Q. The generalised parallel composition P [| A |] P synchronises P and Q on the events in the synchronisation event set A; events that are not listed in A occur independently. The alphabetised parallel composition P [A || B] Q, runs P and Q in parallel, allowing P to only perform events from A, Q to only perform events from B and forcing P and Q to synchronise on the intersection of A and B. The interleaving P1 ||| P2 runs the processes independently. The guarded process g & P behaves like P if the predicate g is true; it deadlocks otherwise. The interrupt operator P /\ Q behaves like P except that at any time Q may perform one of its initial events and take over. Finally, using the hiding operator P \ cs, we may hide all events in cs from the environment.

2.2   VHDL

The VHDL language was created to provide a tool for designing and documenting the VHSIC, a project of the Department of Defense of the United States of America. After some evolution, it became possible to use VHDL to document, describe, synthesise, test and verify digital circuit designs. It was standardised by the Institute of Electrical and Electronic Engineers (IEEE) in 1987, but in 1992 some changes were proposed and a revision of the standard was published, VHSIC Std 1076-1993 (VHDL-93), which brought new features and more flexibility.

Unlike conventional languages that are generally based on sequentially executing instructions, VHDL operates in parallel, making it more suitable for working with digital hardware devices that operate in this way. Some advantages that

```
1   ENTITY circuit
2   IS PORT (  sx : OUT INTEGER;
3              vx : OUT INTEGER );
4   END circuit;
5
6   ARCHITECTURE hardware OF circuit IS
7       SIGNAL sa : INTEGER := 1;
8   BEGIN
9       sig: PROCESS
10      BEGIN
11          sa <= sa + sa;
12          sx <= sa;
13          WAIT FOR 10 ns;
14      END PROCESS sig;
15
16      var: PROCESS
17          VARIABLE va : INTEGER :=1;
18      BEGIN
19          va := va +va;
20          vx <= va;
21          WAIT FOR 10 ns;
22      END PROCESS var;
23  END hardware;
```

Code 1.1: VHDL Example

we can cite from its use are technology-independent design, ease of updating projects, reduction of project time and cost, elimination of low-level errors and simplicity in the documentation.

A VHDL program is based on 3 blocks: package, entity and architecture. The package block, also called a library, is a subprogram that creates components to be reused. In the entity block, the input and output ports of the described circuits must be defined. The architecture block contains the project implementation, describing the relationships between the ports defined in the entity block.

VHDL has a series of concurrent commands which are executed in parallel. This allows the description of circuits with greater complexity. An example of concurrent commands is processes, where each process block will be executed concurrently, but the commands that are inside the process block will be executed sequentially.

In VHDL a signal is an element that can store some value. We can define signals in both sequential code regions and concurrent regions. When we define a signal and assign a value to it, this assignment occurs after a time delay. Another way of storing values is through variables, which are objects that only can be declared in sequential code regions. Unlike the signals, for the variables there is no delay in the time of assignment. In Code 1.1, we present an example of a

VHDL code using signals and variables that describes an entity `circuit` with two output ports, `sx` and `vx`.

The architecture declares a signal `sa` and two processes, `sig` and `"var`, which run in parallel. In the process `sig`, we double the value of the signal and sends the incremented value to the output port `sx`. Finally, we wait 10 nanoseconds before continuing the process execution. The process `var` declares a local variable `va`, doubles the value of the variable and sends the incremented value to the output port `vx`. Finally, it also waits 10 nanoseconds before continuing the process execution.

3   CSP to VHDL Translation

Our translation strategy was based on Oliveira and Woodcock's [9] approach for generating hardware projects based on a high-level formal description, which is illustrated in Fig. 1. In the proposed methodology, we start from a high-level specification, which contains the main properties of the system. This specification needs to be refined (possibly using many refinement steps) to a CSP implementation of the system, which contains only translatable features. Using FDR, the correctness of these refinement steps may automatically be carried out. Finally, the translation is applied to yield a VHDL code, which can then be compiled into an executable FPGA. All files related to this work, including the source CSP scripts of our examples and their corresponding, generated VHDL code, the automatic translator and its source code are available on the project's website[1].

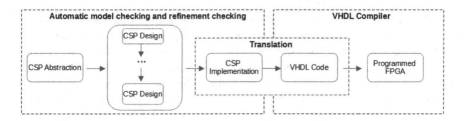

Fig. 1. Development methodology

3.1   Translation Overview

The first translated constructor was the prefixing `c -> P`, in which `c` is an event that must happen for process `P` to be executed. Its translation is presented in the Code 1.2.

---

[1] www.dimap.ufrn.br/~marcel/research/csp2vhdl/.

```
1   library ieee;
2   use ieee.std_logic_1164.all;
3   ENTITY my_entity IS PORT (
4           c       : IN BIT;
5           reset   : IN STD_LOGIC
6   );
7   END my_entity;
8   ARCHITECTURE my_architecture OF my_entity IS BEGIN
9           P: PROCESS (c, reset) BEGIN
10              IF(reset ='1') THEN
11              ELSIF(c'event and c='0') THEN
12                  -- process P commands
13              END IF;
14          END PROCESS P;
15  END my_architecture;
```

Code 1.2: Translation of the prefix operator

Lines 1 and 2 of the translation import the IEEE library, which provides several basic IEEE-defined functions and types. In line 3 a new entity is defined, where it is possible to define the input and output ports of the circuits we are describing. In our case, we assume c as an input port and assign the type bit.

From line 8 we have the definition of an architecture, where the implementation of the processes is defined, describing the relationships between the circuit ports. Within an architecture, we can write the processes, which can optionally be preceded by a label. In our translation, this label will always have the name of the process described in the CSP input script.

Following the declaration of a process, we may add in parentheses a sensitivity list containing ports. Changes to the values of the ports from the sensitivity list lead to a reassessment of the outputs, that is, the process will be executed again. Thus, port c was added to the sensitivity list of process P, so that whenever the value of c is changed, P will be executed. The reset port was also added to the sensitivity list because it works as a lock that blocks the execution of processes. In this way, if it is evaluated as 1 (off) nothing will be offered and the process will be stopped, but if it is evaluated as 0 (on) the processes were waiting for a value change event to occur in c and only then the commands P will be executed.

The CSP process below recursively writes the value 10 on channel c.

```
channel c : Int
P = c!10 -> P
```

In Code 1.3, we see the translation of this CSP, where the value v is written, through channel c, represented by a input port.

Another possible variation is reading a channel. Its translation is similar to the one presented above, inverting the elements of the c <= v line, where the signal will receive the value obtained from the port, and it will have its declaration changed from an output port to an input port.

```
1   ENTITY my_entity IS PORT (
2           c              : IN BIT;
3           reset, clock   : IN STD_LOGIC
4   );
5   END my_entity;
6   ARCHITECTURE my_architecture OF my_entity IS BEGIN
7           P: PROCESS (c, reset, clock) BEGIN
8               IF(reset ='1') THEN
9
10              ELSIF(clock'event and clock='0') THEN
11                  c <= 10;
12              END IF;
13          END PROCESS P;
14  END my_architecture;
```

Code 1.3: Translation of the prefix operator (with output value)

The translation of STOP (Code 1.4) reads a channel that executes a process that goes nowhere and that does not synchronise with any other process, hence deadlocking. The translation of SKIP simply generates no code, hence it simply ignores the SKIP resulting in a "code" that just terminates.

```
1   ENTITY my_entity IS PORT (
2           c                : IN BIT;
3           reset, clock   : IN STD_LOGIC
4   );
5   END my_entity;
6
7   ARCHITECTURE my_architecture OF my_entity IS BEGIN
8           P: PROCESS (c, reset, clock) BEGIN
9               IF(reset ='1') THEN
10              ELSIF(clock'event and clock='0') THEN
11              END IF;
12          END PROCESS P;
13  END my_architecture;
```

Code 1.4: Translation of STOP

The external choice offers to the environment the choice between two (or more) events, as in the CSP script below in which it is possible to choose to enter a value either through keyboard_a or keyboard_b.

```
channel keyboard_a, keyboard_b : {0..3}
P = keyboard_a?number -> P
    [] keyboard_B?number -> P
```

Our translation creates an array of ports called external choice, which when synthesised on an FPGA can be mapped to a set of pins, where the environment can switch according to the stream you want to choose. By way of illustration, Code 1.5 presents the translation of the CSP above.

```
1   ENTITY my_entity IS PORT (
2           keyboard_a, keyborad_b: IN STD_LOGIC_VECTOR(2 DOWNTO 0);
3           external_choice        : IN STD_LOGIC_VECTOR(1 DOWNTO 0) := "XX";
4           reset, clock           : IN STD_LOGIC
5   ); END my_entity;
6   ARCHITECTURE my_architecture OF my_entity IS
7       SIGNAL number : std_logic_vector(2 downto 0);
8       BEGIN
9           P: PROCESS (reset, clock, external_choice) BEGIN
10              IF(reset ='1') THEN
11              ELSIF(clock'event and clock='0') THEN
12                  CASE external_choice IS
13                      WHEN "01"   =: number <= keyboard_a;
14                      WHEN "10"   =: number <= keyboard_b;
15                      WHEN OTHERS =: number <= "XXX";
16                  END CASE;
17              END IF;
18          END PROCESS P;
19  END my_architecture;
```

Code 1.5: Translation of external choice

In this code, the choice is achieved by switching the board pins, which will be evaluated in the VHDL CASE block. The choice of keyboard_a is indicated with value 01 and the second of keyboard_b is indicated with value 10.

The internal choice makes a choice between two or more events without external intervention. In our case, we use the same idea of external choice, but as there should be no influence from the external environment, the choice will be based on a signal named internal choice. The signal will receive a value from a function int_choice that will randomly choose between the values available for switching. This is a particular refinement of non-determinism as it considers a uniform distribution. The result in VHDL can be seen in Code 1.6.

Another way to work with conditional choices in CSP is through the if constructor, which has been translated to the equivalent if structure in VHDL. The last form of conditional choice is the guarded process g & P, which behaves like P if the predicate g is true and deadlocks otherwise. This behaviour can be easily mapped to the use of the if constructor that behaves as the translation of P is g is true and deadlocks otherwise.

```
1   ENTITY my_entity IS PORT (
2           keyboard_a, keyborad_b: IN STD_LOGIC_VECTOR(1 DOWNTO 0);
3           reset, clock        : IN STD_LOGIC
4   ); END my_entity;
5   ARCHITECTURE my_architecture OF my_entity IS
6       SIGNAL number, internal_choice : std_logic_vector(1 downto 0);
7       BEGIN
8           P: PROCESS (reset, clock) BEGIN
9               IF(reset ='1') THEN
10              ELSIF(clock'event and clock='0') THEN
11                  internal_choice <= int_choice();
12                  CASE internal_choice IS
13                      WHEN "01"   =: number <= keyboard_a;
14                      WHEN "10"   =: number <= keyboard_b;
15                      WHEN OTHERS =: number <= "XX";
16                  END CASE;
17              END IF;
18          END PROCESS P;
19  END my_architecture;
```

Code 1.6: Translation of internal choice

The sequential composition of processes, presented below, executes the events
of process P2 as soon as the last event of process P1 is executed.

```
channel event1
channel event2: {0..10}
P1 = event1 -> SKIP
P2 = event2?a -> SKIP
P = P1;P2
```

The translation of the sequential composition (Code 1.7) adds the last event of
P1 (event1) in the sensitivity list of the P2. Hence, when this event happens,
the execution of P2 starts.

In VHDL, if an architecture has more than one process, it will be executed
concurrently, without any type of communication between them. Each process
has its commands executed sequentially. This is exactly the behaviour of CSP
interleaving. Therefore, VHDL provides mechanisms to work with parallel digital
systems, but does not directly support aspects such as channel synchronisation.
The correct translation of these behaviours required the use of the protocol
presented in [12] that uses a series of functions and arrays.

In this protocol, a central process uses the function initializeSync to create an array for each group of synchronising processes. Each of these arrays keeps
a list with the event, process and branch ids, as in [12]. From there, a series of
functions are defined that manipulate these arrays to guarantee the synchronisation of the channels: checkSync, syncComplete, waitSync and toSync. The
checkSync function loops while the process is running. It checks whether or

```
1   ENTITY my_entity IS PORT (
2           reset, clock, event1  : IN STD_LOGIC;
3           event2                : IN INTEGER
4   ); END my_entity;
5   ARCHITECTURE my_architecture OF my_entity IS BEGIN
6           P1: PROCESS BEGIN
7               WAIT UNTIL event1 = "1";
8           END PROCESS P1;
9           P2: PROCESS(event1)
10              VARIABLE a : INTEGER;
11          BEGIN
12              IF(event1'event and event1='0') THEN
13                  a := event2;
14              END IF;
15          END PROCESS P2;
16  END my_architecture;
```

Code 1.7: Translation of sequential composition

not the channels that are offered should synchronise with channels of other processes. If so, it calls the waitSync function which hangs the process until all
the processes involved in the synchronisation are ready to offer the channel.
When this happens, the toSync function is called, enabling data communication
through the channels that are synchronising. When the synchronisation is finished, the syncComplete function is invoked and releases the process to continue
its executions, and the checkSync function goes back to checking possible new
synchronisations. This protocol also implements multi-synchronisation in which
more than two processes are involved in the synchronisation.

The translation of the interruption P /\ Q is achieved by extracting the
Labeled Transition System (LTS), with the help of the FDR's provided API. On
the other hand, hiding is simply ignored. This, however, can only be done if the
restrictions presented in the next section are satisfied.

3.2   Restrictions

Some restrictions must be taken into account in our translation process. First,
only CSP integer and boolean types are currently accepted.

Our translation only supports simple communication, hence, complex communications like c?num1?num2 -> P are not supported. Next, all event sets used
in the specification must have the form {| c1, ..., cn |}, where c1, ..., cn
must be declared channels. Additionally, in the case of parallel composition, the
channels used in the synchronisation must contain all channels that are in both
P and Q ($channels(P) \cap channels(Q) \subseteq \{| c1, ..., cn |\}$).

The choice can only be made on visible events. For this reason, processes
like SKIP and internal events τ are not accepted as part of an external choice.

Fig. 2. Tool Operation Flow

Hence, no event offered in an external choice can be hidden. Furthermore, no multi-synchronised events can be offered on an external choice.

Some other restrictions that must be taken into account when working with parallel composition. First, if we hide some channels in one of the parallel branches, these channels can only be channels of this branch. For instance, in (P \ cs1) [| cs2 |] Q, we have that:

- $cs1 \subseteq channels(P)$, and
- $cs1 \cap channels(Q) = \{\}$.

In case, we hide channels in both parallel branches, these conditions must be satisfied for each of the sets of hidden channels.

Regarding interruptions, both processes involved must initially offer visible events. For this reason, processes like Q = SKIP /\ a -> STOP are not currently translatable. Finally, recursive processes cannot have a cycle on internal events only; hence, all processes are livelock-free.

4   Tool Support

In this section, we present csp2vhdl, the automatic translator that receives CSP formal specifications satisfying the restrictions presented in Sect. 3.2 and yields a VHDL code that can be synthesised in an FPGA, hence, automating the hardware generation process, based on our translation strategy.

In Fig. 2 we have an overview of the translation stages sequence: (1) define CSP input file and target FPGA model; (2) Directives check; (3) Restrictions check; (4) VHDL Code Generation, and; (5)Channel/Ports Mapping. The interaction with the user only takes place in the first and in the final stages.

Initially, the tool prompts a window in which the user selects the input CSP script and the target FPGA model.

In the next stage, our tool extracts the additional information needed for the translation process. Like in [9], this information is received in the form of directives that must be written directly into the specification in the form of CSP comment lines (--) prefixed with !!. In this work, we used four directives:

1. --!! main P: this mandatory directive indicates the main process name P of the script. This directive also accepts the composition of processes, indicating the main behaviour of the system. There may be arguments in this process, in which case, the directive **arg** described below must also be used.

2. --!! arg *id T* within *P*: this directive informs the type *T* of the argument *id* of the process *P*. It is mandatory for every process argument.
3. --!! int bits *n*: this directive defined the number *n* of bits needed to represent the integers of the specification in the generated VHDL code. Thus, whenever the Int data type is used, this directive is usually needed. If, however, it is not defined, the tool uses the size 1 as default.
4. --!! channel *c dir* within *P*: this directive indicates the direction *dir* of communication of the channel *c* within the process *P*. When using this directive, *dir* may only assume either value in for inputs or out for outputs, indicating that the process *P* assumes the role of writer or reader, respectively, in the communications made through *c*.

In the next stage, the tool checks if the restrictions imposed in Sect. 3.2 are all satisfied by the CSP specification. The tool also checks if the total ports that are needed for the synthesis of the VHDL file generated by the translation of the CSP file are available on the FPGA device selected in the tool. Thus, if the total number of ports required is greater than the number of ports available, this restriction is not be met, and the code is not generated. All eventual violations are indicated to the user.

If everything is correct with our specification, the VHDL code generation process is executed using the translation strategy presented in Sect. 3. In this stage, csp2vhdl is aided by the FDR API *libfd*. This API consists of a library for 64-bit systems available for the C++, Java and Python programming languages, that makes it possible for external tools to use the internal components of FDR. Using this API, we can load CSP scripts and execute certain assertions, such as deadlock verification. Among several other functions, we can extract some information, such as the Labelled Transition System (LTS) of a process.

The *libfd* was used throughout the process of generating the VHDL code, both to ensure that our specification meets all the necessary checks, and to perform the translation of the code based on the LTS extracted from the CSP process, where there is no syntactic rule applicable in our translation, such as the interrupt operator.

As seen in Fig. 2, after generating the CSP file, the CSP channels must be mapped to the ports available on the chosen FPGA device. At this point, using the GUI provided by csp2vhdl, the user informs, for each CSP channel, which port of the target FPGA device corresponds to it. This process is completed through a configuration file made available by the Quartus II tool, which was used to compile and synthesise our generated code.

5   Case Study

In this section, we present the main case study developed in order to validate our tool, a smart elevator controller. We have provided a specification of the system, translated it into a VHDL code that was synthesised on an FPGA board. The controller has the following requirements:

- It controls 2 elevators of an 8-story building;
- Each floor has a door;
- Each elevator has a door;
- The requests may be made from buttons available on each floor (external requests) or from the buttons available in each elevator (internal requests);
- External requests may have a direction (up or down) except at the bottom floor (up only) and top floor (down only);
- Only one elevator must attend each request;
- If more than one request is made for a given floor before it is attended, only one elevator must attend these requests, and only once.
- The internal requests have priority over the external requests, unless the elevator, to meet the internal request, needs to go through the floor externally requested, and the external request has the same direction of the elevator.

In addition to the functional requirements presented, the following safety requirements should also be taken into consideration:

- When the emergency button is pressed, the elevator must stop immediately and not respond to any further requests, whether external or internal.
- The controller must ensure that the floor door and the elevator door are only opened when the elevator is stopped on the correct floor.
- The doors can only be closed when no one is entering the elevator.
- The elevator should only leave the floor to meet requests when both doors are completely closed.

For a better understanding of the system specification structure, we can observe the diagram presented in Fig. 3, in which we present the components and the interaction channels among them and with the external environment.

The specification has three main components: the elevators, the central controller and the floors. Each of these components has been specified as the parallel composition of internal processes. For conciseness, we omit the full CSP specification, which can be found elsewhere. Using FDR4, we have verified that the specification meets the functional and safety requirements.

Next, The CSP specification of the smart elevator controller was translated into VHDL using csp2vhdl. The generated VHDL code was compiled and analysed in the Altera Quartus II tool and then, with the support of the same tool, recorded in a CYCLONE IV family FPGA board, model EP4CE115F29C7. It was then verified that the behaviour matches what was expected from its formal specification in CSP. The execution of the FPGA board can be seen in videos we made available on the web[2][3][4].

---

[2] https://www.youtube.com/watch?v=xgZQy9IH-KE.

[3] https://www.youtube.com/watch?v=heaKFhljm0c.

[4] https://www.youtube.com/watch?v=xqdOFnWLKrM.

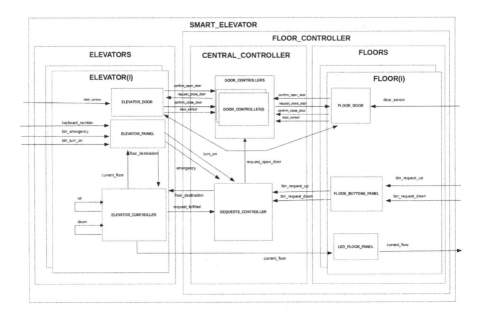

Fig. 3. CSP Specification component diagram

6 Conclusion

The development of concurrent systems is not a trivial task, however, when we work with the hardware we have some peculiarities that make its development even more complex, especially when it involves concurrency. It is extremely important to use methodologies, strategies and tools that assist in each step of this process.

This work developed a translation proposal between CSP and VHDL languages. These languages have different purposes and levels of abstraction, and most commands do not have a direct equivalent, especially concerning process synchronization and multi-synchronization. In this work, a series of translation protocols were developed, so that the behaviour of the specified system is systematically translated.

The translation process is supported by a tool for automatic code generation, called csp2vhdl, also presented in this paper. Our translation approach, together with the developed tool, was validated through some case studies, the main one, presented in this article, being an intelligent elevator control system.

With our results, we facilitate the construction of hardware systems based on a formal specification that can guarantee all the necessary correctness and safety, thus contributing to the automatic generation of verified hardware and making the process of developing concurrent hardware systems safer. In addition, we provide a time gain in the translation process from CSP to VHDL, since csp2vhdl automatically generates the VHDL code, which can already be synthesised in FPGA, without the need to change the generated script. Furthermore, as it is not necessary to make changes to the VHDL script resulting from the translation, the developer does not need to have a deep knowledge of the VHDL language, as well as the concepts of hardware development.

The correctness of our translation was not considered in this paper. We currently rely on the validation of our examples and on the fairly large number of tests we have carried out to validate our translations. We intend to formalise the translation as translation rules, and then prove these rules.

In a near future, we intend to remove some limitations of the tool. For instance, we are currently unable to translate all operators available in CSP. There are also some restrictions in the current translation, where some operators need to respect certain conditions for the translation to take place correctly. For instance, the translation of external choice considers only a restricted form of the operator: the simple choice between distinct events. These restrictions may also be eliminated in the future.

References

1. Burns, A., Wellings, A.: Concurrency in ADA, 2nd edn. Cambridge University Press, Cambridge (1997)
2. Augustin, L.M., Luckham, D.C., Gennart, B.A., Huh, Y., Stanculescu, A.G.: Hardware Design and Simulation in VAL/VHDL. Kluwer Academic Pub, Dordrecht (1991)
3. Brown, S.D., Francis, R.J., Rose, J., Vranesic, Z.G.: Field-Programmable Gate Arrays. Kluwer Academic Publishers, USA (1992)
4. Cavalcanti, A.L.C., Sampaio, A.C.A., Woodcock, J.C.P.: A refinement strategy for *Circus*. Formal Aspects Comput. **15**(2–3), 146–181 (2003)
5. Freitas, A., Cavalcanti, A.: Automatic translation from *Circus* to Java. In: Misra, J., Nipkow, T., Sekerinski, E. (eds.) FM 2006. LNCS, vol. 4085, pp. 115–130. Springer, Heidelberg (2006). https://doi.org/10.1007/11813040_9
6. Gibson-Robinson, T., Armstrong, P., Boulgakov, A., Roscoe, A.W.: FDR3 — a modern refinement checker for CSP. In: Ábrahám, E., Havelund, K. (eds.) TACAS 2014. LNCS, vol. 8413, pp. 187–201. Springer, Heidelberg (2014). https://doi.org/10.1007/978-3-642-54862-8_13
7. Hoare, C.A.R.: Communicating Sequential Processes. Prentice-Hall, Hoboken (1985)
8. Hinchey, M.G., Jarvis, S.A.: Concurrent Systems: Formal Development in CSP. McGraw-Hill Inc, New York (1995)
9. Macário, F.J.S., Oliveira, M.V.M.: Hard-wiring CSP hiding: implementing channel abstraction to generate veried concurrent hardware. In: Cornélio, M., Roscoe, B. (eds.) Formal Methods: Foundations and Applications - 18th Brazilian Symposium on Formal Methods. Lecture Notes in Computer Science, vol. 9526, pp. 3–18. The original publication is available at www.springerlink.com, Springer-Verlag (2015)
10. McMillin, B., Arrowsmith, E.: CCSP-a formal system for distributed program debugging. In: Proceedings of the Software for Multiprocessors and Supercomputers, Theory, Practice, Experience, Moscow - Russia, (1994)
11. Oliveira, M., Cavalcanti, A.: From *Circus* to JCSP. In: Davies, J., Schulte, W., Barnett, M. (eds.) ICFEM 2004. LNCS, vol. 3308, pp. 320–340. Springer, Heidelberg (2004). https://doi.org/10.1007/978-3-540-30482-1_29

12. Oliveira, M.V.M., De Medeiros Júnior, I.S., Woodcock, J.: A verified protocol to implement multi-way synchronisation and interleaving in CSP. In: Hierons, R.M., Merayo, M.G., Bravetti, M. (eds.) SEFM 2013. LNCS, vol. 8137, pp. 46–60. Springer, Heidelberg (2013). https://doi.org/10.1007/978-3-642-40561-7_4

13. Oliveira, M., Woodcock, J.: Automatic generation of verified concurrent hardware. In: Butler, M., Hinchey, M.G., Larrondo-Petrie, M.M. (eds.) ICFEM 2007. LNCS, vol. 4789, pp. 286–306. Springer, Heidelberg (2007). https://doi.org/10.1007/978-3-540-76650-6_17

14. Phillips, J.D., Stiles,G.S.: An automatic translation of CSP to Handel-C. In: East, I., Martin, J., Welch, P., Duce, D., Green, M., (eds), Communicating Process Architectures 2004, pp. 19–38 (2004)

15. Raju, V., Rong, L., Stiles, G.S.: Automatic conversion of CSP to CTJ, JCSP, and CCSP. In: Broenink, J.F., Hilderink, G.H., (eds), Communicating Process Architectures 2003, pp. 63–81 (2003)

16. Roscoe, A.W.: The Theory and Practice of Concurrency. Prentice-Hall Series in Computer Science. Prentice-Hall, Hoboken (1998)

17. Schneider, S.: Concurrent and Real Time Systems: The CSP Approach, 1st edn. John Wiley, New York (1999)

18. Sommerville, I.: Software Engineering, 9th edn. Addison-Wesley, Boston (2010)

19. Stepney, S.: CSP/FDR2 to Handel-C translation. Technical report YCS-2002-357, Department of Computer Science, University of York (2003)

20. Welch, P.H.: Process oriented design for Java: concurrency for all. In: Arabnia, H.R., editor, Proceedings of the International Conference on Parallel and Distributed Processing Techniques and Applications, pp. 51–57. CSREA Press (2000)

21. Woodcock, J.C.P., Davies, J.: Using Z-Specification, Refinement, and Proof. Prentice-Hall, Hoboken (1996)

Synthesis of Implementations for Divide-and-Conquer Specifications

Maksym Bortin[✉][ID]

Department of Software Science, Tallinn University of Technology, Tallinn, Estonia
`maksym.bortin@taltech.ee`

Abstract. The paper presents a systematic approach to the derivation of implementations from abstract specifications featuring a few structural properties. The method is applied in a case study concerning weighted finite matroids and the algorithmic construction of their optimal bases.

Keywords: Implementation · Synthesis · Design tactics

1 Introduction

The so-called 'divide-and-conquer' approach is fairly ubiquitous in the algorithmic problem solving. Indeed, decomposing an input into smaller parts, deriving solutions for these parts, and composing these ultimately to a solution of the original problem seems to be a very natural way taken in innumerable procedures since splitting a list into its head and tail, making a recursive call with the tail and using the result to return some composed value particularly fits into this scheme. On the other hand, the choice of such a decomposition is not at all confined to the inverse of some data constructor and a more sophisticated design is used in [8] to obtain a function searching for optimal subarrays.

Another prominent example is sorting: a list becomes split into parts such that one obtains a sorted version of the list by sorting and combining the parts. What makes this technique however exceedingly valuable is that the correctness argumentation follows essentially the same principle. With *quicksort*, for instance, any non-empty input list *xs* gets split into an intermediate representation by an element p and sublists *ls* and *gs* such that all elements of *ls* (*gs*) are smaller (greater) than p. The crucial point is that we may further assume the existence of some *ls'* and *gs'* being respective sorted versions of *ls* and *gs* in order to conclude that *ls'* · p · *gs'* is a sorted version of *xs*. Precisely due to this closure argument, the specification itself (*i.e.* the output is a sorted version of the input) can likewise be regarded as divide-and-conquer, leading to the insight that it can be refined by a certain fixed point which turns out to be the *quicksort* algorithm. If generalised, this observation is the first step towards synthesis.

From a broader perspective it appears however rather coincidental that sorting is specified on the same data type (*i.e.* lists) on which *quicksort* operates: it

Research supported by the Estonian IT Academy under grant 2014-2020.4.05.19-0001.

L. Lima and V. Molnár (Eds.): SBMF 2022, LNCS 13768, pp. 73–88, 2022.
https://doi.org/10.1007/978-3-031-22476-8_5

is a common practice to specify properties on structures such as graphs, monoids or groups involving abstract data types such as sets, multisets, queues *etc.* For example, one normally does not describe what is the power set of a (finite) set in terms of arrays, lists or trees, *i.e.* the data types used to compute one of its representations. The central objective of this work is to establish a sound method that can handle a variety of abstract specifications in a manner, similar to what has been sketched above for sorting.

The paper is structured as follows. Based on the framework described in Sect. 2, Sect. 3 establishes the synthesis method backed by the main theorem given in Sect. 3.1. Further, Sect. 4 presents a case study where the proposed technique is applied to eventually obtain a 'greedy' algorithm constructing optimal bases of weighted finite matroids. Finally, Sect. 5 contains an overview of the related work and Sect. 6 concludes the paper.

2   Preliminaries

To keep the paper largely self-contained, this section briefly presents the foundational framework which is the locally complete allegory [2] of relations **Rel**: for any objects A and B, an arrow $r : A \to B$ indicates $r \subseteq A \times B$, *i.e.* r relates elements of the set A to elements of B. Thus, the inclusion $\subseteq$ partially orders arrows between any such A and B with the empty relation $\bot$ as the bottom element.

Relational Composition and the Converse Operator. Two arrows $r : A \to B$ and $s : B \to C$ can be composed to the arrow $r \diamond s : A \to C$ where $(u, v) \in r \diamond s$ holds iff there exists some w such that $(u, w) \in r$ and $(w, v) \in s$. Moreover, to any arrow $r : A \to B$ we have the *converse* $r^\circ : B \to A$ such that $(u, v) \in r^\circ$ holds iff $(v, u) \in r$ does.

Simple and Entire Arrows. An arrow $r : A \to B$ is called *simple* if $r^\circ \diamond r \subseteq id_B$, and *entire* if $id_A \subseteq r \diamond r^\circ$. An arrow which is both, simple and entire, is called a *mapping*. Any mapping r has a unique representation $r = f^{\mathcal{G}}$ where $f : A \to B$ is an arrow in the subcategory **Set** and $f^{\mathcal{G}}$ denotes the graph of f. As there is no essential difference between a mapping in **Rel** and a function in **Set**, we will use these notions interchangeably whenever it caters better readability.

Arrow Divisions. The local completeness of **Rel** is due to the existence of the least upper bound for any set of arrows between two objects, *i.e.* the union. In particular, this allows us to define the *left division* operator (*cf.* [2]) as follows: if $s : A \to C$ and $r : B \to C$ then $r \backslash s : A \to B$ is defined by $\bigcup \{x \mid x \diamond r \subseteq s\}$ having thus the universal property

$$x \diamond r \subseteq s \quad \Leftrightarrow \quad x \subseteq r \backslash s \tag{1}$$

The *right division* is symmetric: if $r : A \to B$ and $s : A \to C$ then $s/r : B \to C$ is $\bigcup \{x \mid r \diamond x \subseteq s\}$ with the universal property

$$r \diamond x \subseteq s \quad \Leftrightarrow \quad x \subseteq s/r \tag{2}$$

A Variant of the Monotype Factor. For simplicity's sake, a slight variation of the *monotype factor* $s\backslash r$ from [5] is defined in terms of the left division as follows: $s\backslash_{\bullet}r \stackrel{def}{=} s\backslash(s \diamond r)$ for any $s : A \to B$ and $r : B \to B$, sharing nonetheless with the definition in [5] the properties

$$r \subseteq r' \text{ implies } s\backslash_{\bullet}r \subseteq s\backslash_{\bullet}r' \tag{3}$$

$$s\backslash_{\bullet}r \diamond s \subseteq s \diamond r \tag{4}$$

that will be relevant in the sequel.

Relators. These arise as a specialisation of functors to allegories [2,5]. In what follows, only the *endorelators* on **Rel** will be used, *i.e.* those $\mathcal{R}$ that send each arrow $r : A \to B$ to an arrow $\mathcal{R}(r) : \mathcal{R}(A) \to \mathcal{R}(B)$ such that for any r, s and A

(i) $r \subseteq s$ implies $\mathcal{R}(r) \subseteq \mathcal{R}(s)$,
(ii) $\mathcal{R}(id_A) = id_{\mathcal{R}(A)}$,
(iii) $\mathcal{R}(r \diamond s) = \mathcal{R}(r) \diamond \mathcal{R}(s)$,
(iv) $\mathcal{R}(r)^{\circ} \subseteq \mathcal{R}(r^{\circ})$.

Note that $\mathcal{R}(r)^{\circ} = \mathcal{R}(r^{\circ})$ is a consequence of (i)–(iv) since the converse operator is a monotone involution. Thus, any (endo)relator $\mathcal{R}$ sends simple arrows to simple arrows and entire – to entire, *i.e.* it is indeed also an endofunctor on the subcategory **Set**.

The particular relator, employed in the case study in Sect. 4, sends each object X to $R_E(X) \stackrel{def}{=} 1 + E \times X$ (where E is a parameter object and $\mathbf{1}$ shall stand for the singleton $\{\varnothing\}$) and each arrow $r : A \to B$ to

$$R_E(r) \stackrel{def}{=} \{(inl(\varnothing), inl(\varnothing))\} \cup \{(inr(x, a), inr(x, b)) \mid x \in E \wedge (a, b) \in r\}$$

where $inl : L \to L + R$ and $inr : R \to L + R$ as usually refer to the constructor mappings which respectively embed elements of L and R into their co-product $L + R$. The conditions (i)–(iv) are thus simply verified for R_E.

Least Fixed Points. The arrow $\mu F : A \to B$ is defined by $\bigcap\{x \mid F(x) \subseteq x\}$ for any function F that sends each $s : A \to B$ to $F(s) : A \to B$. Thus, μF is the least fixed point of any monotone F. Let $F \stackrel{\cdot}{\subseteq} G$ abbreviate that $F(x) \subseteq G(x)$ holds for all x with the source and the target determined by F and G. The following fixed point fusion property, where $F \circ H$ denotes the usual functional composition $\lambda x.F(H(x))$, will be used later on.

Lemma 1. *If G is monotone and $F \circ H \stackrel{\cdot}{\subseteq} H \circ G$ then $\mu F \subseteq H(\mu G)$.*

Proof. $\mu F \subseteq H(\mu G)$
  $\Leftarrow$ – by the definition of μF
       $F(H(\mu G)) \subseteq H(\mu G)$
  $\Leftarrow$ – by the assumption $F \circ H \stackrel{\cdot}{\subseteq} H \circ G$
       $H(G(\mu G)) \subseteq H(\mu G)$
  $\Leftarrow$ – by the reflexivity of $\subseteq$ since $G(\mu G) = \mu G$.   □

A Notational Convention. For the sake of brevity we will omit the subscripts under identities, like $id_{\mathcal{R}(A)}$ above, and write just *id* from now on since the respective domains will be clear from the context.

3   From Divide-and-Conquer Specifications to Their Implementations

As pointed out in the introduction, the divide-and-conquer principle is basically about decomposition of inputs to some suitable intermediate form, and composition of solutions from the intermediate level to solutions for the original input. In the framework from the preceding section we can model that by means of:

- a relator $\mathcal{R}$ for the intermediate level,
- a *co-algebra* $c : A \to \mathcal{R}(A)$ as decomposition, and
- an *algebra* $a : \mathcal{R}(B) \to B$ as composition.

Then $s : A \to B$ will be called a *divide-and-conquer specification* w.r.t. $\mathcal{R}, c, a$ if $c \diamond \mathcal{R}(s) \diamond a \subseteq s$ holds. This property can also be encountered as a 'problem reduction principle' in [7]. Note further that $D_{\mathcal{R},c,a}(x) \stackrel{def}{=} c \diamond \mathcal{R}(x) \diamond a$ is a monotone function on $x : A \to B$ and any prefixed point of $D_{\mathcal{R},c,a}$ is a divide-and-conquer specification w.r.t. $\mathcal{R}, c, a$. By taking $\bot$ as either c or a, any arrow $x : A \to B$ becomes a prefixed point of $D_{\mathcal{R},c,a}$. In this sense, the proposed synthesis method will be partial because c and a will become subject to certain additional conditions which particularly rule out such corner cases with the empty relations.

Following [6], the source and the target of s, *i.e.* A and B, can be regarded as the *represented* data. As briefly mentioned in the introduction, an eventual function, set out to implement s, would by contrast operate on some *representing* data A' and B', respectively linked to A and B by means of certain arrows $\alpha_1 : A' \to A$ and $\alpha_2 : B' \to B$. These arrows can in principle be viewed as the counterpart of abstraction functions in [6]. Denoting by $Lists(E)$ from now on the set of all lists drawn from the elements of some (ordered) set E, with the already mentioned sorting we in particular would have $A = A' = B = B' = Lists(E)$ and $\alpha_1 = \alpha_2 = id$, *i.e.* one of those special cases when the represented and the representing data coincide so that α_1 and α_2 can be simplified away. Bringing them back, an arrow (not necessarily a mapping in general) $i : A' \to B'$ will be called an *implementation* of s via α_1 and α_2 if $\alpha_1^{\circ} \diamond i \diamond \alpha_2 \subseteq s$ holds.

Further, notice that $\alpha_1^{\circ} \diamond i \diamond \alpha_2 \subseteq s$ is equivalent to $i \subseteq \alpha_2 \backslash s / \alpha_1^{\circ}$ and this 'left-and-right' division $\alpha_2 \backslash s / \alpha_1^{\circ}$ will be central to the proof of Lemma 2 below, being itself the weakest possible implementation of s via α_1, α_2 and hence an upper bound for mappings among these, if any.

Backed by the above contemplation, the basic approach will be that an appropriate co-algebra/algebra pair c, a that enables the prefixed point property $c \diamond \mathcal{R}(s) \diamond a \subseteq s$ could additionally allow us to utilise the 'decompose/compose' pattern in order to derive a mapping in $\alpha_2 \backslash s / \alpha_1^{\circ}$. More precisely, if a co-algebra $c' : A' \to \mathcal{R}(A')$ and an algebra $a' : \mathcal{R}(B') \to B'$ can be provided as the respective counterparts to c and a at the level of representing data then the *synthesised* arrow $\mu D_{\mathcal{R},c',a'} : A' \to B'$ (which is by the way an $\mathcal{R}$-hylomorphism [5]) would give us an implementation of s. If c' and a' can additionally be shown to be mappings then $\mu D_{\mathcal{R},c',a'}$ will also be a function, computationally resolving s provided c' and a' are computable, of course.

The remainder of this section is about elaborating precise conditions under which the outlined synthesis provably results in a mapping that implements the given specification, and commences with the implementational aspect.

Lemma 2. *Let* $s : A \to B$ *and* $\alpha_1 : A' \to A$, $\alpha_2 : B' \to B$. *Further, let* $\mathcal{R}$ *be a relator and* $c : A \to \mathcal{R}(A)$, $a : \mathcal{R}(B) \to B$ *and* $c' : A' \to \mathcal{R}(A')$, $a' : \mathcal{R}(B') \to B'$ *two co-algebra/algebra pairs such that*

(a) $\alpha_1^\circ \diamond c' \subseteq c \diamond \mathcal{R}(\alpha_1^\circ)$,
(b) $a' \diamond \alpha_2 \subseteq \mathcal{R}(\alpha_2) \diamond a$,
(c) s *is a prefixed point of* $D_{\mathcal{R},c,a}$.

Then $\alpha_1^\circ \diamond \mu D_{\mathcal{R},c',a'} \diamond \alpha_2 \subseteq s$ *holds.*

Proof.

$$\alpha_1^\circ \diamond \mu D_{\mathcal{R},c',a'} \diamond \alpha_2 \subseteq s$$
$\Leftrightarrow$ — by (1)
$$\alpha_1^\circ \diamond \mu D_{\mathcal{R},c',a'} \subseteq \alpha_2 \backslash s$$
$\Leftrightarrow$ — by (2)
$$\mu D_{\mathcal{R},c',a'} \subseteq \alpha_2 \backslash s / \alpha_1^\circ$$
$\Leftarrow$ — by the definition of $\mu D_{\mathcal{R},c',a'}$
$$D_{\mathcal{R},c',a'}(\alpha_2 \backslash s / \alpha_1^\circ) \subseteq \alpha_2 \backslash s / \alpha_1^\circ$$
$\Leftrightarrow$ — by (2)
$$\alpha_1^\circ \diamond D_{\mathcal{R},c',a'}(\alpha_2 \backslash s / \alpha_1^\circ) \subseteq \alpha_2 \backslash s$$
$\Leftrightarrow$ — by (1)
$$\alpha_1^\circ \diamond D_{\mathcal{R},c',a'}(\alpha_2 \backslash s / \alpha_1^\circ) \diamond \alpha_2 \subseteq s$$
$\Leftarrow$ — by the definition of $D_{\mathcal{R},c',a'}$ and (a) and (b)
$$c \diamond \mathcal{R}(\alpha_1^\circ) \diamond \mathcal{R}(\alpha_2 \backslash s / \alpha_1^\circ) \diamond \mathcal{R}(\alpha_2) \diamond a \subseteq s$$
$\Leftrightarrow$ — since $\mathcal{R}$ is a relator
$$c \diamond \mathcal{R}(\alpha_1^\circ \diamond \alpha_2 \backslash s / \alpha_1^\circ \diamond \alpha_2) \diamond a \subseteq s$$
$\Leftarrow$ — by (2) and the monotonicity of $\mathcal{R}$
$$c \diamond \mathcal{R}(\alpha_2 \backslash s \diamond \alpha_2) \diamond a \subseteq s$$
$\Leftarrow$ — by (1) and the monotonicity of $\mathcal{R}$
$$c \diamond \mathcal{R}(s) \diamond a \subseteq s$$
$\Leftrightarrow$ — to (c). $\qquad\square$

Reflecting on the above proposition, the assumptions (a) and (b) address the structure preserving properties of α_1 and α_2, and neither of these can simply be omitted retaining soundness. As this point hints to the actual purpose of the assumptions, it will be briefly substantiated by the sketch of a counterexample depicted in Fig. 1 where the three extra copies of the vertex $inl(\varnothing)$ shall merely foster a clearer presentation. In this setting we have $(u, inl(\varnothing)) \notin c$ and $(inr(\ldots), inl(\varnothing)) \notin \mathcal{R}(\bot)$ such that $c \diamond \mathcal{R}(\bot) \diamond a \subseteq \bot$ holds, *i.e.* $\bot$ is a prefixed point of $D_{\mathcal{R},c,a}$. On the other hand we have $(u, v) \in \alpha_1^{\circ} \diamond \mu D_{\mathcal{R},c',a'} \diamond \alpha_2$, *i.e.* $\alpha_1^{\circ} \diamond \mu D_{\mathcal{R},c',a'} \diamond \alpha_2 \nsubseteq \bot$.

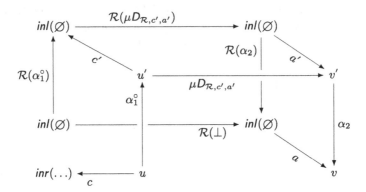

Fig. 1. The sketch of a counterexample.

Next, for the composition $x \diamond f$ (or $f \diamond x$) to be a simple arrow with any possible mapping f, the arrow x has to be simple which basically motivates the assumptions in the following proposition.

Lemma 3. *Let $\mathcal{R}$ be a relator. Then $\mu D_{\mathcal{R},c,a} : A \to B$ is simple for any simple $c : A \to \mathcal{R}(A)$ and simple $a : \mathcal{R}(B) \to B$.*

Proof.
$$(\mu D_{\mathcal{R},c,a})^{\circ} \diamond \mu D_{\mathcal{R},c,a} \subseteq id$$
$\Leftrightarrow$ — by (2)
$$\mu D_{\mathcal{R},c,a} \subseteq id/(\mu D_{\mathcal{R},c,a})^{\circ}$$
$\Leftarrow$ — by the definitions of $\mu D_{\mathcal{R},c,a}$ and $D_{\mathcal{R},c,a}$
$$c \diamond \mathcal{R}(id/(\mu D_{\mathcal{R},c,a})^{\circ}) \diamond a \subseteq id/(\mu D_{\mathcal{R},c,a})^{\circ}$$
$\Leftrightarrow$ — by (2)
$$(\mu D_{\mathcal{R},c,a})^{\circ} \diamond c \diamond \mathcal{R}(id/(\mu D_{\mathcal{R},c,a})^{\circ}) \diamond a \subseteq id$$
$\Leftrightarrow$ — by the fixed point and $\_^{\circ}$ properties
$$a^{\circ} \diamond \mathcal{R}((\mu D_{\mathcal{R},c,a})^{\circ}) \diamond c^{\circ} \diamond c \diamond \mathcal{R}(id/(\mu D_{\mathcal{R},c,a})^{\circ}) \diamond a \subseteq id$$
$\Leftarrow$ — since c is simple
$$a^{\circ} \diamond \mathcal{R}((\mu D_{\mathcal{R},c,a}))^{\circ} \diamond \mathcal{R}(id/(\mu D_{\mathcal{R},c,a})^{\circ}) \diamond a \subseteq id$$
$\Leftrightarrow$ — by the properties of $\mathcal{R}$
$$a^{\circ} \diamond \mathcal{R}((\mu D_{\mathcal{R},c,a})^{\circ} \diamond id/(\mu D_{\mathcal{R},c,a})^{\circ}) \diamond a \subseteq id$$
$\Leftarrow$ — by (2) and the properties of $\mathcal{R}$
$$a^{\circ} \diamond a \subseteq id$$
$\Leftrightarrow$ — a is simple. □

Establishing $\mu D_{\mathcal{R},c,a}$ as an entire arrow is however a bit more intricate since an entire co-algebra $c : A \to \mathcal{R}(A)$ is in general not sufficient to this end so that the reductivity property from [5] in a slightly relaxed form will be additionally presumed. In what follows, a co-algebra $c : A \to \mathcal{R}(A)$ will be called *reductive* if $id \subseteq \mu T_{\mathcal{R},c}$ holds, where $T_{\mathcal{R},c}(x) \overset{def}{=} c\backslash\mathcal{R}(x)$ is monotone due to the monotonicity of $\mathcal{R}$ and (3).

To outline what is behind this abstract concept, let c be a reductive mapping and c^k denote $c \diamond R_E(c) \diamond \ldots \diamond R_E^{k-1}(c)$ for any $k > 0$ where R_E is the relator defined in Sect. 2. Further, let $w \overset{def}{=} \{(v,v) \mid \exists n > 0. \, \forall m \geqslant n. \, c^n(v) = c^m(v)\}$, *i.e.* $w : A \to A$ essentially contains those $a \in A$ for which some $N(a) > 0$ with $c^{N(a)}(a) = c^m(a)$ for all $m \geqslant N(a)$ exists.

Now we can show $T_{R_E,c}(w) \subseteq w$, *i.e.* that w is a prefixed point of $T_{R_E,c}$. To this end suppose $(v,v) \in c\backslash R_E(w)$ which is the same as $\{(v,v)\} \subseteq c\backslash R_E(w)$. By the definition of the monotype factor and (1) this is in turn equivalent to $\{(v,v)\} \diamond c \subseteq c \diamond R_E(w)$, *i.e.* $(c(v),c(v)) \in R_E(w)$. If we have $c(v) = inl(\varnothing)$ then $(v,v) \in w$ holds by setting $N(v)$ to 1. Otherwise let $c(v) = inr(x,v')$ with some x and v'. Then by the definition of R_E and injectivity of inr we have $(v',v') \in w$ so that also in this case $(v,v) \in w$ can be inferred by setting $N(v)$ to $N(v') + 1$.

Summing up, the conclusion $id \subseteq w$ follows by $\mu T_{R_E,c} \subseteq w$ and the assumption that c is reductive. This essentially means that the sequence $a, c(a), c^2(a), \ldots$ eventually reaches a fixed point for any $a \in A$. That is, reductivity rules out successive decompositions *ad infinitum* or, in other words, captures well-foundness.

Lemma 4. *Let $\mathcal{R}$ be a relator. Then $\mu D_{\mathcal{R},c,a} : A \to B$ is entire for any entire and reductive $c : A \to \mathcal{R}(A)$ and entire $a : \mathcal{R}(B) \to B$.*

Proof. $\qquad id \subseteq \mu D_{\mathcal{R},c,a} \diamond (\mu D_{\mathcal{R},c,a})^\circ$

$\qquad\Leftarrow\qquad$ – since c is reductive

$\qquad \mu T_{\mathcal{R},c} \subseteq \mu D_{\mathcal{R},c,a} \diamond (\mu D_{\mathcal{R},c,a})^\circ$

$\qquad\Leftarrow\qquad$ – by Lemma 1 with $D_{\mathcal{R},c,a}$ for G and $\lambda x.\, x \diamond x^\circ$ for H

$\qquad T_{\mathcal{R},c}(x \diamond x^\circ) \subseteq D_{\mathcal{R},c,a}(x) \diamond D_{\mathcal{R},c,a}(x)^\circ$

$\qquad\Leftrightarrow\qquad$ – by the definition of $D_{\mathcal{R},c,a}$ and properties of $\_^\circ$

$\qquad T_{\mathcal{R},c}(x \diamond x^\circ) \subseteq c \diamond \mathcal{R}(x) \diamond a \diamond a^\circ \diamond \mathcal{R}(x)^\circ \diamond c^\circ$

$\qquad\Leftarrow\qquad$ – since a is entire

$\qquad T_{\mathcal{R},c}(x \diamond x^\circ) \subseteq c \diamond \mathcal{R}(x) \diamond \mathcal{R}(x)^\circ \diamond c^\circ$

$\qquad\Leftarrow\qquad$ – by the properties of $\mathcal{R}$ and (4)

$\qquad T_{\mathcal{R},c}(x \diamond x^\circ) \subseteq c\backslash\mathcal{R}(x \diamond x^\circ) \diamond c \diamond c^\circ$

$\qquad\Leftarrow\qquad$ – since c is entire

$\qquad T_{\mathcal{R},c}(x \diamond x^\circ) \subseteq c\backslash\mathcal{R}(x \diamond x^\circ)$

$\qquad\Leftarrow\qquad$ – by the definition of $T_{\mathcal{R},c}$ and the reflexivity of $\subseteq$. $\qquad\square$

3.1 The Synthesis Rule

The following statement summarises everything presented so far.

Theorem 1. *Let $s : A \to B$ and $\alpha_1 : A' \to A$, $\alpha_2 : B' \to B$. Further, let $\mathcal{R}$ be a relator and $c : A \to \mathcal{R}(A)$, $a : \mathcal{R}(B) \to B$ and $c' : A' \to \mathcal{R}(A')$, $a' : \mathcal{R}(B') \to B'$ two co-algebra/algebra pairs such that*

(a) $\alpha_1^\circ \diamond c' \subseteq c \diamond \mathcal{R}(\alpha_1^\circ)$,
(b) $a' \diamond \alpha_2 \subseteq \mathcal{R}(\alpha_2) \diamond a$,
(c) c' and a' are mappings,
(d) c' is reductive,
(e) s is a prefixed point of $D_{\mathcal{R},c,a}$

then there exists a function $f : A' \to B'$ such that $\mu D_{\mathcal{R},c',a'} = f^{\mathcal{G}}$ and, moreover, $\alpha_1^\circ \diamond f^{\mathcal{G}} \diamond \alpha_2 \subseteq s$ hold.

Proof. By Lemma 2 we obtain $\alpha_1^\circ \diamond \mu D_{\mathcal{R},c',a'} \diamond \alpha_2 \subseteq s$, whereas by Lemma 3 and Lemma 4 we can additionally conclude that $\mu D_{\mathcal{R},c',a'}$ is a mapping. □

As a direct consequence of $\mu D_{\mathcal{R},c',a'} = f^{\mathcal{G}}$, the equation visualised by the following diagram in **Set**

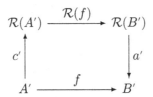

can essentially be viewed as a recursive definition of the synthesised function f fostering inductive reasoning upon further properties of such f.

Finally, it is worth noting that in many practical situations the set A and the domain of the specification s coincide, *i.e.* $s : A \to B$ is entire, so that it is sensible to additionally call for α_1° to be entire (*i.e.* any input has a representation in A') and for the domain of α_2 to cover at least all relevant values in B' (the case study will address this point) in order to ensure that a solution to each element in A can be obtained using f.

4 Case Study: Deriving an Implementation of a Greedy Algorithm

This section presents a case study aiming to derive a function that constructs a list representation of a maximum weight basis of the given finite matroid by applying the method elaborated in the preceding section. In line with the classical 'greedy' approach we will actually obtain an algorithmic solution for a variety of optimisation problems: the abstraction over all further details of the underlying independent family of sets enables this feature.

4.1 Weighted Matroids and Their Bases

Matroids [1] form a class of algebraic structures that has been extensively studied in particular due to its role in algorithmic optimisation. Recalling the definitions and placing these into the context of the preceding sections, let E be some arbitrary non-empty set for the remainder of the paper and let $\mathcal{P}_{fin}(E)$ denote the set of its finite subsets. A family of sets $\mathcal{I} \subseteq \mathcal{P}_{fin}(E)$ is called *independent* if the following conditions hold:

(i) $\varnothing \in \mathcal{I}$,

(ii) if $A \in \mathcal{I}$ and $B \subseteq A$ then $B \in \mathcal{I}$,

(iii) if $A \in \mathcal{I}$ and $B \in \mathcal{I}$ such that $|A| > |B|$ then there exists some $a \in A \setminus B$ with $B \cup \{a\} \in \mathcal{I}$

where (ii) and (iii) are respectively called the *hereditary* and the *exchange* properties. Given some $G \in \mathcal{P}_{fin}(E)$ and an independent $\mathcal{I} \subseteq \mathcal{P}_{fin}(E)$, a set $X \subseteq G$ is called a *basis* of the *matroid* $(G, \mathcal{I})$ if $X \in \mathcal{I}$ and for any $Y \subseteq G$ with $Y \in \mathcal{I}$ we have $|Y| \leqslant |X|$.

If we moreover attach a weight to the elements of E by means of a *weighting function* $w : E \to \mathbb{R}$ then a *maximum weight basis* of $(G, \mathcal{I})$ is consequently a basis X of $(G, \mathcal{I})$ such that we have $\overline{w}(Y) \leqslant \overline{w}(X)$ for any Y which is also a basis of $(G, \mathcal{I})$, where $\overline{w}(A) \overset{def}{=} \sum_{a \in A} w(a)$ for any $A \in \mathcal{P}_{fin}(E)$ subsuming $\overline{w}(\varnothing) = 0$. Note that a maximum weight basis with the opposite weighting $w^{op}(x) \overset{def}{=} -w(x)$ gives a minimum weight basis w.r.t. w.

Aiming to apply Theorem 1, we can summarise the above specification by the family of arrows *max-basis*$_{\mathcal{I}} : \mathcal{P}_{fin}(E) \to \mathcal{P}_{fin}(E)$ defined by

$$\textit{max-basis}_{\mathcal{I}} \overset{def}{=} \{(G, X) \mid X \text{ is a maximum weight basis of } (G, \mathcal{I})\}$$

for each independent $\mathcal{I} \subseteq \mathcal{P}_{fin}(E)$. The assumptions of Theorem 1 with s replaced by *max-basis*$_{\mathcal{I}}$ give us the proof obligations for implementation synthesis, where (e) constitutes the central one: the way it is resolved basically sets the direction and the realisability of all subsequent steps as the next section shows.

4.2   Establishing *max-basis*$_{\mathcal{I}}$ as a Divide-and-Conquer Specification

According to the definition in Sect. 3, this task amounts to showing that *max-basis*$_{\mathcal{I}}$ is a prefixed point of $D_{\mathcal{R},c,a}$ with some relator $\mathcal{R}$, co-algebra c and algebra a.

First of all, for $\mathcal{R}$ we will take the relator R_E defined in Sect. 2. Intuitively, whenever a matroid $(G, \mathcal{I})$ is not empty, R_E allows us to consider $inr(m, G \setminus \{m\})$ with certain $m \in G$ at the intermediate level assuming that a maximum weight basis X of the matroid $(G \setminus \{m\}, \mathcal{I})$ exists, and then specify which bases of $(G, \mathcal{I})$ are composed out of m and X. More precisely, for c we take the co-algebra *decomp* : $\mathcal{P}_{fin}(E) \to R_E(\mathcal{P}_{fin}(E))$ defined by

$$\textit{decomp} \overset{def}{=} \{(\varnothing, inl(\varnothing))\} \cup \{(G, inr(m, G \setminus \{m\})) \mid m \in G \wedge \forall x \in G.\ w(m) \leqslant w(x)\}$$

and pass the parameter $\mathcal{I}$ on to the algebra *compose*$_{\mathcal{I}} : R_E(\mathcal{P}_{fin}(E)) \to \mathcal{P}_{fin}(E)$ defined by

$$\textit{compose}_{\mathcal{I}} \overset{def}{=} \{(inl(\varnothing), \varnothing)\} \cup \{(inr(m, X), \{m\} \cup X) \mid \{m\} \cup X \in \mathcal{I}\}$$
$$\cup \{(inr(m, X), X) \mid \{m\} \cup X \notin \mathcal{I}\}$$

so that Theorem 2 will establish *max-basis*$_{\mathcal{I}}$ as a divide-and-conquer specification w.r.t. R_E, *decomp*, *compose*$_{\mathcal{I}}$ for any independent $\mathcal{I}$ resorting to the three auxiliary lemmas in Appendix A. For the remainder of this section let $\mathcal{I} \subseteq \mathcal{P}_{fin}(E)$ be a fixed arbitrary independent family and we will use the shorthands *max-basis* for *max-basis$_\mathcal{I}$* and *compose* for *compose$_\mathcal{I}$* below.

Theorem 2. *The inclusion*

$$decomp \diamond R_E(max\text{-}basis) \diamond compose \subseteq max\text{-}basis$$

holds, i.e. max-basis is a prefixed point of $D_{R_E, decomp, compose}$.

Proof. Let $(G, X) \in decomp \diamond R_E(max\text{-}basis) \diamond compose$. If $G = \varnothing$ then $X = \varnothing$ and hence we are done because $(\varnothing, \varnothing) \in max\text{-}basis$. Next, let $m \in G$ such that $w(m) \leqslant w(x)$ holds for any $x \in G$. Thus, assuming $(G \setminus \{m\}, X') \in max\text{-}basis$ we have to show $(G, \{m\} \cup X') \in max\text{-}basis$ if $\{m\} \cup X' \in \mathcal{I}$ and $(G, X') \in max\text{-}basis$ otherwise.

In the former case we can first infer that $\{m\} \cup X'$ is a basis of $(G, \mathcal{I})$ by Lemma 7. Further, let Y be another basis of $(G, \mathcal{I})$. If $m \notin Y$ then Y has to be also a basis of $(G \setminus \{m\}, \mathcal{I})$ by Lemma 8, meaning $|\{m\} \cup X'| = |Y| = |X'|$, i.e. a contradiction. Otherwise we can apply Lemma 9 with m for a and Y for X which leads to the following two cases. If $Y \setminus \{m\}$ is a basis of $(G \setminus \{m\}, \mathcal{I})$ then $\overline{w}(Y) = w(m) + \overline{w}(Y \setminus \{m\}) \leqslant w(m) + \overline{w}(X') = \overline{w}(\{m\} \cup X')$. On the other hand, if there exists some $b \in G \setminus Y$ such that $Y \setminus \{m\} \cup \{b\}$ is a basis of $(G \setminus \{m\}, \mathcal{I})$ then we once more get a contradiction: $|\{m\} \cup X'| = |Y| = |Y \setminus \{m\} \cup \{b\}| = |X'|$.

Backtracking to the remaining branch, we can assume $\{m\} \cup X' \notin \mathcal{I}$ in order to show $(G, X') \in max\text{-}basis$. To this end we first note that X' has to be a basis of $(G, \mathcal{I})$ by Lemma 7. Further, let Y be another basis of $(G, \mathcal{I})$. If $m \notin Y$ then by Lemma 8 we have that Y is also a basis of $(G \setminus \{m\}, \mathcal{I})$ and hence $\overline{w}(Y) \leqslant \overline{w}(X')$ because $(G \setminus \{m\}, X') \in max\text{-}basis$. With $m \in Y$ we apply Lemma 9 instantiating m for a and Y for X which leads to the following two cases. If $Y \setminus \{m\}$ is a basis of $(G \setminus \{m\}, \mathcal{I})$ then we have another contradiction: $|Y \setminus \{m\}| = |X'| = |Y|$. Lastly, with some $b \in G \setminus Y$ such that $Y \setminus \{m\} \cup \{b\}$ is a basis of $(G \setminus \{m\}, \mathcal{I})$ we conclude: $\overline{w}(Y) = w(m) + \overline{w}(Y \setminus \{m\}) \leqslant w(b) + \overline{w}(Y \setminus \{m\}) = \overline{w}(Y \setminus \{m\} \cup \{b\}) \leqslant \overline{w}(X')$. $\square$

4.3   Implementations of Decomposition and Composition

Moving from the level of the represented data to one of its representations, sets in $\mathcal{P}_{fin}(E)$ will be linked to $Lists(E)$ by means of α_1 and α_2 as follows:

$$\alpha_1 \stackrel{def}{=} \{(xs, set(xs)) \mid xs \text{ is distinct and sorted by the ascending weight }\}$$
$$\alpha_2 \stackrel{def}{=} \{(xs, set(xs)) \mid xs \text{ is distinct }\}$$

where *set* denotes the function that sends each list to the set containing the elements occurring in the list, and $xs \in Lists(E)$ is called *distinct* if any $x \in E$ occurs at most once in it. Thus both, α_1 and α_2, are in essence surjective partial functions from $Lists(E)$ to $\mathcal{P}_{fin}(E)$.

Decomposition. Let $decomp' : Lists(E) \to R_E(Lists(E))$ be defined by

$$decomp' \overset{def}{=} \{(\epsilon, inl(\varnothing))\} \cup \{(x \cdot xs, inr(x, xs)) \mid x \in E \land xs \in Lists(E)\}$$

where ϵ as usually denotes the empty list and $x \cdot xs$ – the list with the head x and the tail xs. That $decomp'$ is a mapping follows straight by the above definition. Furthermore, that $decomp'$ complies with $decomp$ in the sense of the condition (a) of Theorem 1 is essentially provided by α_1 representing sets by distinct weight-sorted lists. More precisely, if $x \cdot xs$ is sorted by the ascending weight then x is an element with the smallest weight within $set(x \cdot xs)$ and, moreover, xs is weight-sorted as well. Since $x \cdot xs$ is additionally assumed to be distinct, xs is in turn related by α_1 to $set(x \cdot xs) \setminus \{x\}$. The remaining aspect of decomposition to be addressed is therefore the reductivity property.

Lemma 5. *The co-algebra $decomp'$ is reductive.*

Proof. By the definition of reductivity we have to show $(xs, xs) \in \mu T_{R_E, decomp'}$ for any $xs \in Lists(E)$ and proceed by induction on the length of xs. Thus, for all $ys \in Lists(E)$ having a smaller length than the length of xs we can additionally assume $(ys, ys) \in \mu T_{R_E, decomp'}$. Further, noting that $(xs, xs) \in \mu T_{R_E, decomp'}$ is the same as $\{(xs, xs)\} \subseteq \mu T_{R_E, decomp'}$, we can start reasoning as follows:

$$\{(xs, xs)\} \subseteq \mu T_{R_E, decomp'}$$
$$\Leftrightarrow \qquad - \text{ unfolding the fixed point and the definition of } T_{R_E, decomp'}$$
$$\{(xs, xs)\} \subseteq decomp' \backslash R_E(\mu T_{R_E, decomp'})$$
$$\Leftrightarrow \qquad - \text{ by the definition of the monotype factor and (1)}$$
$$\{(xs, xs)\} \diamond decomp' \subseteq decomp' \diamond R_E(\mu T_{R_E, decomp'}).$$

Showing the latter inclusion, let $(xs, v) \in decomp'$ with some v. If $xs = \epsilon$ then $v = inl(\varnothing)$ and hence $(\epsilon, inl(\varnothing)) \in decomp' \diamond R_E(\mu T_{R_E, decomp'})$ is derivable via $inl(\varnothing)$. Otherwise let $xs = x \cdot xs'$ with some x and xs'. Then $v = inr(x, xs')$ so that $(xs, inr(x, xs')) \in decomp' \diamond R_E(\mu T_{R_E, decomp'})$ is derivable via $inr(x, xs')$ because $(inr(x, xs'), inr(x, xs')) \in R_E(\mu T_{R_E, decomp'})$ follows by the hypothesis. $\square$

Composition. Shifting the attention to a list-algebra answering to $compose$, let a decidable set $\mathcal{L} \subseteq Lists(E)$ be given so that

$$\overline{\mathcal{L}} \overset{def}{=} \{set(xs) \mid xs \in \mathcal{L} \land xs \text{ is distinct}\}$$

constitutes a family of sets in $\mathcal{P}_{fin}(E)$ being essentially the image of $\mathcal{L}$ under α_2. Since the elements of $Lists(E)$ can be regarded as the words over the (potentially infinite) alphabet E, we will refer to $\mathcal{L}$ as a *language* in what follows. Further, let $compose'_{\mathcal{L}} : R_E(Lists(E)) \to Lists(E)$ be defined by

$$compose'_{\mathcal{L}} \overset{def}{=} \{(inl(\varnothing), \epsilon)\} \cup \{(inr(x, xs), x \cdot xs) \mid x \cdot xs \in \mathcal{L}\}$$
$$\cup \{(inr(x, xs), xs) \mid x \cdot xs \notin \mathcal{L}\}$$

which evidently gives a simple and entire arrow for any $\mathcal{L}$, being not necessarily injective in contrast to $decomp'$. Hence, it remains to be shown that $compose'_{\mathcal{L}}$ complies with $compose_{\overline{\mathcal{L}}}$ for any $\mathcal{L}$ in the sense of the condition (b) of Theorem 1.

Lemma 6. *If for all distinct xs, $xs' \in Lists(E)$ with $set(xs) = set(xs')$ we have $xs \in \mathcal{L}$ iff $xs' \in \mathcal{L}$ then $compose'_{\mathcal{L}} \diamond \alpha_2 \subseteq R_E(\alpha_2) \diamond compose_{\overline{\mathcal{L}}}$.*

Proof. Note that $xs \in \mathcal{L}$ iff $set(xs) \in \overline{\mathcal{L}}$ follows by the assumption for all distinct $xs \in Lists(E)$, and suppose $(v, X) \in compose'_{\mathcal{L}} \diamond \alpha_2$. If $v = inl(\varnothing)$ then we have $X = set(\epsilon) = \varnothing$ so that $(v, X) \in R_E(\alpha_2) \diamond compose_{\overline{\mathcal{L}}}$ is derivable via $inl(\varnothing)$ by the definition of $compose_{\overline{\mathcal{L}}}$.

For the remainder of the proof we therefore can assume $v = inr(x, xs)$ with some $x \in E$ and $xs \in Lists(E)$. The case $x \cdot xs \in \mathcal{L}$ means that $x \cdot xs$ is distinct and $X = set(x \cdot xs)$. Since we can further infer that $set(x \cdot xs) \in \overline{\mathcal{L}}$ holds and xs is distinct, $(v, X) \in R_E(\alpha_2) \diamond compose_{\overline{\mathcal{L}}}$ is derivable via $inr(x, set(xs))$.

With $x \cdot xs \notin \mathcal{L}$ we have that xs is distinct and $X = set(xs)$. If $x \cdot xs$ is distinct, *i.e.* $x \notin X$, then $\{x\} \cup X = set(x \cdot xs) \notin \overline{\mathcal{L}}$ follows and we can derive $(v, X) \in R_E(\alpha_2) \diamond compose_{\overline{\mathcal{L}}}$ via $inr(x, X)$. Otherwise we have $\{x\} \cup X = X$ so that $(v, X) \in R_E(\alpha_2) \diamond compose_{\overline{\mathcal{L}}}$ is once more derivable via $inr(x, X)$ regardless whether $X \in \overline{\mathcal{L}}$ or $X \notin \overline{\mathcal{L}}$. $\qquad\square$

The Result. We can finally summarise the outcome of the synthesis process:

Theorem 3. *Let $w : E \to \mathbb{R}$ be a weighting function and suppose $\mathcal{L} \subseteq Lists(E)$ is a decidable language such that*

(a) *for all distinct xs and xs' with $set(xs) = set(xs')$ we have $xs \in \mathcal{L}$ iff $xs' \in \mathcal{L}$,*
(b) *$\overline{\mathcal{L}}$ is a family of independent sets.*

Then there is a function $f : Lists(E) \to Lists(E)$ satisfying the equations
(i) *$f(\epsilon) \quad = \quad \epsilon$*
(ii) *$f(x \cdot xs) = $ if $x \cdot f(xs) \in \mathcal{L}$ then $x \cdot f(xs)$ else $f(xs)$*
for any $x \cdot xs \in Lists(E)$ thus constructing a maximum weight basis $set(f(xs))$ of the matroid $(set(xs), \overline{\mathcal{L}})$ for any xs that is distinct and sorted by the ascending weight.

Proof. That the conditions (a)–(d) of Theorem 1 are satisfied by $decompose$, $decompose'$ and $compose_{\overline{\mathcal{L}}}$, $compose'_{\mathcal{L}}$ was the subject of the preceding section, whereas the condition (e) is covered by Theorem 2. This gives us the function f satisfying $\mu D_{R_E, decompose', compose'_{\mathcal{L}}} = f^{\mathcal{G}}$ and $\alpha_1^{\circ} \diamond f^{\mathcal{G}} \diamond \alpha_2 \subseteq max\text{-}basis_{\overline{\mathcal{L}}}$. The former property entails $D_{R_E, decompose', compose'_{\mathcal{L}}}(f^{\mathcal{G}}) \subseteq f^{\mathcal{G}}$ which in turn allows us to infer (i) and (ii). Furthermore, the properties

(c) *$set(f(xs)) \subseteq set(xs)$ for any $xs \in Lists(E)$, and*
(d) *$f(xs)$ is distinct for any distinct $xs \in Lists(E)$*

follow straight, *e.g.* by induction on the list structure using (i) and (ii).

For any distinct and sorted by the ascending weight $xs \in Lists(E)$ we can thus first infer $(set(xs), set(f(xs))) \in \alpha_1^{\circ} \diamond f^{\mathcal{G}} \diamond \alpha_2$ by (d) in order to conclude $(set(xs), set(f(xs))) \in max\text{-}basis_{\overline{\mathcal{L}}}$. $\qquad\square$

The synthesised function f matches the form of a canonical 'greedy' algorithm: a word representing a maximum weight basis is constructed in one run without any backtracking at the expense of the comparably strong assumption that $\overline{\mathcal{L}}$ is independent. From the efficiency perspective, the function f provides a provably correct reference for subsequent code transformations to potentially enhanced implementations of the same task.

One such transformation, specific to the subject of the case study, can tackle the membership tests $x \cdot f(xs) \in \mathcal{L}$ by means of the recursive function

(i) $g(\epsilon)$ $=$ ϵ
(ii) $g(x \cdot xs)$ $=$ *if* $insert(x, g(xs)) \in \mathcal{L}'$ *then* $insert(x, g(xs))$ *else* $g(xs)$

that deploys a function $insert : E \times Lists(E) \rightarrow Lists(E)$ as a parameter alongside a corresponding language $\mathcal{L}'$ satisfying $fold(insert, xs) \in \mathcal{L}'$ iff $xs \in \mathcal{L}$ for any distinct xs, where e.g. $fold(insert, x_1 \cdot x_2 \cdot \epsilon) = insert(x_1, insert(x_2, \epsilon))$ restores an appropriate order such that the language $\mathcal{L}'$ can provide more efficient membership tests than $\mathcal{L}$. Utilising Theorem 3 we first induce that $g(xs)$ is the same as $fold(insert, f(xs))$ for all distinct xs, which in turn allows us to infer that $set(g(xs)) = set(f(xs))$ holds for any distinct xs, and then ultimately $(set(xs), set(g(xs))) \in max\text{-}basis_{\overline{\mathcal{L}}}$ for an xs which is additionally sorted by the ascending weight.

5   Related Work

The presented approach can basically be viewed as a *design tactic* [9] and as a generalisation of the divide-and-conquer design tactic for the theorem prover Isabelle, appeared as an example in [4] strictly following [7].

By contrast to [4], this presentation has been completely lifted to the allegory of relations. The abstract framework allows us to focus on the essentials and to capture the whole design tactic by means of a single general rule in Theorem 1 which particularly avoids the technical overhead that arises from the usage of theory or specification morphisms. However, in order to reify the tactic in all generality for applications in an existing formal system, such as a theorem prover, either full support of type constructor classes at the logic level or some notion of morphism is needed. The reason is that relators in principle form a class of type constructors with the arity 1. However in Isabelle, for instance, non-monomorphic type constructors cannot be quantified within a logical statement because such abstractions are beyond the capabilities of Hindley-Milner polymorphism that extends the underlying simply typed higher-order logic. On the other hand, this is exactly what has been done without much ado in each proposition of Sect. 3. So, to achieve effectively the same as type constructor classes in Isabelle, an axiomatically specified fresh type constructor has been employed in [4] acting essentially as a theory's formal parameter that can be instantiated by actual parameters using a theory morphism.

Another central enhancement to [4] is the conceptual separation between represented data, used in abstract modelling and specification, and representing data, used for computation of solutions to the specified relations so that implementations to specifications built on abstract data types can be synthesised as the case study has shown.

6   Conclusions and Outlook

Taking the locally complete allegory of relations as the foundational framework, the paper first introduced the notions of a divide-and-conquer specification and of an implementation. Based on this, a sound approach to synthesis of implementations from specifications featuring a few required structural properties has been established. The proposed method has been subsequently applied in a case study concerned with the algorithmic construction of optimal bases of weighted finite matroids.

The method is aimed at fostering structured development of provably correct programs: the case study emphasised how we could focus on the core logical reasoning (Theorem 2) detached from the bulk of implementation details which became apparent only in Sect. 4.3 with its largely schematic proofs. The synthesised function gives us a dependable reference for the subsequent software engineering steps, *e.g.* towards improved efficiency.

Although not particularly highlighted in the course of the paper, the presented concept of implementation as a relation between arrows is not at all bound to some specific synthesis approach, being compositional in the following sense: $\alpha_1^\circ \diamond s' \diamond \alpha_2 \subseteq s$ and $\alpha_3^\circ \diamond s'' \diamond \alpha_4 \subseteq s'$ imply $(\alpha_3 \diamond \alpha_1)^\circ \diamond s'' \diamond (\alpha_2 \diamond \alpha_4) \subseteq s$ in agreement with the general stepwise development model, depicted in the introduction to [6]. From the perspective of the divide-and-conquer synthesis, intermediate steps from a specification to a 'loose' implementation (*i.e.* not a simple arrow yet) are covered by Lemma 2: a prefixed point s of $D_{\mathcal{R},c,a}$ leads to $\mu D_{\mathcal{R},c',a'}$ that implements s and is by construction the smallest divide-and-conquer specification w.r.t. $\mathcal{R}, c', a'$. Note that c' and a' shall be selected as weak as possible here to keep $\mu D_{\mathcal{R},c',a'}$ from being too constrained.

Reflecting lastly on the subject of the case study, it is remarkable that by looking for functions constructing list representations of matroid bases we arrive at the notion of languages that has also been extensively studied in the context of *greedoids* [3] which arise as a generalisation of matroids by mere refraining from the hereditary property. This abstraction leads to the less structured families of so-called *feasible* sets rather than independent sets. The function, synthesised in the case study, would not work with such feasible sets in general: the proof of Theorem 2 (via Lemma 7 and Lemma 9 to be more precise) makes use of the hereditary property so that Theorem 3 sensibly does not assert that the synthesised function constructs a basis (not to mention optimality) for a greedoid which is not a matroid. In this sense it would be interesting to investigate on whether there are more sophisticated instantiations of the divide-and-conquer design tactic that would be applicable if not to any greedoid then to some relevant subclasses such as the interval greedoids.

A   The Three Auxiliary Lemmas

Recall that $\mathcal{I} \subseteq \mathcal{P}_{fin}(E)$ is an independent family.

Lemma 7. *Assume that X is a basis of $(G, \mathcal{I})$ and $a \notin G$. Then $X \cup \{a\}$ is a basis of $(G \cup \{a\}, \mathcal{I})$ if $X \cup \{a\} \in \mathcal{I}$ and X is a basis of $(G \cup \{a\}, \mathcal{I})$ otherwise.*

Proof. Suppose $Y \subseteq G \cup \{a\}$ and $Y \in \mathcal{I}$. Then $Y \setminus \{a\} \subseteq G$ holds and, moreover, $Y \setminus \{a\} \in \mathcal{I}$ follows by the hereditary property such that we have $|Y \setminus \{a\}| \leqslant |X|$ because X is a basis of $(G, \mathcal{I})$. If $X \cup \{a\} \in \mathcal{I}$ then $X \cup \{a\}$ is clearly a basis of $(G \cup \{a\}, \mathcal{I})$ since $|Y| \leqslant |Y \setminus \{a\}| + 1 \leqslant |X \cup \{a\}|$. Next, we assume $X \cup \{a\} \notin \mathcal{I}$ and $|Y| > |X|$. Then by the exchange property we could obtain some $b \in Y \setminus X$ with $X \cup \{b\} \in \mathcal{I}$ and consequently the contradiction $|X| \geqslant |X \cup \{b\}| = |X| + 1$ since X is a basis of $(G, \mathcal{I})$ and $b \in G$. $\square$

Lemma 8. *Assume that X is a basis of $(G, \mathcal{I})$ and $a \notin X$. Then X is a basis of $(G \setminus \{a\}, \mathcal{I})$.*

Proof. First, we have $X \subseteq G \setminus \{a\}$ since $a \notin X$. Second, for any $Y \subseteq G \setminus \{a\}$ with $Y \in \mathcal{I}$ we have $|Y| \leqslant |X|$ because X is a basis of $(G, \mathcal{I})$. $\square$

Lemma 9. *Assume that X is a basis of $(G, \mathcal{I})$ and $a \in X$. Then either $X \setminus \{a\}$ is a basis of $(G \setminus \{a\}, \mathcal{I})$ or there exists some $b \in G \setminus X$ such that $X \setminus \{a\} \cup \{b\}$ is a basis of $(G \setminus \{a\}, \mathcal{I})$.*

Proof. We show that $X \setminus \{a\}$ is a basis of $(G \setminus \{a\}, \mathcal{I})$ additionally assuming:

(a) $X \setminus \{a\} \cup \{b\}$ is *not* a basis of $(G \setminus \{a\}, \mathcal{I})$ for all $b \in G \setminus X$.

First, note that we have $X \setminus \{a\} \subseteq G \setminus \{a\}$ and, moreover, $X \setminus \{a\} \in \mathcal{I}$ by the hereditary property. Next, suppose $Y \subseteq G \setminus \{a\}$ and $Y \in \mathcal{I}$. Clearly, $|Y| \leqslant |X|$ holds as X is a basis of $(G, \mathcal{I})$ but we have to show $|Y| \leqslant |X \setminus \{a\}|$. Assuming the opposite, *i.e.* $|Y| > |X \setminus \{a\}|$, we can resort to the exchange property to obtain some $b \in Y \setminus X$ with $X \setminus \{a\} \cup \{b\} \in \mathcal{I}$. Thus, we have $X \setminus \{a\} \cup \{b\} \subseteq G \setminus \{a\}$ and $|X| = |X \setminus \{a\} \cup \{b\}|$ so that $|Y| \leqslant |X \setminus \{a\} \cup \{b\}|$ holds for any $Y \subseteq G \setminus \{a\}$ with $Y \in \mathcal{I}$ in contradiction to the assumption (a). $\square$

References

1. Theory of Matroids. Encyclopedia of Mathematics and its Applications, Cambridge University Press (1986)
2. Bird, R., de Moor, O.: Algebra of Programming. Prentice-Hall, Inc. (1997)
3. Björner, A., Ziegler, G.M.: Introduction to Greedoids. Encyclopedia of Mathematics and its Applications, pp. 284–357. Cambridge University Press (1992)
4. Bortin, M., Johnsen, E.B., Lüth, C.: Structured formal development in Isabelle. Nord. J. Comput. **13**(1–2), 2–21 (2006)
5. Doornbos, H., Backhouse, R.: Induction and recursion on datatypes. In: Möller, B. (ed.) MPC 1995. LNCS, vol. 947, pp. 242–256. Springer, Heidelberg (1995). https://doi.org/10.1007/3-540-60117-1_14

6. Ehrig, H., Kreowski, H.: Refinement and implementation. In: Astesiano, E., Kreowski, H., Krieg-Brückner, B. (eds.) Algebraic Foundations of Systems Specification, pp. 201–242. Springer, IFIP Reports (1999). https://doi.org/10.1007/978-3-642-59851-7

7. Smith, D.R.: The design of divide and conquer algorithms. Sci. Comput. Program. **5**(1), 37–58 (1985)

8. Smith, D.R.: Applications of a strategy for designing divide-and-conquer algorithms. Sci. Comput. Program. **8**(3), 213–229 (1987)

9. Smith, D.R., Lowry, M.R.: Algorithm theories and design tactics. Sci. Comput. Program. **14**(2), 305–321 (1990)

Verification and Solvers

Compositional Verification of Simulink Block Diagrams Using tock-CSP and CSP-Prover

Joabe Jesus$^{(\boxtimes)}$ (iD) and Augusto Sampaio (iD)

Federal University of Pernambuco, Recife, Brazil
{jbjj,acas}@cin.ufpe.br

Abstract. The analysis of timed process networks, such as Simulink multi-rate block diagrams, is challenging, particularly for large and complex diagrams whose verification might easily lead to the state explosion problem. For systems of this nature, with an acyclic communication graph, Roscoe and Dathi conceived a compositional deadlock verification strategy by means of local analyses, where only pairs of components need to have their behaviour analysed. Unfortunately, this strategy is restricted to untimed models. In this paper, we extend this strategy to tock-CSP, a dialect of CSP that allows modelling time aspects using a special tock event. This is implemented as a new package in CSP-Prover, a theorem prover for CSP which is itself implemented in Isabelle/HOL. An example demonstrates the benefits of our approach to deadlock analysis of Simulink block diagrams.

Keywords: CSP · CSP-Prover · Isabelle · HOL · Block diagrams · Deadlock analysis

1 Introduction

The use of *Formal Methods* (FM) is highly indicated to contribute to ensure the correctness and to increase the knowledge of complex systems [10]. For instance, the models created in simulation environments are good targets to to be formally modelled and verified on the earlier stage of the design because they usually lack a formal semantics, as discussed in [4]. In fact, agencies such as NASA, companies such as Airbus, Boeing and Embraer, their partners and suppliers have been applying FM and *Model Driven Development (MDD)* to improve their systems [3,14,19].

In the context of MDD, several works define translations from Simulink [15] models to a formal notation and perform automatic verification using a model

This work was partially supported by the National Institute of Science and Technology for Software Engineering (INES). We would like to thank Pedro Antonino and Bill Roscoe for the discussions on the extension of the approach in [23,24] to handle tock-CSP models and the referees of SBMF 2022 for their comments.

L. Lima and V. Molnár (Eds.): SBMF 2022, LNCS 13768, pp. 91–108, 2022.
https://doi.org/10.1007/978-3-031-22476-8_6

checker [7], whereas other approaches use theorem provers to deal with larger and more complex models [5]. For instance, Simulink provides a theorem prover to deal with some specific classes of problems (see [17]) and a static analyser (see [16]) to check basic model properties.

As discussed in [7,14], the formal behaviour of a Simulink model captured in the *Communicating Sequential Processes* (*CSP*) process algebra [23] can be used for the analysis of different aspects of a system such as reliability and safety. Our previous work in [14] presented an approach to tackle the verification of models as part of larger contexts defining architectural and operational constraints. In Fig. 1, the outer flow (in light grey background) presents an overview of the previous work. Starting at the left-top corner from a Simulink Block Diagram (model), the *Expert* can choose to (1) follow the path down using Matlab/Simulink to obtain simulation results, or (2) follow the right path to translate the model to a specification in CSP_M, the Machine Readable dialect of CSP, by parsing the model and applying *Mapping Rules*. The specification is based on an infrastructure *Toolkit* (a library) encoding *discrete time* Simulink concepts in CSP. So, the CSP_M specification can then be verified with assertions (model properties) specified by the engineer, using FDR. Moreover, the traces produced by FDR can be analysed to modify/correct the original model.

The inner flow (the rectangle entitled "Current Proposal") represents the contribution of this paper: the use of a single notation (CSP) to verify Simulink designs using *model checking, theorem proving* and *simulation*.

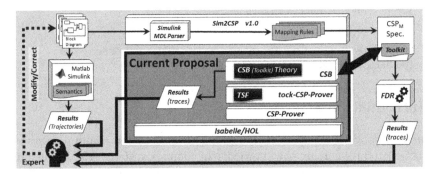

Fig. 1. Overview of previous work and current contribution.

In fact, model checking for complex Simulink diagrams or for diagrams involving complex data can easily become impractical. So, the inner flow in Fig. 1 depicts a new verification path, allowing the *Expert* to choose the appropriate verification technology according to the problem in hand. In this context, we choose to encode our previous work in CSP_{TP} (the *CSP-Prover* [12] dialect of CSP). In Fig. 1, we highlight that the two documents in black color represent theories in *Isabelle/HOL* [22] and *CSP-Prover* that are a contributions of this work. The CSB (Communicating Sequential Blocks) Theory encodes the CSP_M Toolkit in CSP_{TP}, whereas our focus in this work is on the TSF (Time-Stop Free) Theory, that encodes the necessary infrastructure for the purpose of deadlock analysis of tock-CSP processes using *theorem proving* facilities.

Deadlock verification of CSP specifications using refinement is a very powerful technique. Compositional verification approaches such as the one proposed by Roscoe and Dathi in [23,24] for the analysis of networks of processes become candidates for the verification of large and complex systems using local analysis that are restricted to interactions between pairs of components. Nevertheless, although the approach in [23,24] was encoded in CSP-*Prover* [13], this theory restricts the deadlock analysis to systems where no communication is performed by more than two participants. So, this theory is not applicable to verify CSP specifications obtained using our *Mapping Rules* for two main reasons: (1) Simulink's notion of *time steps* was represented as a control event shared by all processes from the network; and (2) the several branches of signals were captured by multiway rendezvous.

To overcome these limitations and be able to benefit from a compositional deadlock analysis approach to verify block diagrams, we have worked in two main directions. First we adopted tock-CSP [23] that allows the representation of time as a special tock event (a way of representing time in untimed CSP). However, since the passage of time in tock-CSP is global, all the processes that embody time aspects need to synchronise on the tock event, giving rise to the problem (1) explained above. We have then extended the theory in [23,24] to allow the synchronisation of more than two processes in the tock event; we have also mechanised the extended theory in CSP-*Prover*. Moreover, the multiway rendezvous, problem (2) above, is avoided in our encoding by representing signals as processes performing interleaved point-to-point communications for each branch, as discussed later. Thus, our main contribution is a compositional strategy for deadlock analysis of *timed process networks* (such as the Simulink multi-rate block diagrams).

This paper is organized as follows. In Sect. 2, we give an overview of background material using a running example. Then, Sect. 3 presents our encoding of tock-CSP in CSP-*Prover* and the extension of the theory in [23,24] to allow the compositional deadlock verification of timed block diagrams. Afterwards, we describe in Sect. 4 the translation from Simulink models to tock-CSP models that give a formal semantics to such diagrams. Finally, Sect. 5 presents our conclusions, related and future work.

2   Background

In this section we briefly introduce, using a running example, Simulink Block Diagrams, tock-CSP, the theory for compositional deadlock analysis in [23,24], and CSP-*Prover*.

2.1 Block Diagrams and MDD

Matlab/Simulink is a *Model-Driven Development* (MDD) *simulation environment* that extends the classic notion of *block diagram* by introducing the notion of *sample time*, defining what Mathworks entitled *"time-based block diagram"* [15]. It's a *de facto* standard for system specification, and the Simulink family of tools support tasks ranging from requirements definition to *code generation*. Creating a Simulink model of a (physical) system can be done in two ways: using the physical relations between variables or using a block that represents the entire equation. The tool provides several libraries and Blocksets (domain-specific block libraries), which group blocks with similar characteristics.

In the context of Simulink, additional functionality is provided by tools such as Simulink Design Verifier (SimulinkDV) [17] and Simulink Verification and Validation (SimulinkVV) [16]. SimulinkDV can formally verify some system properties by defining blocks that specify constraints or temporal properties on Boolean signals as described in [17].

2.2 Running Example - Simple Actuator System (SAS)

To illustrate the concepts, the techniques used and the contributions of this paper, we use a *simple actuation system* (SAS)[1] whose purpose is driving a hypothetical aircraft control surface in order to maneuver an aircraft. The system (see Fig. 2) is composed of an *actuator control electronics* (**ACE**) and the *power control unit* (**PCU**), which is an actuator controlled by a *solenoid valve* (**SOV**) and an *electrical-hydraulic servo valve* (**EHSV**).

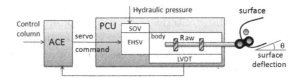

Fig. 2. Simple Actuation System (SAS) - Schematics

The **PCU** actuator has an internal sensor that measures the actuator's **Raw** (piston) position, called *linear variable differential transformer* (**LVDT**). Thus, the **ACE** component receives the *control column* command from the pilots' cabin, and compares this command to the output of the **LVDT** in order to define the current *servo command*. The *solenoid valve* receives the *servo command* to control whether the actuator is engaged or disengaged from power pumps (omitted in the figure) that supply the hydraulic pressure; and the *servo valve* controls how the pressure of the pumps is transformed into the displacement of the actuator's **Raw**. Moreover, when disengaged, the actuator's **Raw** is free to move without any resistance force.

---

[1] Here we adopt the modelling approach using block diagrams. The identification of this system using parametric models can be found in [6].

SAS Block Diagram and Simulation. To model the plant (*power control unit* - **PCU**) of the SAS schematics from Fig. 2, we can first select a *closed loop structure* (for details see [21]) to design the plant using a *block diagram*. The *surface deflection* (measured in degrees) is the *variable to be controlled*, whereas the input *control variable* is the *servo command* (measured in amperes (A)). Figure 3 shows that the controller is composed by a conversion block, a comparator[2] and an error processing block, which inputs the computed error *e* (in degrees) that must be handled by a processing block to correctly drive the raw. Moreover, as long as the **PCU** raw displacement (in centimeters) grows according with the output of the servo controller and the linkage angular velocity is measured in degrees per second, we need to convert these measures and also consider applying any necessary saturation.

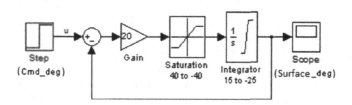

Fig. 3. PCU block diagram in Simulink

The Gain block in Fig. 3 models the hydraulic pressure from the **SOV** controlled by the **EHSV** that produces a constant acceleration of the **Raw** (piston), whereas the Saturation block produces the angular velocity of the linkage to the surface, and the Integrator block produces the displacement of the linkage to the surface, which is physically constrained to -25 to $15°$C. The *simulation* of the presented block diagram can be performed using a Simulink model in which the additional blocks **Scope** (from the Simulink **Sinks** Library) and **Step** (from the Simulink **Sources** Library) are inserted in the model and connected to the desired signals of interest. The Simulink model and the results of the *simulation* are available online[3].

2.3 Formal Verification and CSP

Specialised tools and techniques such as abstract interpretation, data independence and *communication patterns* [1,8,18,20] are very important when verifying complex systems or classes of infinite-state systems. In this context, the process algebra *CSP* (Communicating Sequential Processes) [11,23] is a formal language primarily designed to model the behaviour of concurrent and distributed systems. It has different dialects such as CSP_M (the input notation for

---

[2] In Control Theory, a comparator is usually a sum block that subtracts the feedback signal from the input control variable, producing an error signal.

[3] https://jbjj.github.io/publications/sbmf2022/SASinSimulink/.

the *Failures-Divergences Refinement (FDR) model checker* [9]) and CSP_{TP} (the *CSP-Prover* [12] input notation for the powerful *Isabelle/HOL* [22] *theorem prover*). Nevertheless, both CSP_M and CSP_{TP} use three main elements to describe a system: events (abstractions of real-world actions), processes (flows of events which can be combined to produce complex behaviours), and operators (relating/combining events and processes).

Named processes are defined by giving it a name, a list of parameters, and a body/equation composed of events and processes combined using operators, that determine the order and availability of events. For instance, we highlight some important constructs (in CSP_{TP} dialect): SKIP (termination); STOP (deadlock); ? x:S -> P (external prefix choice, engages on an event x from the set S and then behaves as process P); a -> P (prefix, equivalent to the external prefix choice for the set {a}); P |~| Q (internal choice, that stands for the nondeterministic choice of processes P and Q); P |[S]| Q (parallel composition of two processes P and Q synchronised on events from the set S); P[[a <- b]] (renaming the event a of process P with event b); and P \ A(hiding the events in the set of events A). The main semantic models of CSP are the *traces model*, where a process is denoted by the set of all its possible traces (sequences of events), the *stable-failures model*, which records the events a process can refuse to engage on after each of its traces, and the *failures-divergences model*, which, in addition, records the set of traces after which the process diverges (engages on a loop of internal actions).

To illustrate the usage of CSP for the specification of the Simple Actuator System (SAS), the Listing 2.1 shows the definition of the named process Raw representing the actuator's Raw (piston). The process behaves as a choice between trasmitting its position p using channel rawPos or adjusting the position value according to a value e communicated by channel adjust.

```
1  Raw(p,adj) = rawPos!p -> let d = disp(adj)
2                            within Raw(p+d, adj-d)
3              [] adjust?e -> Raw(p, e)
```

Listing 2.1. CSP_M process representing the Actuator's Raw (piston).

Notably, after every movement of the piston, captured by a rawPos event, the parameter adj is used to compute a displacement (error) d to change the raw position pos value.

A specification of the Simple Actuator System (SAS) in CSP_M, as well as the specification modified to allow *model checking*, and the results of the verification are available online[4]. Although we were able to perform model checking by significantly abstracting the original model, this does not scale. Our main contribution in this paper is to devise a compositional strategy for deadlock verification that scales.

---

[4] https://jbjj.github.io/publications/sbmf2022/SASinCSPM/.

2.4   tock-CSP

Beyond the *CSP* standard notation, some extensions have been proposed to enrich *CSP*. In particular, tock-*CSP* is a variant of *CSP* to deal with discrete time in *CSP* with the following features: (1) the special event tock represents discrete instants, equally separated by any infinitesimal real number value, of the passage of time; (2) TOCKS$^\checkmark$ is a pre-defined process that terminates or performs tock and recurses, TOCKS$^\checkmark$ = (tock -> TOCKS$^\checkmark$) |~| SKIP; (3) processes are considered **well-timed** if, when hiding all their events except for tock, they refine the process TOCKS$^\checkmark$ in the *failures-divergences model* of *CSP*. Beyond that, if a process does not terminate, we can refine TOCKS (equivalent to RUN({tock}), where the process RUN(S) is defined as an external prefix choice on set S followed by a recursive call to itself, i.e., RUN(S) = ? x:S -> RUN(S)).

In tock-*CSP* all the processes with timing constraints must synchronize on the event tock. Thus, we can reason about what each process and the overall system do in specifc time intervals. Violating time constraints indicates a process may be refusing time to pass. Thus, provided a process refuses the tock event, we have a **time-stop**. This is usually a result of inconsistent timing requirements. Indeed, provided a process does not diverge, one can use the refinement of TOCKS$^\checkmark$ in the *stable-failures model* of *CSP* to check for **time-stop**s.

2.5   Roscoe and Dathi's Compositional Deadlock Analysis Theory

The work in [23, 24] defines a compositional theory for the deadlock analysis of networks of processes. Particularly, provided components follow some pre-defined patterns, only pairs of components need to have their behaviours analysed to prove the process network is deadlock free. A process network can be defined as a finite set of atomic tuples, each one representing a basic component of a system. These are triples that contain an identifier for the component, a process of the behaviour of this component and an alphabet that represents the set of events that this component can perform [1].

Definition 1. *(Process Network)   Let* CSP_Processes *be the infinite set of all possible CSP processes,* Σ *the set of CSP events and* IdType *the set for identifiers of atomic tuples. A process network is a finite set V, such that:*

$$V \subset (\text{IdType} \times \textit{CSP\_Processes} \times \wp \, \Sigma)$$

As a concrete illustration, a process network can be concisely specified in *CSP* using the replicated alphabetised parallel composition operator:

|| x:S @ [A(x)] P(x)

which composes, in parallel, processes P(x) synchronising on alphabets A(x) for the values of x in the set S. Moreover, the synchronisation sets can be obtained using the extension sets: {| c |} that contains all events which can be produced by a channel c.

Considering our SAS example, assuming we defined processes for each basic components of the PCU (Power Control Unit), we can describe the actuator behaviour as a process equation defined in terms of an alphabetised parallel composition of processes EHSV, Raw and LVDT, see Listing 2.2. They all synchronise in events of the rawPos channel, whereas EHSV and Raw synchronise in events of the ehsvOut channel. In particular, the LVDT sensor core is physically connected to the raw (piston), so, since they move together, the LVDT process has its events coreMoved renamed to rawPos to be able to synchronise in the alphabet specified in the parallel composition.

```
1  PCU = || (P,A):
2       { ( EHSV ,
3              {| servoCmd, rawPos, ehsvOut |}   ) ,
4          ( Raw [[ adjust <- ehsvOut ]] ,
5              {| rawPos, ehsvOut |}              ) ,
6          ( LVDT [[ coreMoved <- rawPos ]] ,
7              {| rawPos, lvdtOut |}              )
8       } @ [A] P
```

Listing 2.2. CSP_M process representing the PCU component.

In this context, we must distinguish a *live network*, a structure that satisfies three assumptions: (1) busyness - a busy network specifies that there is no trace that is a deadlock state of an atomic process from the network; (2) atomic non-termination - no atomic component can terminate; and (3) triple-disjointness - at most two processes share an event, i.e. the intersection of the alphabet for any three different atomic tuples is the empty set. Particularly, the PCU process in Listing 2.2 violates triple disjointness, since the events from channel rawPos are shared between all sub-processes, generating a multiway rendezvous. The solution is discussed in Sect. 3.

Moreover, semantically, a state of the network is a pair containing a trace and a function from an identifier to the process failures, whereas a deadlock state is a network state in which the union of refusals is equal to the union of the alphabets of the atomic components. Furthermore, as discussed in [1], deadlock states can only arise in a *live network* when two processes have an improper interaction, as long as all components are deadlock free. These misinteractions are captured by the concept of ungranted requests: the conflict between an atom, say a1, offering an event to communicate with another atom, say a2, but a2 refuses any of the events expected by a1. Beyond that, both a1 and a2 must not be able to perform internal/independent actions. Thus, the network is deadlock free provided some given order relation (>) on the set of functions, say f, on the semantics of the components is not violated by an ungranted request.

2.6 *CSP-Prover*

CSP-Prover [12] is an encoding of the *CSP* syntax and semantics as a theory extension of *Isabelle/HOL theorem prover*. Different base theories including the *traces model* T and the *stable-failures model* F are available in *CSP-Prover*. Moreover, deadlock analysis can be performed for processes and networks as presented in [13].

We explain the notations of *Isabelle/HOL* and *CSP-Prover* on demand. *CSP-Prover* is presented in [12] and documentation of *Isabelle/HOL* is publicly available[5]. The CSP_{TP} specification for the SAS is also available elsewhere[6]. However, we highlight three important concepts: (1) most of *CSP-Prover* definitions are based on *Isabelle/HOL* datatypes and syntactical transformations; (2) the type of processes (proc) is parameterised with the types of process names and events; (3) named processes are usually specified in *CSP-Prover* using a datatype for all process names and a (primitive recursive) function (primrec) from this type to the type proc. The Listing 2.3 illustrates the usage of CSP_{TP} for the named process Raw from Listing 2.1, assuming the omitted datatypes PN and Events were correctly defined.

```
1  primrec PNfun :: "PN => (PN,Events) proc"
2  where "PNfun(Raw p adj) = rawPos ! p -> (let d = disp(adj)
3                                             in $(Raw (p+d) (adj-d)))
4               [+] adjust?e -> $(Raw p e)"
```

Listing 2.3. CSP_{TP} process representing the Actuator's Raw (piston).

3 Mechanised Compositional Verification of Timed Process Networks

This section presents our theory for deadlock analysis of Timed Process Networks. In Sect. 3.1, we present the notions of a **time-stop** free process. The definition of **time-stop** free process networks is presented in Sect. 3.2. Finally, in Sect. 3.3 we describe a mechanisation of tock-*CSP* and **time-stop** free process networks in *CSP-Prover*, via *Isabelle/HOL* type classes. All definitions and proofs can be found in the CSP-Prover official GitHub repository[7].

3.1 Time-Stop Free Processes

As discussed in Sect. 2.4, a **time-stop** is usually a result of inconsistent timing requirements. Fortunately, one can check for **time-stop** in a process by analysing if the given process refines the TOCKS$^{✓}$ process (see Sect. 2.4) when hiding all events except for tock, as specified in Lemma 1 (mechanised in Sect. 3.3).

Lemma 1. *(Time-Stop Free Processes) Let P be a tock-CSP process, provided* $P \setminus (\Sigma^{✓} - \{tock\})$ *refines TOCKS$^{✓}$ in the* stable-failures model, *then P is **time-stop** free.*

As one can note, STOP is not **time-stop** free, as long as STOP refuses tock and tick (✔), whereas TOCKS$^{✓}$ can produces traces in one of four patterns: (1) <> (the empty trace); (2) <✔> (the trace for termination); (3) < tock, ..., tock, ... >, traces that record infinite time events (tock) (indicating it is acting as a reactive system); or (4) <tock,...,tock,✔ >, for traces recording time and termination.

---

[5] https://isabelle.in.tum.de/documentation.html.

[6] https://jbjj.github.io/publications/sbmf2022/SASinCSPTP/.

[7] https://github.com/yoshinao-isobe/CSP-Prover/tree/jbjj-phd/.

3.2   Time-Stop Free Process Networks

Based on the work in [23,24] previously presented, we define a timed process network as an extension of a process network as follows.

Definition 2. *(Timed Process Network) Let* `tock-CSP_Processes` *be the set of all possible tock-CSP processes,* Σ *the set of CSP events and* IdType *the set for identifiers of atomic tuples. A timed process network is a finite set V, such that:*

$$V \subset (\ \text{IdType} \times \textit{tock-CSP\_Processes} \times (\wp\ \Sigma \cup \{tock\})\ )$$

We also introduce the following definitions: (1) Time-Stop state is a state in which the `tock` event is a member of the union of refusals of atomic components, hence, some member of the network rejects `tock`, forbidding time to pass; (2) Non-`tock` deadlock state is a state refusing all non-tock events; (3) `tock`-triple-conjoint, i.e., the intersection of the alphabet for any three different atomic tuples is the singleton set {`tock`}; (4) A non-`tock` ungranted request occurs when an atomic component, say a1, is offering a non-tock event to communicate with another atomic component, say a2, but a2 cannot offer any of the events expected by a1 in the given state of the network; and (5) a process of the network is blocked in non-`tock` if the process network is `tock`-triple-conjoint and there is a request such that all other network requests are non-`tock` ungranted requests. Based on these definitions we can estabilish the following lemma and theorems, with mechanised proofs in *CSP-Prover* repository.

Lemma 2. *(**Non-Tock** Blocked Networks) Let V be a Timed Process Network, as in Definition 2, V is in a non-**tock** deadlock state if, and only if, all atomic components of V are blocked in non-**tock**.*

Theorem 1. *(**Time-Stop** Free Network) Let V be a Timed Process Network, as in Definition 2, and consider there exists an order* f *for the atomic components such that there is no cycle of ungranted requests in a non-Time-Stop state, then the process network is a Time-Stop Free Network.*

Theorem 1 allows the verification of timed networks of tock-CSP processes by local analysis of interactions between pairs of components but with a multi-synchronisation of all the processes in the `tock` event.

Beyond the verification of **time-stops**, we aim to check a system for deadlock. The following theorem lifts deadlock verification from CSP to tock-CSP.

Theorem 2. *(Lifting Deadlock Free Analysis)   Consider P a **time-stop** free tock-CSP process and that P \ {tock} is deadlock free, then P is deadlock free.*

Although we state Theorem 2 for an arbitrary tock-CSP process P, it is particularly useful for the verification of timed networks. With this result we can split the deadlock analysis of a timed process network into the verification of **time-stops** (using Theorem 1) and the untimed projection of this network (hiding `tock`). This is an important contribution to allow compositional verification and reuse of existing results for untimed process networks. Moreover, the divergence-free condition does not impose any relevant applicability restriction in the context of deadlock analysis of Simulink Block Diagrams, as their automatically generated semantics are represented by tock-*CSP* processes that do not have divergences, even after hiding the event tock.

Considering our SAS example, we discussed that the process in Listing 2.2 violates triple disjointness constraint, since the events from channel rawPos are shared between more than two components. In this context, to avoid multiway rendezvous, one can use alternative communication patterns such as an interleaved point-to-point communication. Although this is not a general solution, our named process Raw can be modified to produce two different communications of its position in interleaving (|||, where P ||| Q = P |[{}]| Q), see Listing 3.4.

```
1  Raw(p,adj) = ( (rawPos.1!p -> SKIP ||| rawPos.2!p -> SKIP) ;
2                  let d = disp(adj)
3                  within Raw(p+d, adj-d) )
4                [] ( adjust?e -> Raw(p, e) )
```

Listing 3.4. CSP_M modified process representing an Actuator Raw (piston)

Listing 3.5 presents a modified specification of the PCU as a Time-Stop Free Network. The rawPos channel was modified to have an index for the process receiving a copy of its position. So, the synchronisation is now triple-disjoint. Moreover, we declare tock in the synchronisation sets of all components.

```
1  PCU = || (P,A):
2    { ( EHSV ,
3        union( {tock}, {|servoCmd,rawPos.1,ehsvOut|}) ) ,
4        ( Raw [[ adjust <- ehsvOut ]] ,
5        union( {tock}, {|rawPos.1,rawPos.2,ehsvOut|} ) ) ,
6        ( LVDT [[ coreMoved <- rawPos.2 ]] ,
7        union( {tock}, {|rawPos.2, lvdtOut|} )           )
8    } @ [A] P
```

Listing 3.5. tock-*CSP* process representing the PCU as a Time-Stop Free Network.

3.3 Mechanisation in CSP-Prover

To encode the analysis strategy for compositional deadlock analysis of timed process networks, presented in the previous section, in CSP_{TP} we had to extend *CSP-Prover* with a representation for tock-*CSP*, the encoding for the verification of **Time-Stop** Freedom, and the proofs of Theorems 1 and 2.

Mechanisation of tock-*CSP* **in** *CSP-Prover*. Our mechanisation is constructed by defining an *Isabelle/HOL* axiomatic type class[8] for the caracterization of the *tock* event (which represents the drum-beat of the passage of time as an explicit event) and requires the existence of non-tock events (the complement of the singleton set {tock} is non-empty), see Listing 3.6.

---

[8] In *Isabelle/HOL*, an axiomatic type class provides a useful light-weight mechanism for hierarchically-structured abstract theories and allows for a reasonable implementation of overloading as inpired by the Haskell programming language.

```
1  class tockCSP =
2    fixes tock :: "'a"
3    assumes nonempty_Nontock [simp]: "- {tock} ≠ {}"
4  begin
5    abbreviation Nontock :: "'a set"
6    where "Nontock == - {tock}"
7  end
```

Listing 3.6. The `tockCSP` type class in tock-*CSP-Prover*.

In Listing 3.6, our `tockCSP` type class is parameterised by a type variable 'a. To be used, this type needs to be instantiated. As an example, for our process `Raw` from Listing 2.3 we can define a datatype `Events` as in Listing 3.7, which is used in Line 3 to instantiate the type class `tockCSP`. In this example, `Nontock` is the set of event descriptors {`rawPos`, `adjust`}.

```
1  datatype Events = rawPos | adjust | tock
2
3  instance Events :: tockCSP ...
```

Listing 3.7. Instatiating the `tockCSP` type class.

Furthermore, *CSP-Prover* distinguishes event descriptors from proper events. In particular, *CSP-Prover* events are encoded in a datatype `'a event` and assumes values `Ev 'a` or `Tick` (the ✔ from *CSP*). So, the event `Tock` is encoded as an abbreviation to the value `Ev tock`, see Listing 3.8).

```
1  abbreviation Tock :: "'a::tockCSP event"
2  where "Tock == Ev tock"
```

Listing 3.8. The Tock event in tock-*CSP-Prover*.

Indeed, `Tock` (rather than `tock`) is the event that will be present in *CSP-Prover* traces. Thus, as an **abbreviation**, given a *CSP-Prover* event carring values of type class `tockCSP`, *Isabelle/HOL* displays `Ev tock` as `Tock`. As an example, consider the definition of the process TOCKS✔ presented in Sect. 2.4. This process is specified in CSP_{TP} using the type class `tockCSP` as the type of events produced by the process named `TOCKSTick`, as presented in Listing 3.9.

```
1  primrec TOCKSTickfun :: "TOCKSTickPN => (TOCKSTickPN, 'a::tockCSP) proc"
2  where "TOCKSTickfun (TOCKSTick) = (tock -> $(TOCKSTick))
3                                     |~| SKIP"
```

Listing 3.9. The TOCKS✔ (named `TOCKSTick`) process in tock-*CSP-Prover*.

Note that `TOCKSTickfun` is a function specifying the equation for the named process `TOCKSTick`. This process equation has events obeying the `tockCSP` type class and it is defined as an internal choice between: a prefixed recursion (generating `Tock` events from the `tock` descriptor) and SKIP.

Now, according to [23], given a process P, we can check whether it does not have a **time-stop** by hiding all events except for `tock` and checking that it refines TOCKS✔. Listing 3.10 shows an initial encoding of the rule. The lemma states that provided the given process P can be represented as an external prefix choice on a non-empty set S of events, and the refinement holds for the sub-process PXf for all events in S, then it holds when hiding non-tock events of P. It is important to note that hiding does receive values of *CSP-Prover* 'a event type, but works on the type 'a.

```
1  lemma Rule_check_timestops_Roscoe_TOCKSTick :
2      "[| FPmode ≠ CPOmode ;
3          S ≠ {} ;
4          P =F ? x:S -> Pfx x ;
5          ∀ x : S. $TOCKSTick ⊑F (Pfx x -- Nontock) |] ==>
6          $TOCKSTick ⊑F (P -- Nontock))"
```

Listing 3.10. Proved Lemma 1 for Roscoe **time-stop** checking Rule.

Line 2 in Listing 3.10 is a *CSP-Prover* directive to avoid complete partial orders (CPO) for CSP fixed-point induction, see [12] for details.

The Time-Stop Free (TSF) Package. To encode the verification of Time-Stop Free Processes we extend the encoding of deadlock analysis available in *CSP-Prover*, which already provides the definition [X]-DeadlockFree P, stating that a process P is deadlock free for a given alphabet X. So, we define the predicate isTimeStopFree for a given process P provided Tock events are not refused when hiding non-tock events of P, see Listing 3.11.

```
1  definition isTimeStopFree ("_ isTimeStopFree")
2  where "P isTimeStopFree == [{Tock}]-DeadlockFree ( P -- Nontock )"
```

Listing 3.11. The definition of Time-Stop Free in TSF.

As previously mentioned, by refining TOCKS✓ we can check for **time-stops** of a process, so, we can estabilish a theorem (see Listing 3.12) relating Roscoe's Rule encoded in Listing 3.10 to the definition of isTimeStopFree.

```
1  theorem TimeStopFree_TOCKSTick_ref_iff:
2      "( P isTimeStopFree ) = ( $TOCKSTick ⊑F P -- Nontock )"
3      apply (rule iffI)
4      apply (simp add: refTOCKSTick_if_isTimeStopFree)
5      by (simp add: isTimeStopFree_if_refTOCKSTick)
```

Listing 3.12. The equivalence between verifications of TSF.

The proof is performed by checking the implications in both directions.

Mechanisation of Time-Stop Free Networks in TSF Package. Consider a process network V, encoded in *CSP-Prover* as a pair (I,FX), where I is a set of indexes i and FX is a function that associates each i with a pair (PF,A) having a process (or failure set) PF and the communication alphabet A. Also consider a state sigma of the network, encoded as a pair (t,Yf) having the trace t and the function Yf from I to the atom refusals for the trace t.

We encoded in Listing 3.13: (1) isTockNet, as a definition of the predicate that constrains processes to have tock in their communication alphabets; (2) isTimeStopStateOf, as a definition of a state of the network in which Tock belongs to the refusals of the network; and (3) isNonTockDeadlockStateOf, to stand for the states that have refused all network events (the range of Ev on the alphabet of V, given by the function ALP) except for Tock.

```
1   definition "isTockNet V == (∀ i ∈ fst V. tock ∈ (snd (snd V i)))"
2
3   definition isTimeStopStateOf ("_ isTimeStopStateOf _")
4   where "sigma isTimeStopStateOf V == sigma isStateOf V &
5         Tock ∈ ⋃ { ( (snd sigma) i ) | i. i ∈ fst V }"
6
7   definition isNonTockDeadlockStateOf ("_ isNonTockDeadlockStateOf _")
8   where "sigma isNonTockDeadlockStateOf V == sigma isStateOf V &
9         Ev `(ALP V) - {Tock} = ⋃ { ( (snd sigma) i ) | i. i ∈ fst V }"
```

Listing 3.13. The base definitions for proving Time-Stop Free in TSF.

The definition of tock-triple-conjoint, see Listing 3.14, is encoded very similarly to the encoding of triple-disjoint in *CSP-Prover*. But instead of the empty set we have the singleton set containing the tock descriptor. Moreover, a TimeStopFreeNetwork is encoded using definition isTockNet and requires the generalised parallel composition (PAR) of the atomic components to be **time-stop** free.

```
1   definition "tock_triple_conjoint V ==
2       ( ∀ i ∈ fst V. ∀ j ∈ fst V. ∀ k ∈ fst V. i ≠ j & j ≠ k & k ≠ i -->
3       (snd (snd V i) ∩ snd (snd V j) ∩ snd (snd V k)) = {tock} )"
4
5   definition TimeStopFreeNetwork
6   where "TimeStopFreeNetwork V == isTockNet V &
7                       [Ev `(ALP V)]-TimeStopFree (PAR V)"
```

Listing 3.14. Time-Stop Free Networks in TSF.

Finally, the Theorem 1 is encoded in TSF and presented in Listing 3.15. The proof is performed by checking the implications in both directions and is available in *CSP-Prover* GitHub repository.

```
1   theorem Theorem_1_TimeStopFreeNetwork:
2       "[| isTockNet (I,PXf); I≠{}; finite I ; tock_triple_conjoint (I,PXf);
3       (I,FXf) isFailureOf (I,PXf) ; BusyNetwork (I,FXf);
4       ∃ f . ∀ t Yf . (t,Yf) isStateOf (I,FXf) -->
5       (∀ i j. (I,FXf)>> i --tock[(t,Yf),(VocabularyOf(I,FXf))]-->o j -->
6           f j (t --tr (- snd (FXf j)), Yf j) <
7           f i (t --tr (- snd (FXf i)), Yf i)) |] ==>
8   TimeStopFreeNetwork (I,PXf)"
```

Listing 3.15. The Theorem 1 of Time-Stop Free Networks in TSF.

The assumptions in Line 2 are according to Definition 2, whereas in Line 3: isFailureOf allows representing the timed process network using the failures (FXf) function for each atomic component; BusyNetwork guarantees the components are deadlock free. Moreover, in Lines 4 to 7 the existence of the order f implies all states (t,Yf) do not have an atom i with an ungranted non-tock request (--tock[...,...]-->o) to atom j that violates the order in f. Note that the ordering function f receives the trace of the element (obtained by hiding (--tr) from t the complement of the alphabet of the atom). The definitions of isFailureOf, isStateOf and VocabularyOf are available in *CSP-Prover*.

Mechanisation of Deadlock-Free for tock-*CSP* **in TSF Package.** Theorem 2 is encoded in CSP_{TP} as presented in Listing 3.16. Note that the encoding declares P as a tock-*CSP* process (see the type specification using the type class tockCSP). Its proof is available in the *CSP-Prover* GitHub repository.

```
1  theorem Theorem_2_DeadlockFree_tockCSP :
2      "[X]-DeadlockFree (P::('p,'a::tockCSP) proc) ==
3       [X]-TimeStopFree P & [X - {Tock}]-DeadlockFree (P -- {tock})"
```

Listing 3.16. The Theorem of Deadlock-Free for tock-*CSP* in TSF.

4   From Simulink to tock-*CSP*

Simulink models are constructed hierarchically, so we previously proposed in [14] translation rules (equations) (from Simulink to *CSP*) that are compositional; a model is translated in a *bottom-up* order of the hierarchy of Simulink blocks by applying the function Ψ to each element of the model, as depicted in Fig. 4.

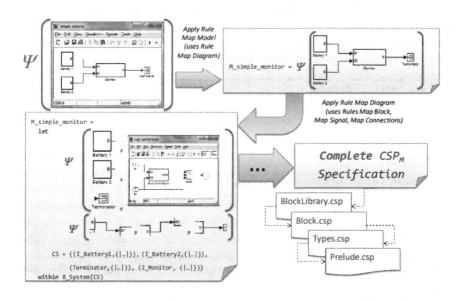

Fig. 4. Applying Translation Rules from Simulink to CSP.

We follow a similar approach to translate to tock-*CSP*; our rules map the entire Simulink model as a unique process and are formatted as $LHS \leftrightarrow RHS$, where LHS stands for the left-hand side and RHS stands for the right-hand side of the rule. Thus, the LHS of the equation represents the application of the translation function Ψ to an element of Simulink, and the RHS is the tock-*CSP* denotation script produced by this particular application of the function. Therefore, our set of mapping rules is an inductive definition of Ψ on the structure of Simulink models.

Recall from the introduction that we raised two main concerns with respect to the translation from Simulink: (1) Simulink's notion of time steps is usually represented as a control event shared by all processes from the network; and (2) the several branches of signals are captured by multiway rendezvous. We highlight that: concerning (1), the Simulink time steps are represented by tock events from tock-CSP and all generated processes in the specification synchronise on tock (now this is no longer a problem since we have extended the original deadlock verification strategy for process networks to allow a full synchronisation on the tock events); regarding (2), Simulink signals, and their branches, are mapped as processes, so that signals receive output from a specific block and perform an interleaving of branches for sending the signal value to each of the signal targets. Indeed, we consider signals as blocks with a single input and multiple outputs. Therefore, our translation solves problems (1) and (2) because the two kinds (block or signal) of atomic components are time-stop free and always synchronise on tock.

The Listing 4.17 presents the encoding of signals and branches in tock-CSP-Prover. A new type class called CSPsig is defined to extend the tockCSP type class with the event descriptor (channel) sig, assuming: sig is an injective function, in order to produce distinct events; and events of sig are not equal to tock.

```
1  class CSPsig = tockCSP +
2  fixes sig :: "PortId => T => 'a"
3  assumes inj_sig         [simp]: "∀ bpid. inj (sig bpid)"
4      and diff_sig_tock   [simp]: "∀ bpid v . sig bpid v ~= tock"
5
6  primrec Signalfun :: "(SignalPN, 'e::CSPsig) pnfun"
7  where
8    "Signalfun(Signal' sn src dstBlks) =
9        (sig src ? v -> ( [||] (i,bpid):set (enumerate 1 dstBlks) ..
10                               ($Branch'sn i v,{|sig (sn,i) v, tock|}));;
11                      $Signal' sn src dstBlks)
12       [+] tock -> $Signal' sn src dstBlks"
13
14  | "Signalfun(Branch' sn i v) =
15        sig (sn,i) ! v -> SKIP
16        [+] tock -> $Branch' sn i v"
```

Listing 4.17. Signals and branches in our tock-CSP-Prover theory for Simulink.

Beyond the new encoding for signals, our Block process is also modified to use tock-CSP. In particular, as long as internal events are hidden, only the input and output events of the processes need to allow tock. This is accomplished by modifying our input and output processes to provide an external choice with tock. Finally, the multirate representation processes Offset and Sampler for the Simulink sample time mechanism had their event tick replaced by tock.

The CSP_{TP} specification for the SAS generated by our translation strategy is also verified deadlock free using Theorems 1 and 2 and available online[9].

---

[9] https://jbjj.github.io/publications/sbmf2022/SASinCSBTP/.

5   Conclusion and Future Works

This work formalises a theory for compositional verification of Simulink Block Diagrams using tock-CSP that is fully mechanised in CSP-$Prover$. In particular, the mechanisation includes: (1) an encoding of tock-CSP in CSP-$Prover$; (2) a mechanised proof for checking **time-stops** using refinement of TOCKS$^{\checkmark}$; (3) a theory of Time-Stop Free Networks; (4) an encoding of the theory and the mechanised proof of Theorem 1 for Time-Stop Free Networks; (5) a compositional strategy for deadlock analysis of timed models by splitting into an untimed and a timed verification; and, finally, (6) a fully automatic translation from Simulink Block Diagrams to tock-CSP.

There are different encodings of tock-CSP in the literature as discussed in [2]. The work in [2] highlights that contemplating **time-stops** is a requirement for the definition of other features in tock-CSP, such as: deadlines; termination; and Zeno behaviour (avoiding infinitely many events between tock events). In particular, their work can be integrated with ours, as long as their theories are also mechanised in $Isabelle/HOL$. Furthermore, no other work has been identified to provide a theory of tock-CSP networks and compositional verification using tock-CSP.

Considering the context of CSP, as already mentioned, this work was inspired by and extends the local deadlock analysis of process networks developed by Roscoe and Dathi [23, 24] and mechanised for FDR in [1] and for CSP-Prover in [13].

Our approach provides a three-way verification path to the *Expert* that can choose between *simulation, model checking* or *theorem proving* when analysing a system model. The set of algebraic rules to systematically translate a Simulink model into a tock-CSP specification is an important contribution. Nevertheless, the soundness proof of this translation is currently under development.

As a further opportunity to scale verification, we plan to consider behavioural patterns as proposed in [23] and implemented in [1], as these also allow local deadlock analysis in particular contexts.

References

1. Antonino, P., Sampaio, A., Woodcock, J.: A refinement based strategy for local deadlock analysis of networks of CSP processes. In: Jones, C., Pihlajasaari, P., Sun, J. (eds.) FM 2014. LNCS, vol. 8442, pp. 62–77. Springer, Cham (2014). https://doi.org/10.1007/978-3-319-06410-9_5

2. Baxter, J., Ribeiro, P., Cavalcanti, A.: Sound reasoning in tock-CSP. Acta Inf. **59**, 125–162 (2022). https://doi.org/10.1007/s00236-020-00394-3

3. Bernard, R., Aubert, J., Bieber, P., Merlini, C., Metge, S.: Experiments in model-based safety analysis: flight controls. In: 1st IFAC Workshop on Dependable Control of Discrete Systems (2007)

4. Bouissou, O., Chapoutot, A.: An operational semantics for Simulink's simulation engine. In: Proceedings of the 13th ACM SIGPLAN/SIGBED International Conference on Languages, Compilers, Tools and Theory for Embedded Systems, pp.

129–138. LCTES 2012, Association for Computing Machinery, New York, NY, USA (2012). https://doi.org/10.1145/2248418.2248437

5. Chen, C., Dong, J.S.: Applying timed interval calculus to Simulink diagrams. In: Liu, Z., He, J. (eds.) ICFEM 2006. LNCS, vol. 4260, pp. 74–93. Springer, Heidelberg (2006). https://doi.org/10.1007/11901433_5

6. Demarchi, F.L.: Modeling and Identification of a Fly-by-Wire Control System. Thesis of master in science, Aeronautical Institute of Technology, São José dos Campos (2005)

7. Didier, A., Mota, A.: Identifying hardware failures systematically. In: Gheyi, R., Naumann, D. (eds.) Formal Methods: Foundations and Applications, pp. 115–130. Springer, Berlin Heidelberg, Berlin, Heidelberg (2012). https://doi.org/10.1007/978-3-030-92137-8

8. Farias, A., Mota, A., Sampaio, A.: Compositional abstraction of CSPZ processes. J. Braz. Comput. Soc. **14**(2), 23–44 (2008)

9. Gibson-Robinson, T., Armstrong, P., Boulgakov, A., Roscoe, A.W.: FDR3 — a modern refinement checker for CSP. In: Ábrahám, E., Havelund, K. (eds.) TACAS 2014. LNCS, vol. 8413, pp. 187–201. Springer, Heidelberg (2014). https://doi.org/10.1007/978-3-642-54862-8_13

10. Gigante, G., Pascarella, D.: Formal methods in avionic software certification: the DO-178C perspective. In: Margaria, T., Steffen, B. (eds.) ISoLA 2012. LNCS, vol. 7610, pp. 205–215. Springer, Heidelberg (2012). https://doi.org/10.1007/978-3-642-34032-1_21

11. Hoare, C.A.R.: Communicating sequential processes. Commun. ACM **21**(8), 666–677 (1978). https://doi.org/10.1145/359576.359585

12. Isobe, Y., Roggenbach, M.: User guide CSP-prover (2004)

13. Isobe, Y., Roggenbach, M., Gruner, S.: Extending CSP-Prover by deadlock-analysis: towards the verification of systolic arrays (2005)

14. Jesus, J., Mota, A., Sampaio, A., Grijo, L.: Architectural verification of control systems using CSP. In: Qin, S., Qiu, Z. (eds.) ICFEM 2011. LNCS, vol. 6991, pp. 323–339. Springer, Heidelberg (2011). https://doi.org/10.1007/978-3-642-24559-6_23

15. Mathworks: Simulink User's Guide. The MathWorks, Inc. (2008). www.mathworks.com

16. Mathworks: Simulink Validation and Verification 2 User's Guide. The MathWorks, Inc. (2008). www.mathworks.com

17. Mathworks: Simulink Design Verifier User's Guide. The MathWorks, Inc. (2019). https://www.mathworks.com/help/pdf_doc/sldv/index.html

18. Mota, A., Farias, A., Sampaio, A.: Efficient analysis of infinite CSPZ processes. In: Workshop de Métodos Formais (2002)

19. Mota, A., Jesus, J., Gomes, A., Ferri, F., Watanabe, E.: Evolving a safe system design iteratively. In: Schoitsch, E. (ed.) SAFECOMP 2010. LNCS, vol. 6351, pp. 361–374. Springer, Heidelberg (2010). https://doi.org/10.1007/978-3-642-15651-9_27

20. Mota, A., Sampaio, A., Borba, P.: Model checking CSPZ: techniques to overcome state explosion. Sociedade Brasileira de Computação (2002)

21. Ogata, K.: Modern Control Engineering. Prentice-Hall, Englewood Cliffs, NJ (1997)

22. Paulson, L.C.: Isabelle: a generic theorem prover. J. Autom. Reasoning **5** (1994)

23. Roscoe, A.: The Theory and Practice of Concurrency. Prentice Hall PTR (1997)

24. Roscoe, A.W., Dathi, N.: The pursuit of deadlock freedom. Inf. Comput. **75**(3), 289–327 (1987). https://doi.org/10.1016/0890-5401(87)90004-6

Excommunication: Transforming π-Calculus Specifications to Remove Internal Communication

Geoff W. Hamilton[1]($\boxtimes$)(ID) and Benjamin Aziz[2](ID)

[1] School of Computing, Dublin City University, Dublin, Ireland
geoffrey.hamilton@dcu.ie
[2] School of Computing, University of Portsmouth, Portsmouth, England
benjamin.aziz@port.ac.uk

Abstract. In this paper, we present a new automatic transformation algorithm called *excommunication* that transforms π-calculus processes to remove parallelism, and hence internal communication. We prove that the transformation is correct and that it always terminates for any specification in which the named processes are in a particular syntactic form we call *serial form*. We argue that this transformation facilitates the proving of properties of mobile processes, and demonstrate this by showing how it can be used to simplify a *leakage analysis*.

Keywords: π-Calculus · Transformation · Simplification · Analysis

1 Introduction

Unfold/fold program transformation techniques were first defined for functional languages by Burstall and Darlington [4] and have since been studied extensively for both functional and logic programs [8,10,14,16–18,20]. However, these techniques have rarely been applied to concurrent languages (some notable exceptions are [5,6,15,19] and the partial evaluation approaches in [3,7,11]). This is partly due to the fact that the non-determinism and synchronisation mechanisms used in concurrent languages substantially complicate their semantics, and thus their corresponding transformation. However, such transformation can be very useful for concurrent languages, since the resulting programs will be easier to analyse and prove properties about as we do not have to deal with the complications of parallel composition and internal communication.

In this paper, we present an automatic transformation algorithm called *excommunication* that transforms π-calculus [12,13] specifications to remove parallelism, and hence internal communication.

Example 1. As a simple example of applying the excommunication algorithm, consider the following π-calculus specification:

$$(\nu m)(B\lfloor l, m\rfloor | B\lfloor m, r\rfloor)$$
$$\textbf{where}$$
$$B \overset{\triangle}{=} (i, o).i(x).\overline{o}x.B\lfloor i, o\rfloor$$

L. Lima and V. Molnár (Eds.): SBMF 2022, LNCS 13768, pp. 109–123, 2022.
https://doi.org/10.1007/978-3-031-22476-8_7

This is the definition of two single cell buffers that are chained together. One cell receives its input at l, and emits this at m. The other cell receives its input at m, and emits this at r. This specification is transformed by the excommunication algorithm to the following:

$$C\lfloor l, r \rfloor$$
where
$$C \stackrel{\triangle}{=} (l, r).l(x).D\lfloor l, r, x \rfloor$$
$$D \stackrel{\triangle}{=} (l, r, x).\bar{r}x.C\lfloor l, r \rfloor + [l = r]D\lfloor l, r, x \rfloor + l(y).\bar{r}x.D\lfloor l, r, y \rfloor$$

The named process C corresponds to a state in which both single cell buffers are empty, and the named process D corresponds to a state in which one of the buffers is full. All parallelism, and hence all internal communication, has been removed by the transformation. The resulting specification is equivalent to the original one, which means that it will have the same observable behaviour within all contexts. This is why the definition of the named process D contains a match between l and r; if the process appears in a context in which the same name is substituted for l and r, then the contents of the second buffer can be passed directly to the first buffer.

The excommunication algorithm for the π-calculus that we present here is inspired by and similar in form to the deforestation algorithm for the λ-calculus [8,20], except that the goal here is to remove parallelism and hence internal communication rather than the intermediate structures that are removed by deforestation. We prove that the transformation is correct and that it always terminates for any specification in which the named processes are in a particular syntactic form we call *serial form*. We argue that this transformation facilitates the proving of properties of mobile processes as we do not have to deal with the complications of parallel composition and internal communication, and demonstrate this by showing how it can be used to simplify a *leakage analysis*.

The remainder of this paper is structured as follows: In Sect. 2, we define the syntax and semantics of the π-calculus. In Sect. 3, we define serial form and the excommunication algorithm, and prove the excommunication theorem which states that excommunication is correct and always terminates for any specification in which the named processes are in serial form. In Sect. 4, we show how excommunication facilitates the static analysis of π-calculus specifications by defining a leakage analysis on the simplified processes resulting from transformation. Section 5 concludes and considers possible further work.

2   The π-Calculus

In this section, we describe the syntax and semantics of the π-calculus.

Definition 1 (Syntax of the π-Calculus). The syntax of the π-calculus is shown in Fig. 1.   □

A specification consists of a process and a number of named process definitions. A process can be null, a prefix action (input, output or silent), match,

$$S \quad ::= P \text{ where } D_1 \ldots D_n \quad \text{Specification}$$

$$D \quad ::= p \stackrel{\triangle}{=} (x_1 \ldots x_n).P \quad \text{Named Process Definition}$$

$P, Q ::=$	$\mathbf{0}$	Null Process
	$\mid x(y).P$	Input
	$\mid \overline{x}y.P$	Output
	$\mid \tau.P$	Silent Action
	$\mid [x = y]P$	Match
	$\mid (\nu x)P$	Restriction
	$\mid P + Q$	Non-Deterministic Choice
	$\mid P \mid Q$	Parallel Composition
	$\mid p \lfloor x_1 \ldots x_n \rfloor$	Named Process Application

Fig. 1. Syntax of the π-Calculus

restriction, non-deterministic choice, parallel composition or named process application. A match $[x = y]P$ only proceeds as process P if the names substituted for x and y are the same; otherwise the process blocks. A named process definition has a number of parameters $x_1 \ldots x_n$ and a process body defined over these parameters. Named process parameters, input variables and restricted variables are *bound* within a process. A name is *free* in a process if it is not bound. We denote the set of names which are free in process P by $fn(P)$. We write $P \equiv Q$ if P and Q differ only in the names of bound variables and are therefore α-equivalent.

Definition 2 (Renaming). We use the notation $\sigma = \{x_1 \mapsto x_1', \ldots, x_n \mapsto x_n'\}$ to denote a *renaming*. If P is a process, then $P\sigma = P\{x_1 \mapsto x_1', \ldots, x_n \mapsto x_n'\}$ is the result of simultaneously replacing the free names $x_1 \ldots x_n$ with the corresponding names $x_1' \ldots x_n'$ respectively, in the process P while ensuring that bound names are renamed appropriately to avoid name capture. □

We define (possibly non-terminating) reduction rules for the π-calculus that reduce processes to the following *normal form* that contains no parallel composition or named processes.

Definition 3 (Normal Form). Normal form is defined as shown in Fig. 2.

Definition 4 (Reduction Rules). The reduction rules for the π-calculus are given in Fig. 3.

These rules closely mirror the denotational semantics for the π-calculus given in [1]. Rule (1) of the form $\mathcal{R}[\![S]\!]$ defines the reduction of the specification S.

Rules (2)-(7) of the form $\mathcal{R}_\mathcal{P}[\![P]\!][\![Q]\!]\ \theta\ \Delta$ define the reduction rules for the parallel composition of the processes P and Q. The parameter θ contains the set of names that are restricted to one of the two processes, and can therefore not be

$$P, Q ::= \mathbf{0}$$
$$| \; x(y).P$$
$$| \; \overline{x}y.P$$
$$| \; \tau.P$$
$$| \; [x = y]P$$
$$| \; (\nu x)P$$
$$| \; P + Q$$

Fig. 2. Normal Form

used as a communication channel between them unless there is a scope extrusion. The parameter Δ contains the set of named process definitions. The reduction rules are followed in a top-down order, so rules (2)-(6) are firstly followed to reduce matching, restriction, choice, parallel composition and named process application.

In rule (2), if matching can be performed then it is removed. If either of the names being matched is restricted then the matching fails, otherwise the match remains. In rule (3), a restriction is removed and the restricted name is added to θ; this is renamed so as not to clash with the free names of the other process. In rule (4), a choice is distributed across the parallel composition. In rule (5), a parallel composition in one process is reduced before further reducing the surrounding composition. In rule (6), a named process application is unfolded. The function $\mathcal{U}$ replaces a named process application with the process body, with the formal names of the body replaced by the actual names in the application. This is defined more formally as follows:

$$\mathcal{U}(p\lfloor x_1 \dots x_n \rfloor, \Delta) = P[x_1/x_1', \dots, x_n/x_n'] \text{ (where } (x_1' \dots x_n').P \in \Delta)$$

When none of the rules (2)-(6) apply, both processes will be either $\mathbf{0}$ or prefixed by an action. Rule (7) is then applied to give a choice of two possible left-prioritised parallel compositions for each possible ordering of the two processes. In a left-prioritised parallel composition, the left process must first perform an action before the residue is composed with the right process. Rules (8)-(12) of the form $\mathcal{R}_{\mathcal{L}}[\![P]\!][\![Q]\!] \; \theta \; \Delta$ define the left-prioritised parallel composition of processes P and Q, where the next action must be performed by process P.

In rule (8), if the left process is prefixed by an output action and the right by an input action, then communication may or may not take place. If the output channel is restricted to the left process, then the communication cannot take place so the result is $\mathbf{0}$. If communication does take place, then the names of the channels in the two actions must be the same so a matching operation is created and the residues of the two processes are composed. Otherwise, the output action is retained and the residue composed with the right process. If the output name is restricted to the left process its scope is extruded, so a restriction is added.

In rule (9), if the left process is prefixed by an output action but the right process is not prefixed by an input action, then if the output channel is restricted to the left process, communication cannot take place so the result is $\mathbf{0}$. Otherwise,

(1) $\mathcal{R}[\![P \text{ where } D_1 \ldots D_n]\!] = \mathcal{R}_P[\![P]\!][\![0]\!] \{\} \{D_1 \ldots D_n\}$

(2) $\mathcal{R}_P[\![[x = y]P]\!][\![Q]\!] \ \theta \ \Delta = \mathcal{R}_P[\![Q]\!][\![[x = y]P]\!] \ \theta \ \Delta$
$$= \begin{cases} \mathcal{R}_P[\![P]\!][\![Q]\!] \ \theta \ \Delta, & \text{if } x = y \\ 0, & \text{if } x \in \theta \vee y \in \theta \\ [x = y](\mathcal{R}_P[\![P]\!][\![Q]\!] \ \theta \ \Delta), \text{ otherwise} \end{cases}$$

(3) $\mathcal{R}_P[\![(\nu x)P]\!][\![Q]\!] \ \theta \ \Delta = \mathcal{R}_P[\![Q]\!][\![(\nu x)P]\!] \ \theta \ \Delta$
$= \mathcal{R}_P[\![P[x'/x]]\!][\![Q]\!] \ (\theta \cup \{x'\}) \ \Delta \ (x' \notin fn(Q))$

(4) $\mathcal{R}_P[\![P_1 + P_2]\!][\![Q]\!] \ \theta \ \Delta = \mathcal{R}_P[\![Q]\!][\![P_1 + P_2]\!] \ \theta \ \Delta$
$= (\mathcal{R}_P[\![P_1]\!][\![Q]\!] \ \theta \ \Delta) + (\mathcal{R}_P[\![P_2]\!][\![Q]\!] \ \theta \ \Delta)$

(5) $\mathcal{R}_P[\![P_1 | P_2]\!][\![Q]\!] \ \theta \ \Delta = \mathcal{R}_P[\![Q]\!][\![P_1 | P_2]\!] \ \theta \ \Delta$
$= \mathcal{R}_P[\![\mathcal{R}_P[\![P_1]\!][\![P_2]\!] \ \{\} \ \Delta]\!][\![Q]\!] \ \theta \ \Delta]\!]$

(6) $\mathcal{R}_P[\![p\lfloor x_1 \ldots x_n \rfloor]\!][\![Q]\!] \ \theta \ \Delta = \mathcal{R}_P[\![Q]\!][\![p\lfloor x_1 \ldots x_n \rfloor]\!] \ \theta \ \Delta$
$= \mathcal{R}_P[\![\mathcal{U}(p\lfloor x_1 \ldots x_n \rfloor, \Delta))]\!][\![Q]\!] \ \theta \ \Delta$

(7) $\mathcal{R}_P[\![P]\!][\![Q]\!] \ \theta \ \Delta = (\mathcal{R}_{\mathcal{L}}[\![P]\!][\![Q]\!] \ \theta \ \Delta) + (\mathcal{R}_{\mathcal{L}}[\![Q]\!][\![P]\!] \ \theta \ \Delta)$

(8) $\mathcal{R}_{\mathcal{L}}[\![\overline{x}y.P]\!][\![x'(z).Q]\!] \ \theta \ \Delta$
$$= \begin{cases} 0, & \text{if } x \in \theta \\ (\nu y)((\mathcal{R}_P[\![[x = x']P]\!][\![Q[y/z]]\!] \ \theta \ \Delta) + \overline{x}y.(\mathcal{R}_P[\![P]\!][\![Q]\!] \ \theta \ \Delta)), & \text{if } y \in \theta \\ (\mathcal{R}_P[\![[x = x']P]\!][\![Q[y/z]]\!] \ \theta \ \Delta) + \overline{x}y.(\mathcal{R}_P[\![P]\!][\![Q]\!] \ \theta \ \Delta), & \text{otherwise} \end{cases}$$

(9) $\mathcal{R}_{\mathcal{L}}[\![\overline{x}y.P]\!][\![Q]\!] \ \theta \ \Delta$
$$= \begin{cases} 0, & \text{if } x \in \theta \\ (\nu y)\overline{x}y.(\mathcal{R}_P[\![P]\!][\![Q]\!] \ \theta \ \Delta), & \text{if } y \in \theta \\ \overline{x}y.(\mathcal{R}_P[\![P]\!][\![Q]\!] \ \theta \ \Delta), & \text{otherwise} \end{cases}$$

(10) $\mathcal{R}_{\mathcal{L}}[\![x(y).P]\!][\![Q]\!] \ \theta \ \Delta$
$$= \begin{cases} 0, & \text{if } x \in \theta \\ x(y').(\mathcal{R}_P[\![P[y'/y]]\!][\![Q]\!] \ \theta \ \Delta), & \text{otherwise } (y' \notin fn(x(y).P|Q)) \end{cases}$$

(11) $\mathcal{R}_{\mathcal{L}}[\![\tau.P]\!][\![Q]\!] \ \theta \ \Delta = \tau.(\mathcal{R}_P[\![P]\!][\![Q]\!] \ \theta \ \Delta)$

(12) $\mathcal{R}_{\mathcal{L}}[\![0]\!][\![Q]\!] \ \theta \ \Delta = 0$

Fig. 3. Reduction Rules for π-Calculus

the output is retained and the residue composed with the right process. If the output name is restricted to the left process, then this is a bounded output, so a restriction is added.

In rule (10), if the left process is prefixed by an input action, then if the input channel is restricted to the left process, communication cannot take place so the result is **0**. Otherwise, the input is retained and the residue composed with the right process where the input name is renamed so as not to clash with the free names of the right process. In rule (11), if the left process is prefixed by a silent action, then the action is retained and the residue composed with the right process. In rule (12), if the left process is null, then no action can be performed so the result is also null.

3   The Excommunication Algorithm

In this section, we present the excommunication algorithm. This is a set of transformation rules (similar in form to the deforestation algorithm for the λ-calculus [8,20]) that convert a given process into an equivalent process from which parallel composition, and hence internal communication, has been removed.

The input to the algorithm is a specification in which all named processes are in *serial form*. Processes in serial form contain no parallel composition and therefore no internal communication.

Definition 5 (Serial Form). Serial form is defined as shown in Fig. 4.

$$
\begin{aligned}
P, Q ::= &\ \mathbf{0} \\
&|\ x(y).P \\
&|\ \bar{x}y.P \\
&|\ \tau.P \\
&|\ [x = y]P \\
&|\ (\nu x)P \\
&|\ P + Q \\
&|\ p\lfloor x_1 \ldots x_n \rfloor
\end{aligned}
$$

Fig. 4. Serial Form

Note that the top-level process in the input specification may still contain parallel compositions and internal communication; it is these that are removed by the excommunication algorithm.

3.1   Transformation Rules

The transformation rules for excommunication are very similar to the reduction rules defined in Fig. 3.

Definition 6 (Excommunication Algorithm). The transformation rules for the excommunication algorithm are shown in Fig. 5.   □

Rule (1) of the form $\mathcal{T}[\![S]\!]$ defines the transformation of the specification S. Rules (2)-(7) of the form $\mathcal{T}_\mathcal{P}[\![P]\!][\![Q]\!]\ \rho\ \theta\ \Delta$ define the transformation rules for the parallel composition of the processes P and Q. The parameter ρ contains a

(1) $T[\![P \text{ where } D_1 \ldots D_n]\!] = T_{\mathcal{P}}[\![P]\!][\![0]\!] \ \{\} \ \{\} \ \{D_1 \ldots D_n\}$

(2) $T_{\mathcal{P}}[\![[x = y]P]\!][\![Q]\!] \ \rho \ \theta \ \Delta = T_{\mathcal{P}}[\![Q]\!][\![[x = y]P]\!] \ \rho \ \theta \ \Delta$
$$= \begin{cases} T_{\mathcal{P}}[\![P]\!][\![Q]\!] \ \rho \ \theta \ \Delta, & \text{if } x = y \\ 0, & \text{if } x \in \theta \vee y \in \theta \\ [x = y](T_{\mathcal{P}}[\![P]\!][\![Q]\!] \ \rho \ \theta \ \Delta), \text{otherwise} \end{cases}$$

(3) $T_{\mathcal{P}}[\![(\nu x)P]\!][\![Q]\!] \ \rho \ \theta \ \Delta = T_{\mathcal{P}}[\![Q]\!][\![(\nu x)P]\!] \ \rho \ \theta \ \Delta$
$= \mathcal{P}[\![P[x'/x]]\!][\![Q]\!] \ (\theta \cup \{x'\}) \ \Delta \ (x' \notin fn(Q))$

(4) $T_{\mathcal{P}}[\![P_1 + P_2]\!][\![Q]\!] \ \rho \ \theta \ \Delta = T_{\mathcal{P}}[\![Q]\!][\![P_1 + P_2]\!] \ \rho \ \theta \ \Delta$
$= (T_{\mathcal{P}}[\![P_1]\!][\![Q]\!] \ \rho \ \theta \ \Delta) + (T_{\mathcal{P}}[\![P_2]\!][\![Q]\!] \ \rho \ \theta \ \Delta)$

(5) $T_{\mathcal{P}}[\![P_1|P_2]\!][\![Q]\!] \ \rho \ \theta \ \Delta = T_{\mathcal{P}}[\![Q]\!][\![P_1|P_2]\!] \ \rho \ \theta \ \Delta$
$= T_{\mathcal{P}}[\![T_{\mathcal{P}}[\![P_1]\!][\![P_2]\!] \ \{\} \ \{\} \ \Delta]\!][\![Q]\!] \ \rho \ \theta \ \Delta]\!]$

(6) $T_{\mathcal{P}}[\![p\lfloor x_1 \ldots x_n \rfloor]\!][\![Q]\!] \ \rho \ \theta \ \Delta = T_{\mathcal{P}}[\![Q]\!][\![p\lfloor x_1 \ldots x_n \rfloor]\!] \ \rho \ \theta \ \Delta$
$$= \begin{cases} P\sigma, \text{if } \exists(P = Q') \in \rho, \sigma.Q'\sigma \equiv (p\lfloor x_1 \ldots x_n \rfloor|Q) \\ p'\lfloor x'_1 \ldots x'_k \rfloor \text{ where } p' \stackrel{\triangle}{=} (x'_1 \ldots x'_k).P', \text{ otherwise} \\ \text{where} \\ \{x'_1 \ldots x'_k\} = fn(p\lfloor x_1 \ldots x_n \rfloor|Q) \setminus \theta \\ P' = T_{\mathcal{P}}[\![\mathcal{U}(p\lfloor x_1 \ldots x_n \rfloor, \Delta)]\!][\![Q]\!] \ (\rho \cup \{p'\lfloor x'_1 \ldots x'_k \rfloor = p\lfloor x_1 \ldots x_n \rfloor|Q\}) \ \theta \ \Delta \end{cases}$$

(7) $T_{\mathcal{P}}[\![P]\!][\![Q]\!] \ \rho \ \theta \ \Delta = (T_{\mathcal{L}}[\![P]\!][\![Q]\!] \ \rho \ \theta \ \Delta) + (T_{\mathcal{L}}[\![Q]\!][\![P]\!] \ \rho \ \theta \ \Delta)$

(8) $T_{\mathcal{L}}[\![\bar{x}y.P]\!][\![x'(z).Q]\!] \ \rho \ \theta \ \Delta$
$$= \begin{cases} 0, & \text{if } x \in \theta \\ (\nu y)((T_{\mathcal{P}}[\![[x = x']P]\!][\![Q[y/z]]\!] \ \rho \ \theta \ \Delta) + \bar{x}y.(T_{\mathcal{P}}[\![P]\!][\![Q]\!] \ \rho \ \theta \ \Delta)), & \text{if } y \in \theta \\ (T_{\mathcal{P}}[\![[x = x']P]\!][\![Q[y/z]]\!] \ \rho \ \theta \ \Delta) + \bar{x}y.(T_{\mathcal{P}}[\![P]\!][\![Q]\!] \ \rho \ \theta \ \Delta), & \text{otherwise} \end{cases}$$

(9) $T_{\mathcal{L}}[\![\bar{x}y.P]\!][\![Q]\!] \ \rho \ \theta \ \Delta$
$$= \begin{cases} 0, & \text{if } x \in \theta \\ (\nu y)\bar{x}y.(T_{\mathcal{P}}[\![P]\!][\![Q]\!] \ \rho \ \theta \ \Delta), & \text{if } y \in \theta \\ \bar{x}y.(T_{\mathcal{P}}[\![P]\!][\![Q]\!] \ \rho \ \theta \ \Delta), & \text{otherwise} \end{cases}$$

(10) $T_{\mathcal{L}}[\![x(y).P]\!][\![Q]\!] \ \rho \ \theta \ \Delta$
$$= \begin{cases} 0, & \text{if } x \in \theta \\ x(y').(T_{\mathcal{P}}[\![P[y'/y]]\!][\![Q]\!] \ \rho \ \theta \ \Delta), & \text{otherwise } (y' \notin fn(x(y).P|Q)) \end{cases}$$

(11) $T_{\mathcal{L}}[\![\tau.P]\!][\![Q]\!] \ \rho \ \theta \ \Delta = \tau.(T_{\mathcal{P}}[\![P]\!][\![Q]\!] \ \rho \ \theta \ \Delta)$

(12) $T_{\mathcal{L}}[\![0]\!][\![Q]\!] \ \rho \ \theta \ \Delta = 0$

Fig. 5. Transformation Rules for Excommunication

set of previously encountered memoised processes. The parameter θ contains the set of names that are restricted to one of the two processes, and can therefore not be used as a communication channel between them unless there is a scope extrusion. The parameter Δ contains the set of named process definitions.

Rules (8)-(12) of the form $\mathcal{T}_{\mathcal{L}}[\![P]\!][\![Q]\!]\ \rho\ \theta\ \Delta$ define the left-prioritised parallel composition of processes P and Q, where the next action must be performed by process P.

Any potentially infinite sequence of transformation steps must involve the unfolding of a named process application in rule (6); these processes are therefore memoised by being added to ρ. A new named process is also defined in which the arguments are the names within the process that are not contained in θ (and must therefore be internal to the process). If a renaming of a memoised process in ρ is subsequently encountered, it is replaced by an appropriate application of the previously introduced named process.

Example 2. Consider the transformation of the specification given in Example 1:

$$(\nu m)(B\lfloor l, m\rfloor | B\lfloor m, r\rfloor)$$
where
$$B \stackrel{\triangle}{=} (i, o).i(x).\bar{o}x.B\lfloor i, o\rfloor$$

During the transformation, the process $B\lfloor l, m\rfloor | B\lfloor m, r\rfloor$ is encountered. A new named process C with parameters l and r is defined for this (the name m is internal to this process, so is not included in the parameters). Later in the transformation, the process $B\lfloor l, m\rfloor | B\lfloor m, r\rfloor$ is re-encountered, so a recursive application of the named process C is added.

Similarly, during transformation the process $B\lfloor m, r\rfloor | \overline{m}x.B\lfloor l, m\rfloor$ is encountered. A new named process D with parameters l, r and x is defined for this (m is again internal). Later in the transformation, the processes $B\lfloor m, r\rfloor | \overline{m}x.B\lfloor l, m\rfloor$ and $B\lfloor m, r\rfloor | \overline{m}y.B\lfloor l, m\rfloor$ are encountered, so they are replaced with the corresponding applications of the named process D. The overall result of the transformation is therefore as follows:

$$C\lfloor l, r\rfloor$$
where
$$C \stackrel{\triangle}{=} (l, r).l(x).D\lfloor l, r, x\rfloor$$
$$D \stackrel{\triangle}{=} (l, r, x).\bar{r}x.C\lfloor l, r\rfloor + [l = r]D\lfloor l, r, x\rfloor + l(y).\bar{r}x.D\lfloor l, r, y\rfloor$$

The excommunication theorem can now be stated as follows.

Theorem 1 (Excommunication Theorem). Every π-calculus specification in which all named process definitions are in serial form can be transformed by the excommunication algorithm into an equivalent process which is in serial form. □

In order to prove that the process generated by excommunication is equivalent to the original process, we need to show the result of reducing the transformed process is the same as that of reducing the original process.

Lemma 1 (On Equivalence). $\mathcal{R}[\![\mathcal{T}[\![P]\!]]\!] \equiv \mathcal{R}[\![P]\!]$ $\hfill\square$

Proof

As the process P may actually be non-terminating, the proof is by co-induction. This is fairly straightforward since the rules for excommunication are almost identical to those for reduction, with only the addition of folding. $\hfill\square$

Lemma 2 (On The Form of Output Produced by Excommunication). The output process produced by the excommunication algorithm is in serial form. $\hfill\square$

Proof

The proof is by structural induction on the transformation rules. This is fairly straightforward since we can see that there is no parallel composition on the right hand side of the transformation rules. $\hfill\square$

Theorem 2 (Termination of Transformation). The transformation algorithm always terminates.

Proof. In order to prove that the algorithm always terminates, it is sufficient to show that there is a bound on the size of processes which are encountered during transformation. If there is such a bound, then there will be a finite number of processes encountered (modulo renaming of variables), and a renaming of a previous process must eventually be encountered. The algorithm will therefore be guaranteed to terminate.

First of all, it must be defined what is meant by the size of a process:

$$\mathcal{S}[\![\mathbf{0}]\!] = 1$$

$$\mathcal{S}[\![x(y).P]\!] = 1 + \mathcal{S}[\![P]\!]$$

$$\mathcal{S}[\![\overline{x}y.P]\!] = 1 + \mathcal{S}[\![P]\!]$$

$$\mathcal{S}[\![(\nu x)P]\!] = 1 + \mathcal{S}[\![P]\!]$$

$$\mathcal{S}[\![P + Q]\!] = \mathcal{S}[\![P]\!] + \mathcal{S}[\![Q]\!]$$

$$\mathcal{S}[\![p\lfloor x_1 \ldots x_n \rfloor]\!] = n$$

$$\mathcal{S}[\![P|Q]\!] = \mathcal{S}[\![P]\!] + \mathcal{S}[\![Q]\!]$$

We then define the level of composition of a process as follows:

$$\mathcal{C}[\![\mathbf{0}]\!] \qquad\qquad = 1$$

$$\mathcal{C}[\![x(y).P]\!] \qquad = \mathcal{C}[\![P]\!]$$

$$\mathcal{C}[\![\overline{x}y.P]\!] \qquad = \mathcal{C}[\![P]\!]$$

$$\mathcal{C}[\![(\nu x)P]\!] \qquad = \mathcal{C}[\![P]\!]$$

$$\mathcal{C}[\![P+Q]\!] \qquad = max(\mathcal{C}[\![P]\!], \mathcal{C}[\![Q]\!])$$

$$\mathcal{C}[\![p\lfloor x_1 \ldots x_n \rfloor]\!] = 1$$

$$\mathcal{C}[\![P|Q]\!] \qquad = \mathcal{C}[\![P]\!] + \mathcal{C}[\![Q]\!]$$

We then prove, for an input process with level of composition c and maximum named process size s, that the size of processes encountered during transformation is bounded by $c \times s$. This is done by structural induction on the transformation rules.

4   Example Application: A Leakage Analysis

The excommunication transformation provides us with a simple serial form for the π-calculus on which we can define static analyses to detect any interesting properties of the resulting observable process behaviour. In this section, we give an example of one such analysis that can detect leakages of sensitive data given a security partial ordering relation.

We start first by assuming a partial order of security labels, $(\Xi, \leq_\ell)$, where the set Ξ is ranged over by labels, $\ell, \ell', \ldots$, and is ordered by a partial ordering relation, $\leq_\ell$. We use these labels to annotate all channel names to reflect the trustworthiness of the sub-process owning those channels. Hence, we annotate as $x^\ell(y).P$ and $\overline{x}^{\ell'} z.Q$. In a real scenario, this annotation would be subject to some predefined multi-level security policy derived using a requirements analysis.

We next define an input/output data analysis on an annotated specification as the interpretation function, $\mathcal{A}_S[\![S]\!] \phi_I \phi_O \in (\Phi_\perp \times \Phi_\perp)$, where $\Phi_\perp : \mathcal{N} \to \wp(\Xi)$ is the domain of mappings, ϕ, from names to sets of security labels. The bottom element mapping in this domain, $\perp_\Phi$, is defined as the element that maps every name to an empty set of labels:

$$\forall x \in \mathcal{N} : \perp_\Phi(x) = \{\}$$

We also define the union of such mappings, $\uplus_\phi : \Phi_\perp \times \Phi_\perp \to \Phi_\perp$, as follows:

$$\forall x \in \mathcal{N}, \phi_1, \phi_2 \in \Phi_\perp : (\phi_1 \uplus_\phi \phi_2)(x) = \phi_1(x) \cup \phi_2(x)$$

and the pairwise union, $\uplus_{\phi,\phi}$, distributes $\uplus_\phi$ over a pair of mappings:

$$\forall \phi_1, \phi_1', \phi_2, \phi_2' \in \Phi_\perp : (\phi_1, \phi_1') \uplus_{\phi,\phi} (\phi_2, \phi_2') = ((\phi_1 \uplus_\phi \phi_2), (\phi_1' \uplus_\phi \phi_2'))$$

We distinguish between two types of such mappings: $\phi_I \in \Phi_\perp$, which maps input variables to the security labels of the channels over which their input actions happen, and $\phi_O \in \Phi_\perp$, which maps message names to the labels of the channels over which they are sent.

The formal rules defining the analysis are shown in Fig. 6. The two most notable rules in this analysis are (3) and (4), which update the input and output mappings, respectively, with new elements that pair the input variable, y in Rule (3), and output message, y in Rule (4), with the security label of the channel x over which the input and output actions happen.

(1) $\mathcal{A}_S[\![P \text{ where } D_1 \ldots D_n]\!] \, \phi_I \phi_O = \bigsqcup \mathcal{F}$
$$\text{where}$$
$$\mathcal{F} = \{(\phi_I, \phi_O), \mathcal{A}_P[\![P]\!] \, \phi_I \phi_O \, \{D_1 \ldots D_n\}\}$$

(2) $\mathcal{A}_P[\![\mathbf{0}]\!] \, \phi_I \phi_O \, \Delta \qquad\qquad = (\phi_I, \phi_O)$

(3) $\mathcal{A}_P[\![x^\ell(y).P]\!] \, \phi_I \phi_O \, \Delta \qquad = \mathcal{A}_P[\![P]\!] \, \phi_I[y \mapsto \{\ell\}]\phi_O \, \Delta$

(4) $\mathcal{A}_P[\![\overline{x}^\ell y.P]\!] \, \phi_I \phi_O \, \Delta \qquad = \mathcal{A}_P[\![\overline{x}^\ell y.P]\!] \, \phi_I \phi_O[y \mapsto \{\ell\}] \, \Delta$

(5) $\mathcal{A}_P[\![\tau.P]\!] \, \phi_I \phi_O \, \Delta \qquad\quad = \mathcal{A}_P[\![P]\!] \, \phi_I \phi_O \, \Delta$

(6) $\mathcal{A}_P[\![[x = y]P]\!] \, \phi_I \phi_O \, \Delta \qquad = \begin{cases} \mathcal{A}_P[\![P]\!] \, \phi_I \phi_O \, \Delta, \text{ if } x = y \\ \phi, \qquad\qquad\qquad \text{otherwise} \end{cases}$

(7) $\mathcal{A}_P[\![(\nu x)P]\!] \, \phi_I \phi_O \, \Delta \qquad = \mathcal{A}_P[\![P]\!] \, \phi_I \phi_O \, \Delta$

(8) $\mathcal{A}_P[\![P + Q]\!] \, \phi_I \phi_O \, \Delta \qquad = \mathcal{A}_P[\![P]\!] \, \phi_I \phi_O \, \Delta \, \uplus_{\phi,\phi} \, \mathcal{A}_P[\![Q]\!] \, \phi_I \phi_O \, \Delta$

(9) $\mathcal{A}_P[\![p\lfloor x_1 \ldots x_n \rfloor]\!] \, \phi_I \phi_O \, \Delta \quad = \mathcal{A}_P[\![\mathcal{U}(p\lfloor x_1 \ldots x_n \rfloor, \Delta)]\!] \, \phi_I \phi_O \, \Delta$

Fig. 6. An I/O Analysis of Normalised Processes

The remaining rules are described as follows. Rule (1) interprets a specification using the operator, $\bigsqcup \mathcal{F}$, which computes the least fixed point of $\mathcal{A}_P$. Rule (2) returns the same pair of mappings for a null process. Rules (5) and (7) remove input and silent actions and name restrictions as they have no effect on the two mappings. Rule (6) will continue analysing the process if its conditional matching evaluates to an equality, otherwise, it returns the same pair of mappings. Rule (8) distributes the analysis onto the two sides of a choice and combines the results. Finally, Rule (9) unfolds a named process application.

Based on the above analysis, it is possible to define the property that a system is *leaky*, as follows.

Property 1 (A Leaky System). Define a leaky system as one whose specification, S, has an analysis result, $\mathcal{A}_S[\![S]\!]\ \phi_I\phi_O = (\phi'_I, \phi'_O)$, that satisfies the following condition:

$$\exists x \in bn(S), \ell_1 \in \phi'_I(x), \ell_2 \in \phi'_O(x) : \ell_2 \leq_\ell \ell_1$$

A leaky system is therefore characterised as being unable to keep sensitive data received over high-level channels, from being output over low-level channels.

4.1   An Application of the Leakage Analysis

We next show how this analysis can be applied in the context of *Example 1* in the Introduction to model an Internet-of-Things (IoT) publish-subscribe (pub-sub) server, such as the one defined in [2]. A pub-sub server receives data from various IoT devices, e.g. sensors, and outputs those data onto the relevant *topics*. Interested applications, which have already subscribed to those topics, receive the data either through a pull or a push mode of communication. Figure 7 shows an example of an IoT system set-up running an MQTT broker [2] collecting atmospheric humidity data.

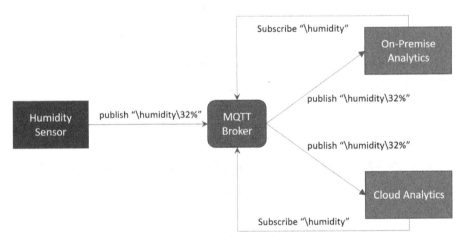

Fig. 7. Example of an IoT (MQTT-based) System Set-up for Collecting Humidity Data

The humidity sensor collects this data and then publishes the data (e.g. humidity level of 32%) to a topic called "humidity". This topic is subscribed to by two software applications: an on-premise (local) analytics application and a cloud-based analytics application that stores data remotely.

In general, a pub-sub server can be modelled as the parallel composition of n-number of pairs of data-processing chained cells:

$$Server \overset{\triangle}{=} \prod_{i=1}^{n} (\nu topic)(Data\lfloor sensor, topic \rfloor \mid Data\lfloor topic, application \rfloor)$$
where
$$Data \overset{\triangle}{=} (i, o).i(x).\bar{o}x.Data\lfloor i, o \rfloor$$

Each first cell receives data from a *sensor* and outputs those data to an internal *topic*. The second cell then takes the data from that *topic* and outputs it to a subscribed *application*. Every data cell will have similar but distinguished behaviour due to the uniqueness of topics. As was demonstrated in *Example 1*, any of the above individual pairs of cells can be excommunicated into a single cell, as follows:

$Data\lfloor sensor, application \rfloor$
where
$Data \overset{\triangle}{=} (l, r).l(x).D\lfloor l, r, x \rfloor$
$D \overset{\triangle}{=} ((l, r, x).\bar{r}x.Data\lfloor l, r \rfloor + [l = r]D\lfloor l, r, x \rfloor + l(y).\bar{r}x.D\lfloor l, r, y \rfloor)$

Returning to the humidity data system of Fig. 7, we can model the server in this system as follows:

$$Server \overset{\triangle}{=} (\nu humidity)(Data\lfloor Humidity\ Sensor, humidity \rfloor \mid$$
$$Data\lfloor humidity, On\text{-}Premise\ Analytics \rfloor \mid$$
$$Data\lfloor Humidity\ Sensor, humidity \rfloor \mid$$
$$Data\lfloor humidity, Cloud\ Analytics \rfloor)$$

with the excommunicated version modelled as follows:

$$Server \overset{\triangle}{=} (\nu humidity)(Data\lfloor Humidity\ Sensor, On\text{-}Premise\ Analytics \rfloor \mid$$
$$Data\lfloor Humidity\ Sensor, Cloud\ Analytics \rfloor)$$

The latter allowing the humidity sensor to sometimes pass the data to the on-premise analytics application, and sometimes to the cloud-based analytics application, without necessarily revealing the topic being subscribed to.

If we assume that $\ell_2 \leq_\ell \ell_1$ and $\ell_3 =_\ell \ell_1$, and we adopt the following security labelling scheme:

$$Data\lfloor Humidity\ Sensor^{\ell_1}, On\text{-}Premise\ Analytics^{\ell_3} \rfloor,$$
$$Data\lfloor Humidity\ Sensor^{\ell_1}, Cloud\ Analytics^{\ell_2} \rfloor$$

Then by applying our static analysis, $\mathcal{A}_S[\![Server]\!]\ \phi_I\phi_O$, we obtain the result, $(\phi_I[x \mapsto \{\ell_1\}, y \mapsto \{\ell_1\}], \phi_O[x \mapsto \{\ell_2, \ell_3\}])$, which indicates the presence of information leakage according to Property 1, since $\exists x : \phi_O(x) \leq_\ell \phi_I(x)$.

We note here that our analysis of the excommunicated specification is simpler than if we were analysing the original specification, since we do not have to deal with internal communication, in this case over the *humidity* topic internal channel. In addition, including the *humidity* channel may hide the leakage in the case where there are multiple *Humidity Sensors* and one of these sensors is annotated with a lower label than the *humidity* channel, but still higher than either the *On-Premise Analytics* or *Cloud Analytics* channels. In this case, no leakage would be detected between the *Humidity Sensor* and the *humidity* topic channels, only between *humidity* and the *Cloud Analytics* channels, the latter being too strong a condition as to exclude all *sensor* communication to *application* in our more general definition of the pub-sub system.

5 Conclusion and Further Work

In this paper, we have presented an automatic transformation algorithm which removes all parallel composition, and hence all internal communication, from π-calculus specifications in which all named processes are in a specialised form we call serial form. We have proved that the transformation preserves equivalence, and also that it always terminates. We argue that this transformation facilitates the proving of properties of concurrent systems, and have demonstrated this by showing how it can be used to simplify a leakage analysis.

There are a number of possible directions for further work. Firstly, as was done for the deforestation algorithm [9], an extended version of the excommunication algorithm could be developed that can be applied to all π-calculus specifications. This would involve the identification of terms that could prevent the termination of the algorithm so they are transformed separately. In [9], this required the identification of intermediate data structures within function definitions. Here, it would involve the identification of parallel compositions within named process definitions.

Secondly, a transformation analogous to the supercompilation transformation [16,18] for functional languages could be developed for the π-calculus. This would involve the use of a homeomorphic embedding relation on processes to determine when generalisation should be performed. Positive information propagation could also be performed using the results of matching operations.

Finally, a transformation algorithm analogous to the distillation algorithm [10] for functional languages could be developed for the π-calculus. Just as the distillation algorithm builds on top of the supercompilation algorithm, this algorithm could build on top of the transformation corresponding to supercompilation for the π-calculus.

References

1. Aziz, B., Hamilton, G.: A denotational semantics for the π-calculus. In: Proceedings of the 5th Irish Conference on Formal Methods, pp. 37–47 (2001)
2. Banks, A., Gupta, R.: MQTT Version 3.1.1 Plus Errata 01. Technical report, OASIS (2015)

3. Bensaou, N., Guessarian, I.: Transforming constraint logic programs. Theoret. Comput. Sci. **206**(1–2), 81–125 (1998)
4. Burstall, R., Darlington, J.: A transformation system for developing recursive programs. J. ACM **24**(1), 44–67 (1977)
5. Etalle, S., Gabbrielli, M., Meo, M.C.: Transformations of CCP programs. ACM Trans. Program. Lang. Syst. (TOPLAS) **23**(3), 304–395 (2001)
6. De Francesco, N., Santone, A.: Unfold/fold transformations of concurrent processes. In: Kuchen, H., Doaitse Swierstra, S. (eds.) PLILP 1996. LNCS, vol. 1140, pp. 167–181. Springer, Heidelberg (1996). https://doi.org/10.1007/3-540-61756-6_84
7. Gengler, M., Martel, M.: Self-applicable partial evaluation for the π-calculus. In: Proceedings of the ACM SIGPLAN Symposium on Partial Evaluation and Semantics-Based Program Manipulation, pp. 36–46 (1997)
8. Hamilton, G.W.: Higher order deforestation. In: Proceedings of the Eighth International Symposium on Programming, Logics, Implementation and Programs, pp. 213–227 (1996)
9. Hamilton, G.W.: Extending higher order deforestation: transforming programs to eliminate even more trees. In: Trends in Functional Programming (Volume 3), pp. 25–36. Intellect Books (2002)
10. Hamilton, G.: Distillation: extracting the essence of programs. In: Proceedings of the ACM SIGPLAN Symposium on Partial Evaluation and Semantics-Based Program Manipulation, pp. 61–70 (2007)
11. Hosoya, H., Kobayashi, N., Yonezawa, A.: Partial evaluation scheme for concurrent languages and its correctness. In: Bougé, L., Fraigniaud, P., Mignotte, A., Robert, Y. (eds.) Euro-Par 1996. LNCS, vol. 1123, pp. 625–632. Springer, Heidelberg (1996). https://doi.org/10.1007/3-540-61626-8_83
12. Milner, R., Parrow, J., Walker, D.: A calculus of mobile processes. I. Inf. Comput. **100**(1), 1–40 (1992)
13. Milner, R., Parrow, J., Walker, D.: A calculus of mobile processes. II. Inf. Comput. **100**(2), 41–77 (1992)
14. Pettorossi, A., Proietti, M.: Rules and strategies for transforming functional and logic programs. ACM Comput. Surv. **28**(2), 360–414 (1996)
15. Sahlin, D.: Partial evaluation of AKL. In: Proceedings of the First International Conference on Concurrent Constraint Programming (1995)
16. Sørensen, M.H., Glück, R., Jones, N.D.: A positive supercompiler. J. Funct. Program. **6**(6), 811–838 (1996)
17. Tamaki, H., Sato, T.: Unfold/fold transformations of logic programs. In: Second International Conference on Logic Programming, pp. 127–138 (1984)
18. Turchin, V.: The concept of a supercompiler. ACM Trans. Program. Lang. Syst. **8**(3), 90–121 (1986)
19. Ueda, K., Furukawa, K.: Transformation rules for GHC Programs. Institute for New Generation Computer Technology Tokyo (1988)
20. Wadler, P.: Deforestation: transforming programs to eliminate trees. Theoret. Comput. Sci. **73**, 231–248 (1990)

Level-Up - From Bits to Words

Matthias Güdemann$^{(\boxtimes)}$ and Klaus Riedl

University of Applied Sciences Munich HM, Lothstrasse 64, 80335 Munich, Germany
`matthias.guedemann@hm.edu`

Abstract. Model checking based on SAT solving has been successfully applied to hardware and software verification. Most of the time the verification is done on the single bit-level using Boolean logic to represent operations on atomic data types.

With the extension of SAT solving to SMT solving, there exist solvers which can use more abstract reasoning on the word-level. SMT solvers support richer theories and allow for adding additional lemmas that can speed up verification.

In this paper we show how a combination of bit and word-level analysis can speed up the verification of hardware models specified on the word-level. We combine the analysis efficiency of SAT solvers to identify bit-level information that is added to the word-level model. Effectively we use different bit-level invariant generation to augment word-level models. We validate the approach on the HWMCC word-level benchmarks using different integration strategies and state-of-the-art model-checkers.

1 Introduction

SAT-based model-checking is an established technique in hardware verification. It is also used to formally verify reactive systems written in synchronous languages like Lustre [18] or HLL [24] used in safety critical domains like rail or avionics. In contrast to approaches based on reduced ordered binary decision diagrams (ROBDD) or enumeration, these approaches do not construct the full state space but use inductive reasoning to verify properties. While this generally limits the properties to invariants or reachability analysis, it also allows for the verification of larger state spaces.

SMT enhances SAT with additional decidable theories. The basic principles of the verification algorithms stay very similar to SAT-based verification. SMT allows for a richer modelling language and also for higher level lemmas, which can speed up verification. For example, where SAT-based model-checking uses Boolean circuits for arithmetic, SMT can add mathematical theorems like commutativity, which can be hard to deduce for a SAT solver. In contrast to SAT-based verification, SMT-based verification is done on the word-level where several bits are combined into bitvectors to represent data-types like integers, arrays, etc.

In recent years, word-level verification has seen an increased interest. SMT solvers got more efficient and with SMTLIB2 [1] there exists a common exchange

© The Author(s), under exclusive license to Springer Nature Switzerland AG 2022
L. Lima and V. Molnár (Eds.): SBMF 2022, LNCS 13768, pp. 124–142, 2022.
https://doi.org/10.1007/978-3-031-22476-8_8

format, which allows to use the same model with different solvers without changes to a verification framework. The hardware model-checking contest (HWMCC) [4] now has a successful word-level track as part of its competition. While bit-level model-checking is still often more efficient, word-level model-checking is better suited for models with memory and arrays [2].

As both bit-level and word-level verification uses similar approaches for verification, e.g., bounded model-checking, k-induction or PDR/IC3 [10], it seems possible that a combination of both approaches can be useful. For example, partial results from the low-level approach should be able to increase the efficiency of the higher level approach. For bit-level verification there exist algorithms that aim at reducing the size of the model by finding equivalent or constant state variables. These methods are generally used to preprocess bit-level models prior to verification.

In this work we analyze the research question **Can bit-level information about equivalence bits and additional bit-level clauses be used to speed-up word-level verification?** A positive answer to this question would allow for combining the efficiency of SAT-based verification with the increased abstract reasoning power of SMT-based verification for an overall increase in efficiency of word-level formal verification.

To achieve this we implemented a tool that takes both word-level model descriptions and bit-level information as its input. From this the tool creates models which are extended with the bit-level information. This extension is done in different ways. These extended models are then analyzed using state-of-the-art word-level model-checkers. The results show that bit-level information can often decrease the required time for the analysis of the systems.

The paper is structured as follows: Sect. 2 gives some background on model-checking using satisfiability solvers, on the word-level format we used and the benchmarks we analyzed. In Sect. 3 we explain which bit-level information we use and it is integrated into the word-level model. We evaluate the approach and show the results in Sect. 4. In Sect. 5 we discuss some related work and conclude the paper with a summary and outlook in Sect. 6.

2   Background

Both SAT and SMT-based approaches to formal verification use very similar building blocks and techniques. In both cases a solver is used to decide a satisfiability problem. The problem is formulated in such a way that a SAT result corresponds to disproving a property and UNSAT corresponds to proving that a property holds.

2.1   Verification Using Satisfiability Solvers

In the following we use the following notation: s or s_j with index j represent a state, s' or s'_j represent the *next* state after the system completes a step. States, next states and inputs i are related via a transition relation $T(i, s, s')$.

The predicate $I(s)$ holds for all *initial* states s (generally s_0) of a model and $P(s)$ and $Q(s)$ are invariant properties that should be verified.

Bounded Model-Checking. Bounded Model-Checking (BMC) was introduced in [3]. It allows for finding violations of an invariant by iteratively unrolling the transition relation and checking whether a bad state is reachable within a given number of time steps.

$$I(s_0) \wedge \bigwedge_{j=0}^{k-1} T(i_j, s_j, s'_j) \wedge \neg P(s'_j) \text{ with } s'_i = s_{i+1} \tag{1}$$

BMC can show either that a property does not hold (Eq. (1) is SAT) or that it cannot be violated within a given number of time steps (Eq. (1) is UNSAT). It cannot generally prove that a property is invariant, only for systems with known diameter.

K-Induction. K-induction [25] is a direct extension of BMC, which additionally allows for verification of invariant properties. BMC is used as base step and then a second *induction step* is added. The induction step uses as induction hypothesis that the property holds for a sequence of k states and then analyzes whether it is possible to reach a successor state s_{k+1} with $\neg P(s_{k+1})$ in step $k + 1$.

$$(\bigwedge_{j=0}^{k} P(s_j) \wedge T(i_j, s_j, s'_j)) \wedge \neg P(s_{k+1}) \text{ with } s'_i = s_{i+1} \tag{2}$$

If, in addition to BMC, Eq. (2) is SAT, then there exists a counterexample to induction, if Eq. (2) is UNSAT the property holds.

A property $P(s)$ which can be proven invariant using k times unrolling the transition relation is called *k-inductive*. The above shows the most commonly used form of k-induction, although it is actually incomplete. The problem with the above is that a property can be too weak to be provable that way. In order to get complete k-induction one would have to add the constraint that all states of the sequence of states are pairwise different. Most often this constraint is not used because it increases the formula quadratically in k.

Property Directed Reachability—IC3. Property Directed Reachability (PDR) was first proposed in [10] and called IC3. In contrast to k-induction, PDR is a complete algorithm and also does not unroll the transition relation of a system. PDR overapproximates the states reachable within k steps and computes a 1-inductive strengthening if an invariant holds. It can also be used to find violations of an invariant like BMC does.

```
module counter(input clk,
               output reg [7:0] counter);
  reg [7:0] counter;

  always @(posedge clk)
    if(counter<5)
      counter <= counter + 1;

  initial counter <= 0;

  p1: assert property (counter < 6);
endmodule
```

Listing 1. System Verilog Example counter

$$(Q(s) \wedge P(s) \wedge T(i, s, s')) \wedge \neg(Q(s') \wedge P(s')) \tag{3}$$

PDR computes an *inductive strengthening* $Q(s)$ for $P(s)$ as shown in Eq. (3). If $Q(s_0 \wedge P(s_0))$ holds and Eq. (3) is UNSAT then $Q(s) \wedge P(s)$ is 1-inductive and holds in all reachable states. $Q(s) \wedge P(s)$ strengthens $P(s)$ in the sense that it implies $P(s)$. $Q(s)$ is computed iteratively; starting with *true* PDR successively refines the strengthening while Eq. (3) is SAT until $Q(s) \wedge P(s)$ becomes 1-inductive. It is this feature which is used in this paper to get information from a partial run of PDR on the bit-level to exploit this information on the word-level.

PDR can be extended to include k-induction [19] and even encode k-induction without unrolling of the transition relation [17]. It can also be extended to systems with infinite state spaces [13], using SMT solvers and predicate abstraction for software verification [12,14].

2.2 Word-Level Verification

There exist different word-level specification languages. This includes languages like VHDL or System Verilog for hardware but also Lustre [18] or HLL [24] for reactive software development. BTOR (more precisely in the version BTOR2 [23]) is a simple description language for word-level sequential circuits. Tools like yosys [28] allow for converting from higher level formalisms to BTOR2.

The simple System Verilog example in Listing 1 will be used to illustrate the approach presented in this paper. It consists of a counter variable with 8 bits. Initially its value is 0 and while it stays below 5, it is incremented at each step.

The model contains a single property, which states that the value of the state variable is less than 6. This property is obviously invariant because once the counter reaches the value 5 it is not incremented any more.

```
1 sort bitvec 1
2 input 1 clk ; ebmcEx1.sv:1.18-1.21
3 sort bitvec 8
4 const 3 00000000
5 state 3 counter
6 init 3 5 4
7 sort bitvec 3
8 const 7 110
9 uext 3 8 5
10 ult 1 5 9
11 const 1 1
12 not 1 10
13 and 1 11 12
14 bad 13 p1 ; ebmcEx1.sv:13.4-13.37
15 uext 3 11 7
16 add 3 5 15
17 const 7 101
18 uext 3 17 5
19 ult 1 5 18
20 ite 3 19 16 5
21 next 3 5 20
```

Listing 2. counter Example in BTOR2 Format

BTOR2 Model Format. The BTOR2 format was developed as a common format to compare different tools for word-level analysis. It is an extension of the AIGER [5] format for bit-level sequential circuits. BTOR2 allows for defining sorts based on bitvectors and arrays. It provides different operators on bitvector arguments like Boolean logic, arithmetic etc. It also allows for the specification of state variables by defining a next state function for each such variable.

The Listing 2 is the example System Verilog model converted into BTOR2 format via the yosys tool. The system has one input signal clk, one state variable counter and one property (expressed as negated *bad state* in BTOR2) in line 14. There are two sorts, bitvectors of width 1 (Booleans/bits) and bitvectors of width 8 (bytes).

HWMCC. The Hardware Model Checking Contest (HWMCC)[1] was first held in 2007. Similar to other competitions the goal is to incentivise enhancement of tools by comparing the tools on a given benchmark and publishing the results. Originally it was limited to bit-level systems using the AIGER format. The most recent event included a word-level track, too.

---

[1] http://fmv.jku.at/hwmcc20/.

The benchmarks of HWMCC[2] include different system models. It also provides the systems in different formats. It consists of BTOR2 models with and without use of arrays and also bit-blasted AIGER versions of each model.

Some examples are safe, i.e., the bad state is not reachable, some are unsafe, i.e., there exist counterexamples that show that a bad state can be reached and for others it is unknown. Counterexamples can require very long input sequences and some analysis tools are more efficient to prove an invariant while others are more efficient in the case of reachable bad states.

Word-Level Model Checking Tools. There exist different tools, which can read and analyze word-level systems, most support different input formalisms, including BTOR2. Some of them participated in the HWMCC contest. We chose three actively developed tools to validate our approach.

The overall winner of the 2020 HWMCC was the Abstractly Verifying Reachability (AVR)[3] tool. AVR provides different verification engines. Its standard engine is a PDR-like verification algorithm using predicate abstraction techniques. It can also be used in *proof race* mode where different engines (e.g., PDR, interpolation, k-induction, BMC) are started in parallel and the result of the first engine to finish is reported.

The second tool is `btormc` [23], which supports BMC and incomplete k-induction as shown in Eq. (2). It is part of the `btortools` package. `btormc` can be used in BMC only mode or with k-induction.

The third tool we used in this paper is `pono` [21][4] which is the successor of `cosa` and `cosa2` [22]. It is developed in the Upscale project[5] at Stanford University. The `pono` tool placed third at HWMCC 2020. It allows for different formal verification engines to be used. It provides different PDR-like verification engines in addition to BMC and k-induction.

3   Using Bit-Level Information on Word-Level

There are different approaches to get bit-level information about a model. These approaches are often used as reduction methods to remove redundant state bits and combinatorial gates in a sequential circuit. The general heuristic is that a smaller circuit is easier to analyze than a larger one. While this is not strictly true, there is often a real benefit to eliminate redundant information before an analysis.

The challenge with word-level models is that one cannot simply remove some bits from the model as signals and state variables consist of more information than single bits. In this section we describe first how bit-level information can be found and then how it can be added to a word-level model.

---

[2] http://fmv.jku.at/hwmcc20/hwmcc20benchmarks.tar.xz.
[3] https://github.com/aman-goel/avr.
[4] https://github.com/upscale-project/pono.
[5] https://upscale.stanford.edu/.

3.1 Computing Bit-Level Information

One way to identify redundant bits is to find equivalences in sequential circuits as described in [9]. It uses Stålmarck's algorithm [26] to find equivalences in a circuit by refining equivalence classes.

This method allows for finding equivalences in a circuit, which can be quite hard to find for a SAT solver that does not have the structural information about the state variables of the circuit. It also has the advantage that Stalmarck's algorithm can be executed partially, i.e., it can find a subset of all equivalences efficiently without any risk for exponential runtime. This property makes it a very useful algorithm for preprocessing a circuit before an analysis.

In this form, the algorithm can identify constant state bits and state bits that are equivalent to other state bits (or equivalent to the negation of other state bits). It also identifies equivalences in the combinatorial circuit, but this information cannot be used on the word-level.

A different method to find bit-level information about a sequential circuit is based on PDR/IC3. As described in Sect. 2.1 the algorithm finds an inductive strengthening [10] for an invariant. This inductive strengthening is refined during a run of the algorithm. It is possible to extract a partial refinement while the algorithm is running.

This approach produces clauses, which may or may not be invariant. PDR only guarantees that the clauses hold for a certain number of steps. But it is possible to analyze inductiveness of these clauses in parallel to PDR. This approach produces a list of invariant clauses, which represent a refinement of the reachable states of the system and are a partial result in finding an inductive strengthening of the system property.

3.2 Bit-Level Information for the Example

Using `btor2aiger` we converted the BTOR2 version of *counter* model (Listing 1) into bit-level AIGER. In this format, each state bit is treated as a separate single bit. Using the equivalence analysis, we can deduce directly that the upper 4 bits of the `counter` state variable are always false. Below is the output of our analysis tool.

```
true <-> ~counter[4]
true <-> ~counter[5]
true <-> ~counter[6]
true <-> ~counter[7]
```

This output means that the negation of the bits 7 to 4 of the `counter` bitvector are equivalent to *true*, i.e., the constant value of these bits is *false*. For AIG, these 4 bits are independent, the connection to the original bitvector is only present in the name of the state bits. Knowning that these 4 bits are equal to *false* reduces the state space of the word-level model, potentially simplifying the verification of the property.

3.3   Integration Strategies

Bit-level information can be integrated into word-level models in different ways. The first decision is how the single bits are extracted from the bitvectors.

Single Bit Extraction. One approach is using bitmasks and bitwise logical operations to check whether a specific bit of a bitvector has value 0 or 1. For example for stateBit[10] where stateBit is a bitvector of width 16, the following BTOR2 code is used:

```
1   sort bitvector 1
2   sort bitvector 16
..
11  state 2 stateBit
12  constant 2 0000010000000000
13  and 2 11 12
14  zeros 2
15  neq 2 13 14
...
```

This code declares a 16 bit constant in line 12 with the single bit 10 set to 1. This constant is used to mask the corresponding bit in the state variable stateBit (line 11) using the bitwise *and* in line 13. This result is then tested for non-equality (or equality using eq) to the 16 bit constant zero declared in line 14.

BTOR2 also has a direct way to extract bits from bitvectors by using the slice indexed operator. The following code is therefore equivalent to the above:

```
1   sort bitvector 1
...
10  sort bitvector 16
11  state 2 stateBit
12  slice 1 11 10
...
```

The slice operator extracts a bitvector from the first to the second index. In this case this selects exactly one bit with the sort Boolean defined in line 1.

Our experiments have shown that using the bitmask is slower on average than using slice, although there are some examples where using the bitmask is faster. Therefore, in this work we used the slice operation to extract bits from bitvectors for the benchmarks (cf. Sect. 4).

Bitvector Combination. As BTOR2 models are based on bitvectors, often there are more than single bits of a bitvector for which we can find an invariant clause. An extreme example is the buggy_ridecore.btor example in the HWMCC benchmark. In this model, there are 512 bitvectors of width 128 bits for which all bits are stuck at a constant value. In total, 78.9% (65645 out of 83119) of all state bits of the model cannot change their values.

Using single bit integration via slicing as described above leads to an almost 6 fold increase in file size of the original model. Experiments showed that this increased significantly the run time of the solvers by requiring more time to parse the file and also because of the more complex model structure. Because of this we also implemented a combination of bits that belong to a single bitvectors.

Any continuous sequence of bits of a bitvector for which a bit-level equivalence is found is combined into a single slice and comparison operation on the bitvector level. For the `buggy_ridcore` example, this reduces the overhead from 6 fold file size to just an additional 2.1%. Figure 1 shows the relation of the number of bits in combined bitvectors to the total number of constant bits for the models of the benchmark (cf. Sect. 4). For some models no bitvector combination at all was possible, and for some almost all constant bits could be combined into bitvectors. Models with the same ratio represent different variants of the same model, wither slight model variation or with different properties.

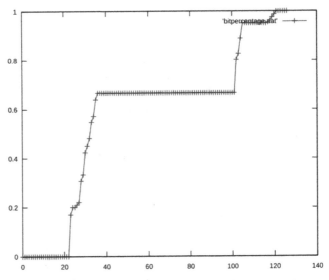

Fig. 1. Relation of bits in bitvector combination to total number of bits

The code in Listing 3 shows the integration of the bit-level information of the equivalence analysis into the BTOR2 model of *counter*. The first part of this model is identical to the original model but has additional 4 lines (l. 22–25).

In the original model there were only the sorts of bitvectors of width 1 and 8. As there are 4 consecutive constant bits in the state variable `counter`, we first declare a new sort of bitvectors of width 4 (l. 22). We then declare a new constant of this sort, which contains only zero valued bits (l. 23). In line 24 we extract the uppermost four bits (7 to 4) from the state variable and compare (l. 25) this new bitvector to the 4-bit constant zero.

```
...
5  state 3 counter
...
22 sort bitvec 4
23 const 22 0000
24 slice 22 5 7 4
25 eq 1 24 23
```

Listing 3. counter Model with Bit-Level Information

3.4 Integration Strategies for Bit-Level Information

Once the conjunction of the additional clauses are added to the model, there are two main ways to use them to speed up the verification process. The first is to add the additional clauses to the property, i.e., to strengthen the property itself. The second way is to add the additional clauses as constraints to the system model.

Strengthening Properties. A stronger property is generally easier to prove by induction as it better approximates the set of reachable states in the system. So, instead of property $P(s)$, the verification tries to prove $Q(s) \land P(s)$, which obviously implies $P(s)$.

A stronger property can be easier to prove using induction or PDR or related approaches because this better describes the reachable states of a system. Because of this, strengthening a property can reduce the number of steps required for k-induction or can reduce the number of iterations of PDR until inductiveness can be decided.

In the BTOR2 format this means that each bad state B_i of the original model is replaced by a new bad state $B_i \lor \neg C$. This corresponds to the property $\neg B_i \land C$, i.e., the conjunction of the added clauses and the negation of reaching the bad state.

For the running example this integration looks as shown in Fig. 2a. The new bad state is defined in l. 28 as the disjunction of the original bad state (l. 13) and the negation of the conjunction of added clauses (l. 26).

```
...
25 eq 1 24 23
26 not 1 25
27 or 1 26 13
28 bad 27
```
(a) Bad State Property

```
...
25 eq 1 24 23
26 constraint 25
```
(b) Model Constraint

```
...
25 eq 1 24 23
26 not 1 25
27 bad 26
```
(c) Validation Model

Fig. 2. Different integration strategies

System Constraints. As each of the additional clauses is implied by the system, adding these clauses as constraints does not change the system. Explicitly adding the constraints to the systems reduces the search space for the SMT solvers as a larger part of the system becomes fixed. This can reduce the time required to deduce that a property becomes inductive as can become easier for the solver to show that the resulting formula is unsatisfiable.

In the BTOR2 format this means that the node C, which corresponds to the conjunction of the added clauses is added as `constraint`. For the running example this looks as shown in Fig. 2b, i.e., the upper part of the bitvector `counter` and the new bitvector of zeros are equal.

3.5   Implementation and Tool Chain

The approach to add bit-level information to sequential BTOR2 models was implemented as a Haskell tool. The tool can parse output from other tools that produce bit-level (AIGER) models and extend BTOR2 files with the additional information from the different strategies for integration.

Model Completion. The initial source model is in BTOR2 format (most often converted from System Verilog or similar). Each node has an optional string as identifier. The first step is completing the BTOR2 model to ensure that each state variable has an associated name. This is important to keep the link in the bit-level model to the BTOR2 model. If no name is specified in the original model, then a new name is synthesized for this node. This results in the *completed model*.

Model Conversion. The second step is converting the BTOR2 model to a bit-level AIG model. This is done using the `btor2aiger` tool, which is part of the `btortools` package[6]. Any state variable without an associated name would get a default name consisting of a sequential number on the AIG level and this would break the association to the word-level here.

Bit-Level Analysis. The third step is the analysis of the AIG model. This is done using standard tools for reduction using the approach as described in Sect. 3.1. We also use the reference implementation of IC3[7] to extract the partial information about the inductive strengthening computed by IC3. In practice, this is done by running `IC3ref` with a timeout and then checking which of the candidate clauses of the frames is inductive. This bit-level information is saved in a JSON file.

Word-Level Model Extension. In the fourth step the information in the generated JSON file is integrated into the completed BTOR2 model to form the *extended* model. The extended model is then written in 3 different variants: the *validation model*, which contains the added information as property that can be validated,

---

[6] https://github.com/boolector/btor2tools.
[7] https://github.com/arbrad/IC3ref.

the *stronger property/invariant* model in which the properties are conjoined with the additional information and the *constraint model*, which contains the additional information as constraints.

The overall approach is shown in Fig. 3. The word-level models are shown in blue, the bit level model is shown in green and the different extended models are shown in yellow.

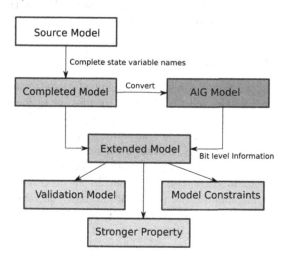

Fig. 3. Overall approach (Color figure online)

The implemented tool internally keeps track of each new sort that is introduced to the extended model for combining constant or equivalent bitvectors. It also keeps track of new constants so that the minimal amount of new constants and sorts is added to the extended model.

For the running example the *validation models* looks as shown in Fig. 2c, i.e., the bad state property is the negation of the conjunction of the added clauses. This allows for independent validation that the additional information is correct.

4   Evaluation Experiments

For the evaluation of the approach we used the benchmarks of HWMCC 2020. Each model has a single bad state property to check. As the published `btortools` package, in particular `btor2aiger`, does currently not support arrays, we only used the model variants without arrays.

4.1   Experimental Setup

For each model we used our equivalence checking tool and our variant of the `IC3ref` implementation to check for equivalences of state bits and for inductive clauses. The runtime for `IC3ref` to generate candidate lemmas for the inductive strengthening was 60 s. We then selected the 164 models for which at least one invariant clause was identified and the validation model was verified within

1200 s. All experiments and the comparison was done on a i7-8665U CPU (4 cores) at 1.90 GHz and 32 G of RAM with a timeout setting of 1200 s. The single threaded tools were run in parallel on the 4 physical cores using GNU `parallel` [27]. All models are available[8].

For the verification of the extended BTOR2 models we used `btormc` 3.2.2, the HWMCC 2020 version of `AVR`[9] and the git version of `pono`[10]. For `pono` we used two different engines: `ic3sa`, which implements IC3 with syntax-guided abstraction [15] and model based IC3 `mbic3`.

4.2 Experimental Results

For each result plot, the x-axis shows the number of models solved, the y-axis is the time required to find the solution (safe or unsafe). `orig` marks the results of the original BTOR2 model without any added information (but with completed state variable names). `inv` marks the results for which the property is strengthened using the additional clauses. `constraint` marks the results for which the additional information is added as constraints to the model.

The results for `btormc` are shown in Fig. 4a. In the case of `btormc`, it is interesting to see that strengthening the properties actually *decreased* the number of solved models. Why this happens is unfortunately not clear as it is counterintuitive. For the unsafe models it seems to be a statistical artifact because of slightly varying run-times. But for the safe models, the reason is not known. The analysis of the logs shows that the models with the stronger property use much larger values of k and apparently do not manage to show UNSAT. It also only happens with this solver and not the others in the experiments. In contrast, adding additional constraints increased the total number of solved models significantly.

Figure 4b shows the results of the benchmarks using `avr` in its single thread mode, i.e., by running `avr.py`. Here, strengthening the properties allows for slightly more models to be verified than the original models. Adding the additional information as constraints solves significantly more of the models than the unchanged models or the models with strengthened properties.

Figure 4d shows the results for `pono` using the `mbic3` engine and Fig. 4e for the `ic3sa` engine. In both the additional information leads to a clear increase analyzed models compared to the original system model. For `mbic3` adding constraints solves significantly more models than strengthening the invariant. For `ic3sa`, adding constraints only results in a single additional successful system analysis.

Figure 4c shows the results of the benchmarks using `avr` in proof race mode. The exact mode is the one defined for the HWMCC 2020 version of `avr`, running `avr_pr.py`. This runs 16 different configurations and engines in parallel and stops either on timeout or when the first engine finds a result. The runtimes in

---

[8] https://www.dropbox.com/s/ny9fu0va1bz2zls/extended_models.tar.xz?dl=0.

[9] tag `HWMCC` of https://github.com/aman-goel/avr.

[10] `8b2a94649f5ea1161260a611de4b49e6f5d92b98`   of   https://github.com/upscale-project/pono.

the figure are the times reported by the engine that finished first. As the test system has only 4 physical cores these results do not allow for 1200 s wall time to run for each engine. For the proof race mode the results of the original models, the strengthened properties and the constrained system are much closer than for the other tools. While the added information lead to more analyzed models, the overall number is only 3 more.

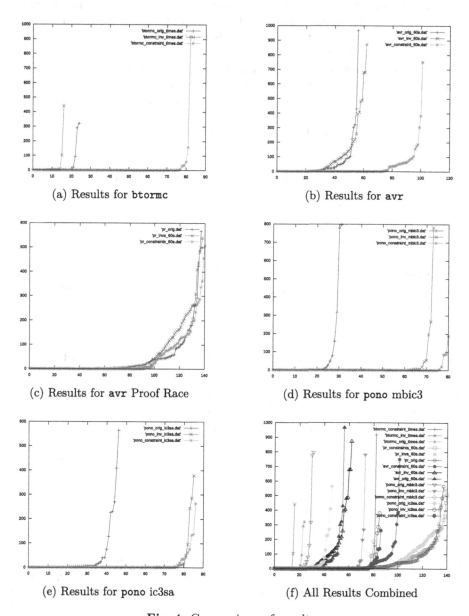

Fig. 4. Comparison of results

Figure 4f shows a plot of all results together. Table 1 gives a more detailed overview of the results. They are split into tools (and engines where applicable), as well as in safe and unsafe models. The total number refers to successful analyses, i.e., either safe or unsafe out of 164 models. Generally, safe models benefit more from the additional information than unsafe ones. The number of models that can be shown as unsafe changes much less than the number of safe models.

Finding deep counterexamples that show that a property is violated can be a hard problem. Most algorithms are based on PDR/IC3, which can be used as bug finder. But the most successful tools in HWMCC for unsafe models are more often based on pure BMC.

In general, it seems that PDR/IC3 style algorithm can benefit from additional information. These algorithms use refinement to overapproximate states reachable within k steps. Adding more invariants can make the overapproximation more precise which seems to be the reason for the speed-ups. The engine portfolio of avr proof race benefits less than the other tools.

Table 1. Number of results for each variant (164 models in total)

Tool	Integration	Safe models	Unsafe models	Total solved
btormc	–	17	8	25
btormc	Strengthened property	10	7	17
btormc	Constraints	75	8	**83**
avr single mode	–	55	2	57
avr single mode	Strengthened property	57	6	63
avr single mode	Constraints	97	5	**102**
avr proof race mode	–	129	9	138
avr proof race mode	Strengthened property	130	9	139
avr proof race mode	Constraints	132	9	**141**
pono mbic3	–	26	6	32
pono mbic3	Strengthened property	69	5	74
pono mbic3	Constraints	75	6	**81**
pono ic3sa	–	42	5	47
pono ic3sa	Strengthened property	81	5	86
pono ic3sa	Constraints	82	5	**87**

5   Related Work

In [7] Bjesse uses word-level information on memory to abstract to bit-level system models. This reduces the number of memory slots and time steps which have to be analyzed in contrast to the analysis of a direct bit-level version of the system models which allows for analysis of larger models than with standard bit-level algorithms.

Similarly, in [6,8] Bjesse uses bit-level verification for word-level systems by using different abstraction techniques. This approach guarantees that the resulting bit-level models are at most as big as directly bit-blasted versions of the word-level systems. This approach is orthogonal to our approach, as the bit-level information could be extracted from these bit-level models, too. Due to abstraction one would need to validate that the additional information is not spurious in the word-level model. The corresponding validation model is easy to generate using our approach.

Gacek et al. Describe the model-checker JKind in [14], which can verify the synchronous language Lustre [18]. JKind uses different engines in parallel to verify the models, including a template based invariant generation. While JKind allows for analysis of unbounded models, practical Lustre programs generally use bounded data-types, e.g., machine width integers. In such a case, our approach to invariant clause generation could also be integrated to speed up verification. The same applies to the kind2 [12] model checker for Lustre.

In [29], Zhang et-al. Present a syntax guided invariant generation technique that uses a grammar to produce candidate lemmas to strengthen the property of an PDR-like word-level formal verification tool. They compare their results to constrained Horn clause (CHC) solvers and hardware model checkers, including btormc, avr and pono. There is no integration of the lemmas into the word-level models as in our approach. But this would be an interesting further source of generated invariants. In [16] Gurfinkel et-al. Use approximations in different logics to find inductive invariants that can then be added to the bitvector model in order to speed up the analysis. This is also an interesting additional source for invariants albeit not necessary property directed ones like when using PDR.

Similar techniques as in [9] are used to generate additional clauses in the HLL [24] model checker S3 [11]. There exist translators from Lustre/SCADE to HLL and HLL is translated into its low-level-language (LLL) form, which is more or less equivalent to bit-blasted AIG models. The main difference is that LLL contains Stålmarck triplets while AIG uses and-inverter nodes. Our techniques could be applied to HLL/LLL analogously. In [20] Khasidashvili and Nadel propose using a simultaneous verification of proof obligations, which can be used to find invariants and speed up run-time of multiple, similar SAT queries which arise in IC3/PDR. This approach includes the invariant generation into the SAT solving and prevents increasing the CNF size.

6   Conclusion and Outlook

In conclusion, we can positively answer whether bit-level information can speed up word-level verification. Integration is not trivial because lots of bit-level clauses can blow up the size of the model, but combining the information into larger bitvectors can reduce the necessary overhead in most cases considerably.

From the experiments it seems that adding explicit constraints is the most effective approach. This reduces the search space of the SMT solvers and can reduce the time necessary to deduce that a problem is unsatisfiable or to find a satisfying assignment.

It also became clear that different algorithms benefit differently from more information. The single thread version of avr uses a PDR/IC3 like algorithm and it seems that adding information for such an algorithm can be very beneficial. Similarly, this holds for the PDR/IC3-like engines of pono. As some additional clauses are taken from the candidate clauses of a partial run of bit-level IC3, this is probably not too surprising. This holds similarly for btormc using k-induction. For the proof race version of avr the benefit is smaller. For the btormc solve we got some counter-intuitive results with respect to property strengthening which we will further analyze.

For future work it would be interesting to analyze further, which engines benefit more from additional information and how to generate useful invariants. It would also be interesting to evaluate other, more diverse sources of additional bit-level information, e.g., invariant patterns that are generated and tested for inductiveness, or extending the variant of Stålmarck's algorithm to also generate implications instead of only equivalences [9].

One interesting open question is how to treat superfluous state bits. In bit-level information one can use a cone of influence (COI) analysis to remove all state bits that do not influence the value of the bad state property. This can often remove some state bits and input signals. On the word-level this is more complicated. Of course, a bitvector can be removed if all its state variables are not used at all in the COI of a bad state property, but generally one cannot simply remove single bits from bitvectors as this would change their sort and make them incompatible with some operations.

It seems reasonable to further integrate the proposed approach into word-level model-checking. One possible way would be to allow for on-the-fly addition of clauses to a model. This would require support for adding information while the verification is running, i.e., adaptation of the software of avr, pono or similar model-checkers. This would allow for running the bit-level and word-level analysis in parallel while generating information usable for the word-level verification.

References

1. Barrett, C., Fontaine, P., Tinelli, C.: The SMT-LIB standard: version 2.6. Technical report, Department of Computer Science, The University of Iowa (2017). www.smt-lib.org/
2. Biere, A.: Tutorial on world-level model checking. In: 2020 Formal Methods in Computer Aided Design (FMCAD) (2020)
3. Biere, A., Cimatti, A., Clarke, E., Zhu, Y.: Symbolic model checking without BDDs. In: Cleaveland, W.R. (ed.) TACAS 1999. LNCS, vol. 1579, pp. 193–207. Springer, Heidelberg (1999). https://doi.org/10.1007/3-540-49059-0_14
4. Biere, A., Claessen, K.: Hardware model checking competition. In: Hardware Verification Workshop (2010)
5. Biere, A., Heljanko, K., Wieringa, S.: AIGER 1.9 and beyond (2011)
6. Bjesse, P.: A practical approach to word level model checking of industrial netlists. In: Gupta, A., Malik, S. (eds.) CAV 2008. LNCS, vol. 5123, pp. 446–458. Springer, Heidelberg (2008). https://doi.org/10.1007/978-3-540-70545-1_43

7. Bjesse, P.: Word-level sequential memory abstraction for model checking. In: 2008 Formal Methods in Computer-Aided Design (2008)

8. Bjesse, P.: Word-level bitwidth reduction for unbounded hardware model checking. Formal Methods Syst. Des. **35**(1), 56–72 (2009). https://doi.org/10.1007/s10703-009-0080-2

9. Bjesse, P., Claessen, K.: SAT-based verification without state space traversal. In: Hunt, W.A., Johnson, S.D. (eds.) FMCAD 2000. LNCS, vol. 1954, pp. 409–426. Springer, Heidelberg (2000). https://doi.org/10.1007/3-540-40922-X_23

10. Bradley, A.R.: SAT-based model checking without unrolling. In: Jhala, R., Schmidt, D. (eds.) VMCAI 2011. LNCS, vol. 6538, pp. 70–87. Springer, Heidelberg (2011). https://doi.org/10.1007/978-3-642-18275-4_7

11. Breton, N., Fonteneau, Y.: S3: proving the safety of critical systems. In: Lecomte, T., Pinger, R., Romanovsky, A. (eds.) RSSRail 2016. LNCS, vol. 9707, pp. 231–242. Springer, Cham (2016). https://doi.org/10.1007/978-3-319-33951-1_17

12. Champion, A., Mebsout, A., Sticksel, C., Tinelli, C.: The KIND 2 model checker. In: Chaudhuri, S., Farzan, A. (eds.) CAV 2016. LNCS, vol. 9780, pp. 510–517. Springer, Cham (2016). https://doi.org/10.1007/978-3-319-41540-6_29

13. Cimatti, A., Griggio, A.: Software model checking via IC3. In: Madhusudan, P., Seshia, S.A. (eds.) CAV 2012. LNCS, vol. 7358, pp. 277–293. Springer, Heidelberg (2012). https://doi.org/10.1007/978-3-642-31424-7_23

14. Gacek, A., Backes, J., Whalen, M., Wagner, L., Ghassabani, E.: The JKIND model checker. In: Chockler, H., Weissenbacher, G. (eds.) CAV 2018. LNCS, vol. 10982, pp. 20–27. Springer, Cham (2018). https://doi.org/10.1007/978-3-319-96142-2_3

15. Goel, A., Sakallah, K.: Model checking of Verilog RTL using IC3 with syntax-guided abstraction. In: Badger, J.M., Rozier, K.Y. (eds.) NFM 2019. LNCS, vol. 11460, pp. 166–185. Springer, Cham (2019). https://doi.org/10.1007/978-3-030-20652-9_11

16. Gurfinkel, A., Belov, A., Marques-Silva, J.: Synthesizing safe bit-precise invariants. In: Ábrahám, E., Havelund, K. (eds.) TACAS 2014. LNCS, vol. 8413, pp. 93–108. Springer, Heidelberg (2014). https://doi.org/10.1007/978-3-642-54862-8_7

17. Gurfinkel, A., Ivrii, A.: K-induction without unrolling. In: FMCAD (2017)

18. Jahier, E., Raymond, P., Halbwachs, N.: The lustre V6 reference manual. Verimag, Grenoble (2016)

19. Jovanović, D., Dutertre, B.: Property-directed K-induction. In: 2016 Formal Methods in Computer-Aided Design (FMCAD), pp. 85–92 (2016)

20. Khasidashvili, Z., Nadel, A.: Implicative simultaneous satisfiability and applications. In: Eder, K., Lourenço, J., Shehory, O. (eds.) HVC 2011. LNCS, vol. 7261, pp. 66–79. Springer, Heidelberg (2012). https://doi.org/10.1007/978-3-642-34188-5_9

21. Mann, M., et al.: Pono: a flexible and extensible SMT-based model checker. In: Silva, A., Leino, K.R.M. (eds.) CAV 2021. LNCS, vol. 12760, pp. 461–474. Springer, Cham (2021). https://doi.org/10.1007/978-3-030-81688-9_22

22. Mattarei, C., Mann, M., Barrett, C., Daly, R.G., Huff, D., Hanrahan, P.: CoSA: integrated verification for agile hardware design. In: Formal Methods in Computer-Aided Design, FMCAD 2018, Austin, Texas, USA, 30 October–2 November 2018. IEEE (2018)

23. Niemetz, A., Preiner, M., Wolf, C., Biere, A.: BTOR2 , BtorMC and Boolector 3.0. In: Chockler, H., Weissenbacher, G. (eds.) CAV 2018. LNCS, vol. 10981, pp. 587–595. Springer, Cham (2018). https://doi.org/10.1007/978-3-319-96145-3_32

24. Ordioni, J., Breton, N., Colaço, J.L.: HLL v. 2.7 modelling language specification (2018)

25. Sheeran, M., Singh, S., Stålmarck, G.: Checking safety properties using induction and a SAT-solver. In: Hunt, W.A., Johnson, S.D. (eds.) FMCAD 2000. LNCS, vol. 1954, pp. 127–144. Springer, Heidelberg (2000). https://doi.org/10.1007/3-540-40922-X_8

26. Sheeran, M., Stålmarck, G.: A tutorial on stålmarck's proof procedure for propositional logic. In: Gopalakrishnan, G., Windley, P. (eds.) FMCAD 1998. LNCS, vol. 1522, pp. 82–99. Springer, Heidelberg (1998). https://doi.org/10.1007/3-540-49519-3_7

27. Tange, O.: GNU parallel 20220322 (2022). https://doi.org/10.5281/zenodo.6377950

28. Wolf, C., Glaser, J.: Yosys-a free verilog synthesis suite. In: Proceedings of the 21st Austrian Workshop on Microelectronics (Austrochip) (2013)

29. Zhang, H., Gupta, A., Malik, S.: Syntax-guided synthesis for lemma generation in hardware model checking. In: Henglein, F., Shoham, S., Vizel, Y. (eds.) VMCAI 2021. LNCS, vol. 12597, pp. 325–349. Springer, Cham (2021). https://doi.org/10.1007/978-3-030-67067-2_15

Author Index

Printed in the United States
by Baker & Taylor Publisher Services